THE SELF-RESPECTING CHILD

CLASSICS IN CHILD DEVELOPMENT

THE BIOGRAPHY OF A BABY
by Milicent Washburn Shinn
Introduction by T. Berry Brazelton, M.D.

THE CONTINUUM CONCEPT
by Jean Liedloff

THE CHILD, THE FAMILY, AND THE OUTSIDE WORLD
by D. W. Winnicott
Introduction by Marshall H. Klaus, M.D.

BABIES AND THEIR MOTHERS
by D. W. Winnicott
Foreword by Benjamin Spock, M.D.

THE SELF-RESPECTING CHILD
by Alison Stallibrass
Foreword by John Holt

THE SELF-RESPECTING CHILD

Development through
Spontaneous Play

ALISON STALLIBRASS

FOREWORD BY JOHN HOLT

 A MERLOYD LAWRENCE BOOK

PERSEUS PUBLISHING
Cambridge, Massachusetts

Many of the designations used by manufacturers and sellers to distinguish their products are claimed as trademarks. Where those designations appear in this book and   was aware of a trademark claim, the designations have been printed in initial capital letters (e.g., Tuftape).

Library of Congress Cataloging-in-Publication Data

Stallibrass, Alison.
    The self-respecting child : development through spontaneous
    play / Alison Stallibrass.
       p. cm.—(Classics in child development)
    Reprint. Originally published: London: Thames and
Hudson, c1974.
    Bibliography: p.
    Includes index.
    ISBN 0-201-19340-X
    1. Play. 2. Child development. I. Title. II. Series:
Classics in child development (Reading, Mass.)
    [HQ782.S7   1989]
    155.4'18—dc20   89-34325

First published 1974 by Thames and Hudson, London

Cover design by Steve Snider
Cover photo by Jerry Howard/Positive Images
Set in 10-point Plantin by Compset, Inc., Beverly, MA

Published by Perseus Publishing
A Member of the Perseus Books Group

Visit us on the World Wide Web at www.perseuspublishing.com

10 9 8 7 6 5 4

Contents

Acknowledgments

My heartfelt thanks are due to the many kind friends who encouraged and criticized, and helped me to present my material in a readable form.

The genesis of the *matter* of the book was the Pioneer Health Centre in Peckham, London. This family-club-cum-research-station was famous all over the world in the years immediately before and after the 1939–45 war. The aim of its director, Dr G. Scott Williamson, was to discover the nature and quality of the activity of healthy human beings and the environment created by them, and the kind of facilities it is necessary to provide in order that ordinary people living in ordinary urban areas may cultivate health and wholeness in themselves, their families and society.

I had the good fortune to be for three years a junior assistant to the small but talented and enthusiastic team of research-workers led by Scott Williamson. I was able not only to sit at their feet but, as I went about my job of making available to the children of the member-families of 'the Centre' the space and equipment that they needed for their chosen activities, I was able to watch whole families growing in health and happiness and effectiveness.

It was the best possible way in which to obtain an understanding of the process of healthy physical, emotional and mental growth in children, and of the importance to growth of play. I am particularly grateful to Dr Innes H. Pearse who offered me the position of student-assistant, and to Lucy Crocker who was my patient mentor, and also to my parents who encouraged me to do this training.

I am also very grateful to my husband for being consistently indulgent of my enthusiasm and preoccupation, and for willingly sharing his home with a pre-school playgroup for many years.

Running my own playgroup and research among the relevant literature have clarified and developed in me the ideas encountered and absorbed at the Pioneer Health Centre.

Foreword
by John Holt

Most books written about how to rear or teach children miss the point. They talk about what we should make children do, and the best or easiest ways to make them do it. Some talk about how to make children into geniuses, others only about how to make them obedient. But they all talk as if children must be and can only be what adults *make* them. They rarely if ever talk about what children can make of themselves, about the powers that from the day or moment of birth are present in every child.

This book does. One of the many excellent photographs in it shows a child, only sixteen months old, who has climbed unaided to the top of a jungle gym and, holding on with one hand, is using the other to wave away imperiously her mother (the author) who (so the child fears) is coming up to "help." The gesture says, more clearly than words, "Thank you, but I don't need and don't want your help. I am managing fine on my own." The picture sums up what this book is about. It is by far the best, the most detailed and vivid account I have yet read of the extraordinary energy, persistence, independence, courage, and resourcefulness with which young children, even babies, gradually explore, master, and make sense of the world about them. It is also about the ways in which adults, at home or in child-care centers, nursery schools, or playgroups, can make it possible for them to do this.

Nothing in this delightful book is more delightful and revealing than the many detailed descriptions, by the author, or by Milicent Shinn, Jean Piaget, and others, of the activities of babies. Milicent Shinn was an American biologist who, around 1900, describe minutely, in *The Biography of a Baby* and other writings, the daily doings of her baby niece, Ruth. At one point she described Ruth, less than a year old and not yet walking, slowly and for the first time climbing the stairs in her house (her mother's hands close behind).

> For the rest of the month she was not satisfied without going up several times daily, and *having people who believed in letting her do things, and ensuring her safety by vigilance while she did them, instead of holding her back*, she soon became expert and secure in mounting. She made assaults too on everything that towered up and looked in the least climbable.

I have put those words in italics because they seem to me to express the heart of this book. This is, above all else, what children need, people who will let them do things and ensure their safety by vigilance rather than by holding them back. There is endless talk these days about children needing love, love, love. What this means, or should mean, is made clear by Mrs. Stallibrass:

> To a child, approval of his spontaneous activity means love. Love that is expressed in care for his safety or for his future happiness, or even in constant attention or in *unsolicited* demonstrations of affection, means little or nothing to him. He needs the manifestations of love that increase his self-respect.

As with the climbing baby, approval means support, not praise. People who call themselves "humanistic educators" are busily pushing the idea that the way to help children gain a sense of their own dignity, competence, and worth (what educators call "positive self-concept") is by deluging them, and trying to make them deluge each other, with an endless flood of praise. Nothing could be more absurd and harmful. Mrs. Stallibrass points out that a baby learning, say, to climb, will learn less well if he is doing it to get a smile or a piece of candy than if he is doing it because he wants to be able to climb. Later she writes of the children, anywhere from four-year-olds to teenagers, at the Peckham Center, a unique and wonderful community and family activity center:

> It became apparent, as time passed, that the children were mainly motivated by a desire to acquire skills of all kinds. It was also evident that they wanted to master a skill for its own sake; they showed no desire to compete with their fellows — to want to do things better than the next child. One never noticed any jeering of the less competent. . . . Sometimes they would play games of skill that would entail winning or losing, but it was obvious that competition, in the sense of wanting to measure their ability with that of another, was not at all important to them. The pleasure lay in acquiring the skill; and when a child had achieved success in something *to his own satisfaction* (italics mine) and had for a while reveled in his newly acquired skill, he would move on to the mastery of something else, even if it meant changing his playfellows.

It is sad to compare this description with the mean-spirited competitiveness one can see in almost all schools. Indeed, one of the most important results, and probably *purposes*, of schools is to kill in children the idea of doing things as well as they can just for the pleasure of doing them, and to make them think instead that the only reason for doing anything is to escape a penalty, gain some kind of praise or reward, or show that you can do it better than someone else. Even in those extremely rare schools that do not encourage this way of thinking, the peer group itself usually does.

As a result, whether they go to soft schools that smother them in praise, or hard schools that set every child in grim competition with every other, children soon lose whatever faint sense they may have had of their own worth. For we do not gain much self-esteem either from praise or from winning competitions. The more praise we get, the less it is worth; the more we win, the less we can stand the thought of losing. We gain true self-esteem in one way only, by doing to our own satisfaction things that we have chosen to do because they seem to us worth doing. In the case of children, this often means the things they see bigger children do, or even adults themselves.

Here I may be ready to go further even than Mrs. Stallibrass. In recent months I have come to know, in one case through letters, in another through a personal meeting, two mothers of children who, *since before they were two,* have been cooking, on a real stove, real food that they and their parents then ate. To do this, these tiny children had to move chairs to the sink or stove, and then climb on them to put water in a pot or do the cooking itself. For all my deep respect for the seriousness and ability of children, I would not have thought this possible for children much under five. Such examples, of which there are probably many others, show clearly not only that children are able to be far more competent and careful than we think, but also that they need far more opportunities than we give them not just for adventurous play *but for serious work.* From a very early age they want and need, not just to explore, but to help, to fit in, to take part, to be and feel useful and needed.

Though most directly concerned with play, this is a very important book about teaching and learning. A number of recent books have told us that we can teach babies to do this or that, including respond to certain written words, by showing them what to do and rewarding them every time they do it. With respect to this, Mrs. Stallibrass quotes Piaget as saying that imitation secured by training of this sort is very different from the spontaneous imitation that is the result of what he calls "assimilation," i.e., the baby understands what we are doing and sees it as something he wants to do for its own sake. In the case of the former, the baby soon loses the skill or ability if the training stops, because he does not yet have a body of knowledge and skill into which this new knowledge can fit. It is the difference between parrot imitation and real speech. Only the latter can be used in new situations and can lead to new learning.

Only a few days ago I spent a day with two friends and their altogether delightful eighteen-months-old son. Like many children of that age, he talks what sounds to us like a kind of pseudo-speech, full of rhythms, tones, and sounds of adult speech, but almost no recognizable words. Near the end of the day this baby fell into what can only be called a conversation with me. Anyone who understood no English could not have told the difference between it and "real" conversation. The baby, looking right at me, would make a long utterance that sounded exactly like real talk. When he stopped, I would reply. In this case I was talking, exactly as I would to an adult, about my need to make a plane reservation, why I had to get to the airport ahead of time, and why I wanted to return to Boston that evening rather than the next day. Back and forth we went, at least half a dozen times. His mother was astonished; though the baby likes to chatter away to himself, she had never seen or heard him have such an extended "conversation" with another person. My point here is that his wordless utterances were in fact much closer to true speech than the accurately imitated "talk" of a parrot. Even though I could not understand his words, the baby was *talking* to me; even when I *can* understand his words, the parrot is not.

Mrs. Stallibrass puts it very well:

> The amount of knowledge that a child can digest at any time depends upon the number of growing shoots that have been put forth by his tree-of-knowledge. In other words, it depends on what he has already, through his activity, digested. . . . A healthy child will want to do what he has become newly capable of learning to do.

And I would add, not just "do," but find out. Here we see why it is not only futile but harmful to try, as the schools do, to impose a curriculum on children, to say, you must learn *what* we tell you to learn, *when* we tell you to learn it. Even those children who quickly learn to parrot what they have been told cannot use most of what they learn or build new knowledge on it. People who like to plan and control children's learning say, "But how can children know what they need to learn?" Of course they don't know what they may need or want to learn ten years from now. But they do know, far better than anyone else knows or can know, what they want to learn, need to learn, and can learn *right now*. On their own, children do not and will not try to do what we are always trying to make them do — grow knowledge buds where there are no twigs. Unlike us, they do not think we can turn a stick into a living plant by glueing leaves on it. Their curiosity is never idle. They do not ask questions that have no meaning, interest, or significance to them, but only

4

those that at any moment they think or hope will most help them make sense of some part of the world. If our answers help them do this, they may ask more questions, until they have as much food for thought as they think they can digest. If our answers make no sense, they drop the matter, or try a different line, or look for someone else to ask. But everything they learn on their own grows out of what they already know and leads to further learning.

Mrs. Stallibrass makes, in passing, an important point about teaching. The people who worked in the Peckham Center learned to their surprise that in the Center professional teaching, done by experts whose main work was teaching, almost always inhibited and prevented rather than helped learning. Children and adults are most inspired to do something when they can see someone else, otherwise much like themselves, doing it *a little bit better than they can*. The most effective teaching at the Center was done by ordinary people who, while doing something for their own pleasure, took a minute or two to show someone else how to do it, or even in some cases said nothing at all, and taught only by their example.

I have seen this in informal school sports, in those rare schools where such things still exist. Eight-year-olds playing baseball for fun with ten-year-olds learn much more about that difficult and complicated game from the older children than they ever do from professional stars or coaches. Children teach other children to read far better than even good adult teachers do. Indeed, I have come to believe that the greatest single fault of full-time teachers is precisely *that they teach full time*, instead of incidentally, in the course of doing other things. Being full-time teachers, they tend to think that learning happens only if and when they make it happen, and that they have to be busy all the time making it happen — which more often than not results only in preventing it from happening at all.

Mrs. Stallibrass believes, and shows convincingly, that one of the important functions of playgroups is to help young children learn not just physical but also social skills — patience, generosity, kindness, tact, forgivingness, helpfulness, and a sense of what it is like to be in the other persons' shoes. One might get the impression, however, that she thinks that if children do not learn these social skills early in life, in a large group of people their own age, they may never learn them at all. I don't believe this. People have grown up without the company of children their age without becoming social or spiritual cripples or monsters. It may be easiest or even best for us to learn the rules of the social game when very young, from people our own age, but it is surely not the only way.

Nor am I convinced that children need or are much helped by

having large numbers of playmates. When in control of their own lives, children like to play with one or two friends, rarely even as many as three. If we gather children together in larger numbers than these, it is mostly for reasons of economics or our own convenience. With very young children, such as the ones Mrs. Stallibrass describes, this may not create great problems. The children have very little sense of the group *as a group*, and do not worry much about their rank or standing in it. But even by first grade, this changes. The peer group begins to form, with its intrigues and jealousies, insiders and outsiders, leaders and followers, winners and losers. Before long it becomes for many or most children as competitive, oppressive, and destructive an institution as school itself. Even with very young children, though it is good for them to spend some time with others of their age, it does not follow that the more of these there are, or the more time they spend with them, the better. Young children (and not so young) need much more time for and by themselves than most of them ever get. I strongly agree with Paul Goodman's judgment that most of them are over rather than undersocialized.

But this is, after all, only a minor disagreement with what seems to me a most exciting and important book. I hope a great many people will read it, and be cured once and for all of the idea that when children are doing what they have freely chosen to do, this activity cannot be purposeful, disciplined, or constructive. We need to understand, and this book should help us to understand, that children do not need to be made (or "motivated") to learn, told what to learn, or shown how. What they need from us is not orders, and usually not even much advice or help, but *access* to the world — to places and experiences (like the baby climbing the stairs, or the children cooking), to people (children and adults, above all adults whose full-time work is *not* looking after children), and to tools and resources, including books, music, and the raw materials of art and science.

Our task is to make such things available, and finally, to understand, as Mrs. Stallibrass says, that babies (and I would add all children) "can be seriously harmed by being starved of food for their faculties and by the disregard of their wishes." May we learn this lesson soon.

John Holt

Introduction

The purpose of this book is to deepen our understanding of the spontaneous and voluntary activity of normal healthy children. It is written for parents and for all those people who are interested in the possibility of increasing the happiness and wisdom of future generations.

It does not contain a comprehensive list of all the games that children play, or of all the skills or kinds of knowledge that they acquire through their activity. But it does try to get to the bottom of play – to discover the basic needs that children satisfy through play, and to answer such fundamental questions as:

Why do children need to play and what sort of play do they choose?

Do children learn through their self-chosen play, and if so – what?

Is this learning necessary for their full and healthy development, and why?

Does the present-day environment of a child allow him to develop the basic human faculties and a healthy, integrated personality and, if not, what can be done about it?

We live increasingly in surroundings that are almost entirely man-made. Knowing this, we may try to plan the environment for the good of all; but we are working in the dark as far as children are concerned if we do not know the answers to these questions.

I believe that the present state of our knowledge enables us to answer them. Lifelong students of various branches of human and animal biology in different parts of the world have independently come to very similar conclusions concerning the process of growth and the developmental needs of young creatures. Together they provide the theory; others have done practical work, trying out various play and learning environments and observing the results, and these can be seen to provide confirmation of the scientists' hypotheses. There is no need to call for further research. We can act now. Governments, planning authorities and groups of families can all help to create an environment in which children may, through their activity, realize their potential powers, individuality and integrity.

It may be doubted if one can provide – or even conceive of – an environment that suits all children, for we know that every child has a unique genetic make-up and therefore unique potential powers. Indeed, not only does one child have a potentially quicker intelligence, a potentially stronger emotional power, or a potentially finer sensibility than another, but each has a different physique, a different metabolism, a different temperament and different tastes from every other. Mothers of large families know that from birth each child looks at the world and responds to it in a different manner. This being the case, one child's meat may be another child's poison, and one could maintain that it is impossible to find an environment that suits all children.

However, this is only partly true because babies are all – or almost all – alike in possessing the potentiality to become mature and complete *human beings*; they contain within themselves at birth the seeds of the powers that together constitute an effectively functioning member of the species 'Mankind' – but only the dormant seeds: all new-born babies are quite ignorant and almost completely helpless; their physical, emotional and mental powers must grow from nothing.

If this is to happen, the seedling powers must be exercised in an appropriate manner, at the appropriate time, in appropriate surroundings. Like all living things, powers grow by the digestion of nourishment from the environment. How and why this happens – or does not happen – will be explained in Part II, with particular reference to the work of Professor Jean Piaget and of Dr Robert W. White.

The basic powers of a human being, the ability to see and recognize objects, to move precisely when and where and how he will, to plan a course of action, to put his thoughts and feelings into words or to respond to events with spontaneity, integrity and realism, must be *used* if they are to develop. If a young creature lacks nourishment for its body, its physical growth will be stunted; similarly, if opportunities to exercise its powers are lacking, its mental and emotional growth will be stunted.

I believe we should make it our business to find out what kind of food is required by the basic powers that are common to all children, and to provide it.

We must be quite sure what we are looking for. What exactly, for example, is meant by the statement that a child's faculties and his individuality develop through the digestion of nourishment from the environment?

8

In Walter de la Mare's *Peacock Pie* there is a poem called 'Miss T':

> It's a very odd thing –
>   As odd as can be –
> That whatever Miss T eats
>   Turns into Miss T;
> Porridge and apples,
>   Mince, muffins and mutton,
> Jam, junket, jumbles –
>   Not a rap, not a button
> It matters; the moment
>   They're out of her plate,
> Though shared by Miss Butcher
>   And sour Mr Bate;
> Tiny and cheerful,
>   And neat as can be,
> Whatever Miss T eats
>   Turns into Miss T

Exactly the same thing happens when experience is thoroughly digested; it becomes part of a person; it nourishes his body-of-knowledge and his judgment, but, at the same time, it is acted upon by his unique digestive juices, so to speak, so that the resulting emotional and mental growth is peculiar to himself. Whatever an individual does as a result of the digestion of experience is specific to himself and therefore to some extent new and original.

A further point – not mentioned in the poem – was the fact that Miss T did not digest all of what she ate. She assimilated only what was needed by her body at the time for energy, growth and renewal. In the same way a wholly healthy child will *select* from his environment the experiences that his powers need at the time for growth. Just as the tissues of the body absorb what they currently need for growth and renewal from the circulating blood, so the child takes the particular nourishment needed by his basic human powers at any moment *if* it is present in his environment and he is *free* to choose for himself. What is meant by freedom in this context will be made clear – I hope – later in the book.

The kind of knowledge and skill for which a small child has an appetite at any moment may be entirely different from the kind that adults consider valuable. But, in an environment that is appropriate to his needs, what a child *wants* to do is what he *needs* to do in order to develop his potential wholeness as a human being – if not to acquire the skills of the civilization into which he has been born. That is why, in the sense of the word used in this book, play is as important as schooling, or more so.

Our task is to create an environment in which children may digest the functional food they all need. Once we are agreed on the nature of this environment, it should be possible – even now – to provide it.

AUTHOR'S NOTE

In most cases
   for 'he' read 'he or she'
   for 'boy' read 'boy or girl'
   for 'man' read 'man or woman'
   for 'playgroup' read 'playgroup or nursery school'.
Toddler = a child between nine and thirty months who is learning to walk and run efficiently.

PART I

The Spontaneous Play of Healthy Children

CHAPTER ONE

What do we mean by Play?

I use the word 'play' in the sense in which it is commonly used when children are the subject of conversation. Almost anything a child does when it is not obliged to be doing something else is called 'play'; for instance, the baby shaking his rattle or 'kicking' before the fire after his bath, the toddler slowly and carefully climbing up the stairs and down over and over again, or discovering how to make water come out of the tap, the five-year-old making patterns with his fruit juice and custard, or 'islands' with his potatoes and gravy, the ten-year-olds playing gang games on the common, or kicking and heading a football to each other in some handy corner between buildings.

All the things that children do purely for the joy of it are quite rightly called play. But at the same time – apart from acts necessary to physical existence like eating – play is, both to and for the child, his most important and serious activity. This truth has been asserted from time to time over the centuries – but it is still not generally understood and accepted. A professor of philosophy at the university of Basle at the end of the nineteenth century called Karl Groos, who specialized in the study of the play of animals and man, had a more acute understanding of children's play than subsequent writers on the subject. He is often summarily dismissed by the latter with some – suspiciously similar – remark to the effect that he considered the play of animals and children to consist of the practice of skills they will need as adults. In fact, he realized that young creatures develop their faculties – including their intelligence, and their ability to be aware of things as they really are, and to respond to them appropriately – through play. In *The Play of Man* (p. 374) he said,

> From the moment when the intellectual development of the species becomes more useful in the struggle for life than the most perfect instinct, will natural selection favour those individuals that play. . . . The human child comes into the world an absolutely helpless and undeveloped being, which must *grow in every other sense* as well as physiologically in order to become an individual of independent capabilities.

But adults tend to think of this spontaneous activity as if it were like their own 'play' – a relatively unimportant part of living. For them, play is relaxation, distraction from worries or merely a means of passing the time; it is secondary to their main occupation, their work or vocation, and a similar attitude is often shown by adults to the play of a child. They say, 'He is *only* playing.' On the whole, people do not sufficiently respect the play of children.

Luckily for society, there have always been exceptions: many parents, and others, have intuitively understood what children are about, have let them be, and even had the wisdom to provide them with timely opportunities for functional nourishment.

The quality of a child's play, and therefore of his functional growth, will depend upon (a) his inherent character and temperament and (b) his environment – including the human part of it – and on the interaction of (a) and (b). We can better understand how a child's ability in a particular field of activity at any moment depends on the quantity and quality of the interaction between himself and his environment which has already taken place in that field of activity by looking at certain relatively simple examples.

Our eyes and whatever else it is that makes up our sight organs may or may not be completely formed at birth, but they are certainly not immediately in working order, and they only become so as they are used. The baby has to learn how to make them serve a useful purpose, and this takes some time and a great deal of practice. It has been found that people born blind, and given their sight by means of an operation when adult, take a long time to learn to use their eyes effectively. Beatrix Tudor-Hart quotes a scientific writer as recording that one such previously blind man, when shown an orange and asked to say what shape it was, said: 'Let me touch it and I will tell you.' This man had developed very fully his power to know the world through his sense of touch, whereas his only recently acquired sense of sight was unused and therefore, so to speak, ignorant: he had not yet developed his ability to see. Groos quotes a description of '. . . a certain Johan Ruben, who was born blind and, when operated on at the age of nineteen, at once started to learn how to judge distances. He would, for instance, pull off his boot, throw it some distance and then try to guess how far off it was, walking so many paces towards it, trying to pick it up, and finding that he had to go farther . . .'

To take another example, a boy may come of a long line of distinguished cricketers or baseball players and may himself inherit a potential talent for such games – the right temperament, physical build, natural speed of reaction, and so on; and yet he cannot be a good player or even in the least skilled at throwing and catching a ball until he has thrown and caught a considerable number of them. He must learn through the experience of throwing and catching balls how to judge the trajectory and speed of a ball through the air so as to be able to place himself in the correct position for catching it, and also to know which muscles to relax and which to contract, and by how much, at the moment of contact, in relation to the speed, weight and direction of the ball. In the same way, he can only learn, by doing it, how to adjust his weight and his balance and how to co-ordinate his movements in space and time in order to be able to throw the ball exactly as far as and in the direction he wishes. Through experimenting and through repetition of the successful actions, he becomes capable of doing the appropriate thing in an increasing number of circumstances and situations.

Through the simultaneous activity of his senses, muscles and mind, the child acquires a body-of-knowledge of the nature and characteristic behaviour of the physical forces, the objects and the creatures that compose his environment, and a knowledge of how to respond to them effectively. At the same time he is learning what his physical, mental and emotional powers are to date, and therefore what he is capable – at the present moment – of achieving. He develops judgment, or what, in some fields of activity, is called wisdom. Judgment cannot be taught. Children acquire it through their spontaneous and voluntary activity.

Some of the child's potential powers, such as the power to read and write and juggle with figures, are only of use in a literate and numerate society, and he may not feel the need to develop them until he is old enough to appreciate the value of such skills (and if his elders exercise the skills of civilization with enjoyment). But a baby has potentially a great many powers that, ever since mankind became a distinct species, have been part of the make-up of a mature and competent human being. It is these that he has a biological urge to exercise and develop. They include the powers that enable a human being to be aware of and to respond to other human beings satisfactorily, and the powers that enable him to be delicately aware of his physical surroundings and in precise control of his limbs. His body is a tool that has acquired its present form and potential characteristics in the course of evolution, and a child appears to experience a need to use it to the best possible advantage, and to develop all its basic functional potentialities – including some of those that may no longer be used by the majority of adults in the course of everyday living, such as the ability to leap ditches and to pull oneself up into the overhanging branches of a tree.

Observation (see chapters 2 and 3) shows that a child of *any* age, who has not become inhibited through too frequent experiences of failure and the fear of rediscovering his incompetence, will want to become able to use his body in as agile, controlled, co-ordinated and – to use an archaic word – feat a manner as a monkey or an acrobat. It is therefore not surprising that walking – though such a milestone to parents – is not the only end at which a toddler is aiming. It must be very dull – and therefore dulling – to a child to live where there is nothing to climb on or to jump from – not even a doorstep.

Stepping and jumping down from things is something every baby has to learn by degrees, sequentially. As he makes use of every available opportunity to step and jump from various heights, he gradually learns, not only how much and in which direction to lean his body, to flex his knees and ankles and to move his feet, but to judge by eye the distance to the ground in every case and to make exactly the movements that he has learned it is necessary to make in response to that particular distance. He is developing sensory-motor judgment through exercising it.

The adjective 'sensory-motor' smacks to some people irritatingly of jargon, but it is a very useful term and I shall be obliged to use it frequently. One could perhaps use 'sensory' by itself if it were understood that we have senses of movement, and 'proprioceptive' senses and nerves which keep the brain informed of the position of the body and of its parts relative to each other and to the whole, and also that our senses are not purely receptive. We actively use our senses; and we can only use them in a very limited manner without the simultaneous use of muscles – and vice versa.

Through the exercise of the skill of jumping in a variety of circumstances, a child's judgment of how to jump down from, over or across obstacles becomes increasingly reliable, and soon he will be able to make jumps in entirely new terrain with precision and grace – and therefore satisfaction and joy.

Jumping is a natural function of the human body. It is one of the powers that a small child feels the need to nourish through appropriate and timely exercise. And, if it is starved of exercise, it will fail to grow, and the child will be handicapped, like a blind or deaf child. But there is a difference: a blind child uses the senses he does possess very effectively; he can never try to use his eyes, and failing, feel inadequate and incompetent. A child, on the other hand, whose power to jump has remained undeveloped, will frequently be conscious of his inadequacy. He will suffer from the fear of not being capable of responding aptly to the circumstances that he may at any moment encounter, and his self-confidence and self-respect will be diminished to an extent that an adult may find difficult to understand.

After a time, however, he may accept the fact that he cannot jump skilfully and successfully – that he is minus the power. Consequently he will avoid activities that require the use of it; with the result that, like the blind child, he will be barred from a great many enjoyable and satisfying activities and experiences.

From the very beginning, the baby wriggles and squirms as he did in the womb, and his legs and arms jerk about. Probably the only way in which he is able to control these movements at first is momentarily to stop them. However, as the days go by, he becomes increasingly capable of directing his movements until, after months of ever more voluntary activity, he is overjoyed to find that he is able to bring his feet within reach of his hands and keep them there while he plays with those intriguing objects, his toes.

If a young human being continues to practise movements that require more and more judgment, co-ordination and control, he will throughout his youth, experience the delight in easy, swift, precise movement that is evident in the young of other species,, and also the growth of that self-confidence and self-respect, serenity and poise that comes of knowing that his senses are acute and that his limbs will do precisely what he intends them to do. Furthermore, the possession of these powers and qualities will strengthen any tendency he has to be outward-looking and so aware of and responsive to his surroundings, and his potentiality for mental adventure and creativity will stand more chance of being realized.

A child's play can be the means whereby he develops not only his potential powers but also his awareness of reality – of things and people as they really are. This is well illustrated by the examples of children's activity included later in the text.

Last but not least: a child can develop his individuality and integrity through his play. But in order to develop *himself*, he must have the company of other children. A student of animal behavior has remarked "One chimpanzee is *no* chimpanzee"; a human being, particularly a young one, cannot fully develop his humanity or his potential abilities and talents if he is left all day alone or among people who are completely strange to him.

It is recognized that one should try to be fairly consistent in one's responses to a small child, otherwise he will be all at sea, and unable to form any judgment of how one wishes him to behave. It is equally important that a young child should have the opportunity to become thoroughly familiar with a particular physical environment and what goes on in it, and with a number of children and adults. Only then will he be able to exercise his sensory-motor and social judgment with increasing accuracy and thus have the courage to be spontaneously and consistently himself within that territory and in relation to those people – and later elsewhere.

It must be briefly noted here that people may be prevented from realizing the true nature of play because a child may use play for other purposes than the basic one described above. A child may use play therapeutically; as a means, for instance, of compensating for long-term deficiencies in his emotional experience. Also any child may, from time to time, restore his emotional equilibrium by, for instance, painting a large black splodge onto a piece of paper and informing those present that this is 'Mummy very cross', after which he turns happily to real play – play that promotes growth; or the child may suddenly throw a doll to the ground and stamp on it with evident satisfaction. But activities of this kind form a very small part of the play of a child who feels accepted and on the whole enjoyed in his family circle, and who knows that in some fields of activity he can be effective and powerful.

Play can even be, on occasion, nothing more than the expenditure of surplus energy; for example, when schoolchildren are released from the classroom to the *bare* asphalt of the school playground, their play may consist entirely of running around aimlessly and shouting.

Compulsory games and athletics in schools do not come into the category of children's play – although they may be play for certain individuals at certain moments. If anyone doubts this, he has only to recall that play to a child is something that he does for its own sake, and not something that he does to order, to avoid censure or for the sake of honour or renown.

Psychologists writing on the subject of play have, during the last fifty years, tended to concentrate on its therapeutic or compensatory aspect. The subject of the present study, on the other hand, is the spontaneous and freely chosen play of *healthy* children, that is, children who have retained their babyhood interest in the environment and their love of being effective.

So what is play, or rather what is it that play can be? It can be the means whereby children develop their basically human potentialities and a spontaneity and individuality of response to reality, and therefore also self-respect and a healthy appetite for experience, knowledge and skill.

In the following pages I hope to demonstrate the truth of this statement. If it *is* true, it is surely important to provide adequate opportunity for play. How do we do this?

It is not easy to discover exactly what to provide, for young children cannot tell us what their play needs are, and older ones do not know what they have missed. The only possible way of finding out what play opportunities to provide, is to watch children playing. But how can we be sure that what they are doing is what they need to do for the healthy development of their faculties? Is what they want to do the same as what they need to do? It is possible to be relatively sure of an affirmative answer to the last question in the case of babies that are too young to have become inhibited by fear of disapproval or failure, and are still satisfied by a very small field of excursion. But one can also learn from watching older children playing under certain conditions.

The most important of these conditions are: (1) a wide variety of play activities from which to choose, and (2) complete freedom of choice. The children's choice must be absolutely spontaneous and uninfluenced by any ulterior motives such as pleasing mother or teacher or escaping from boredom: a 'don't mind if I do' attitude on their part is not good enough, neither is asking them to choose between two alternatives of our choosing. They must feel free to do nothing if that is what they prefer, and they must feel that what they are able to choose to do is what they want to do more than anything else at the moment. They must be able to respond directly and quite unselfconsciously to the environment. If there is an adult supervising the children's play who has a preconceived idea of what the children should be doing, or guides them and directs them in any way, however gently, little will be discovered.

The freedom of children is more easily safeguarded if the play facilities provided are of a kind that they can learn to use successfully without help or instruction. Secondly, since children cannot exercise choice in any real sense in a strange environment, they must be able to play regularly in a familiar place or with a familiar group such as the one that in the past might have gathered on the village green or in a quiet street.

CHAPTER TWO

Choice of Play at the Pioneer Health Centre

At the Pioneer Health Centre in Peckham, London, the school-age children were free to occupy their leisure time as they chose. For one thing, they were not obliged to enter the building at all if they did not want to, except on the occasion of their yearly 'health overhaul', or in order to accompany their parents. The membership was a family one; the weekly family subscription covered all the activities of the children under the age of sixteen, and the building was open every day, except Sunday, from 2 to 10.30 p.m.

Mothers coming to the Centre in the afternoons could, if they wished, leave their babies or their children under five in the nurseries, which were well equipped for play, and where the warm polished-cork floors were ideal surfaces upon which to crawl and to play barefoot – while they themselves swam, played badminton, attended 'Keep Fit' classes or met their friends over a cup of tea. Since the Centre was within walking distance of the members' homes and the primary schools, many children would come from school at four o'clock and join their mothers there, or families might all come together after tea. But the majority of the school-children came and went on their own between the hours of 4 and 8 p.m. or on Saturdays and holidays from 2 p.m. onwards. Some of the older ones did their homework at the Centre, bringing a sandwich from home or buying a snack at the cafeteria.

The children were free to use most of the facilities for recreation and for the acquisition of physical, mental and social skills that were available to the adult members. Besides this, equipment was made available especially for the children's use during the after-noons and early evenings. As great a variety as possible of oppor-tunities for physical, mental and social activity was provided, but anything that was not regularly used was discarded.

The children were able to share with the adults two or three ping-pong tables, a trampoline, a large swimming pool equipped with a full complement of diving boards, a small 'learners' pool' and a gymnasium. The last was used between 4 and 7 p.m. entirely and very fully by the schoolchildren for free and unsuper-vised play.

There were also enthusiasts in various arts and sports who would make regular visits to the Centre for a time. One of these would sit down in a corner and play his concertina, having set out beside him an assortment of his home-made wind and percussion instruments, such as bamboo pipes and wooden xylophones. In front of him he had an apparatus consisting of poles which he could lever up in turn by means of pedals; the tops of the poles were painted in various colours which corresponded to colours painted on the keys or around the stops of the instruments. Children observing the rules of the game could in this way make music with him, making sounds that harmonized with the melody that he was playing.

No one, unless it were their own parents, stopped the children from moving round the building or choosing quite spontaneously what they would do. No one stopped them either from what might have been considered 'doing nothing', that is, from sitting around in groups chatting, or standing all alone and watching what was going on.

The building was designed on a flexible 'open plan' system with a minimum of inside walls, the floors and roof being supported by reinforced concrete pillars. This was not common practice at the time and the building was planned this way in order to encourage easy movement around the building. It was on three floors, with a staircase at each end of the rectangular building and at one end a large hall two storeys high – the theatre/badminton court – and at the other end the equally high-ceilinged gymnasium. On the top floor was the 'medical department', where the members' health overhauls and the 'family consultations' with the doctors took place; also there was a games area containing billiards and ping-pong tables and darts boards; and along the front of the building a long sunny hall that was used in the afternoons as the babies' and toddlers' nurseries, and often in the evening for dancing. The swimming pool occupied the centre of the building, the deep end resting on the ground and the high diving board being close to the central glass roof. The surface of the water was level with the floor of the wide galleries that made up the 'social floor' (the first floor), plus the kitchen, cafeteria and bar counter and a small office. From these galleries one could look down into the gymnasium and the badminton hall through glass walls, as well as into the swimming pool and on to the children's outdoor play-space in front of the building.

Two or three hundred children came to the Centre every day, and more could have been accommodated, yet the only staff necessary was the 'curator' of the 'apparatus for health' used by both adults and children; assisted by a student, she saw to it that the various pieces of equipment were in good repair and available to all those who wished to use them. At the same time she observed and, when possible, recorded the manner in which they were used.

After the first few months there were no classes provided for the children. Although the activities with which they chose to occupy themselves involved skill, no one was employed to give them instruction. This had proved to be the way the children wanted it. They had shown that they preferred to learn by trying on their own and by watching others – older and more skilled children or adults. Their reasons may have been various and complex, but the *effect* was to safeguard their freedom of choice and their freedom to move from one activity to another, for, as their interests changed, they were able to follow them where they led. They were not put off from trying to learn something because of having to commit themselves to attend regular classes or to put themselves into a teacher's power and learn it in *his* way.

From the point of view of research into play needs, the absence of instructors and classes was useful, for we knew that the children were not influenced in their choice of activity by the attractiveness – or otherwise – of the teacher.

The child wandering round the building and noting the available apparatus and its possibilities, and watching the activities of the others, would become aware of what he wanted to do and would set about doing it. The use to which a piece of apparatus could be put was often immediately evident to the child – as in the case of a climbing frame or a bat and ball – but if not, it soon became so, as he watched others using it. Watching what they chose to watch was therefore an extremely important part of the activity of the children at the Centre.

It became apparent, as time passed, that the children were mainly motivated by a desire to acquire skills of all kinds. It was also evident that they wanted to master a skill for its own sake; they showed no desire to compete with their fellows – to want to do things better than the next child. One never noticed any jeering at the less competent; neither was there any 'daring' of each other to do things – perhaps because they were always in the position of being severally responsible for their own safety or because, being quite free to move around and to do a variety of attractive things, they were never bored, or for both these and other reasons. Sometimes they would play games of skill that would entail winning or losing, but it was obvious that competition, in the sense of wanting to measure their ability with that of another, was not at all important to them. The pleasure lay in acquiring the skill;

and when a child had achieved success in something to his own satisfaction and had for a while revelled in his newly acquired power, he would move on to the mastery of something else, even if it meant changing his playfellows.

The children were endlessly occupied in the acquisition of sensory-motor co-ordinations of all kinds, and of mental and social skills. Energy and purposiveness were strikingly characteristic of their behaviour. Many were engaged in one activity after another for four or five hours at a stretch on a Saturday afternoon and during the school holidays. And the capacity shown by some of them – even the youngest – for sustained attention and dogged perseverance was astonishing. The following example is taken from the notes that I made at the time:

> January 22nd. Brian O —— [aged just 4] was away from school owing to a cold* – asked for skates, insisted in keeping them on for 3 hours. The next day he had them on for 4 hours and the same every day for a week. By the end of the week he could skate fast and well and turn corners with skill.
>
> Brian was a bit anti-social in the nursery and uncontrolled in his behaviour. Now that he goes to school, comes to the Centre on his own and goes when and where he likes, he is a responsible person. No one bothers about him and he bothers no one else. There was a very short period at first when he was up to mischief.

An extremely interesting phenomenon was the behaviour of the children in the gymnasium. The latter was conventionally equipped, with ropes suspended from the high ceiling, ribstalls along two walls, a 'window frame' reaching to the roof at one end; booms, vaulting-horses, balancing forms, parallel bars, a punch-ball, coconut-matting etc., and a beautifully sprung cork-covered floor. The one rule enforced was 'bare feet'.

The gym was, however, used in a very unconventional manner: there were sometimes as many as thirty children in it at one time, but no instructor. The children would be running after each other, sliding down the balancing forms, jumping from everywhere, swinging on the ropes, playing with balls, doing handsprings or wrestling. One of the favourite activities was to swing on the ropes between the ribstalls and a vaulting-horse, which they had previously positioned so that they could land neatly upon it, let the

---

* Children in Peckham at that time all started school during their fifth year and many as early as three and a half. Perhaps this was owing to a population 'hollow' of the infant school-age group.

rope swing away and leap on to it again on its return swing. To do this successfully required very accurately timed and co-ordinated movements or, in other words, sensory-motor judgment; and yet skill in this particular activity was not confined to a few gifted individuals. The ropes were constantly being used for this purpose (much more rarely for climbing), and the children made knots at the ends of the ropes, sometimes several knots – a thing that must have made a teacher of conventional gymnastics shrivel up with horror.

(More recently, I have seen boys and girls, including fourteen- and fifteen-year-olds, enjoying an exactly similar activity in the GLC 'playpark' in Battersea Park, London. They had a long rope suspended from the limb of a very tall tree, and they were swinging the rope away and leaping on to it on its return swing from the top of a high wooden platform, which they had constructed with the help of the playleader from poles lashed together.)

In the gymnasium at the Centre, at the same time as some children were swinging on ropes, others might be chasing each other – playing 'off-ground' or some similar game – or running after balls; and yet collisions were very rare. (Incidentally, there was only one instance in four and a half years of a child breaking a bone in the gym. This, I am told, would have been considered an exceptionally good record in a gymnasium used for the same number of child-hours for organized classes.) The children not only exercised judgment in moving in relation to the apparatus, but also in moving in relation to the movements of the other children. They threaded their way with accuracy and at speed among their constantly moving companions, and in order to do this they had to be aware of what all the children in their vicinity were doing and to anticipate what they were likely to do in the next few seconds. This awareness of the total situation was observed to be a quality of the activity in many parts of the Centre: for instance, in the children's outside play-space, which might be shared at one time by, for example, roller-skating twelve-year-olds and five-year-olds learning to ride small bicycles and scooters.

The following is part of an analysis of the activity in the gym, from *The Peckham Experiment* (p. 192):

Let us study this hub of activity from the point of view of a child who goes into it. He goes in and learns unaided to swing and to climb, to balance, to leap. As he does all these things he is acquiring facility in the use of his body. The boy who swings from rope to horse, leaping back again to the swinging rope, is learning by his eyes, muscles, joints and by every sense organ he has, to judge, to estimate, to *know*. The other twenty-nine boys and girls in the gymnasium are all as active as he, some of them in his immediate vicinity. But as he swings he does not *avoid*. He swings *where there is space* – a very important distinction – and in so doing he threads his way among his twenty-nine fellows. Using all his faculties, he is aware of the total situation in that gymnasium – of his own swinging and of his fellows' actions. He does not shout to the others to stop, to wait or to move from him – not that there is silence, for running conversations across the hall are kept up as he speeds through the air.

But this 'education' in the live use of all his senses can only come if his twenty-nine fellows are also free and active. If the room were cleared and twenty-nine boys sat at the side silent while he swung, we should in effect be saying to him – to his legs, body, eyes – 'You give all your attention to swinging; we'll keep the rest of the world away' – in fact – 'Be as egotistical as you like'. By so reducing the diversity in the environment we should be preventing his learning to apprehend and to move in a complex situation. We should in effect be saying – 'Only this and this do; you can't be expected to do more.'

In the Centre gymnasium each child was acting in mutuality with the environment and therefore a diversity of spontaneous actions resulted in a harmonious whole.

Although there was no supervisor in the gymnasium itself, the 'curator of the apparatus for health' was aware of what was going on there for two reasons: she was able to see the whole of the gymnasium from the window on the social floor, and secondly she knew which children were in the gym because she controlled the entry to it. This she achieved by issuing 'tickets' to the children, authorizing them to enter the changing rooms by means of which the gym and the swimming bath were reached. Usually the earlier half of the 4–7 p.m. period was reserved for the younger, less skilled, or 'newer' children.

The issuing of tickets was also a part of an ingenious self-service system which enabled the children to help themselves to the equipment they required. The equipment was kept in especially designed cupboards or racks with, wherever possible, appropriately shaped spaces or niches for each article – pair of roller-skates with boots attached, small bicycle, chess set or whatever it might be. The child placed his ticket in the place from which he had taken the object. When the ticket was issued to him he was required to write his name on it, or his initials if that was all he could manage at his age, and if possible what he was going to do and the time. Then, having used it to obtain his objective, or having returned the piece of apparatus to its place, he would deposit his ticket in a box provided. Thus, at the end of each day, the boxes contained a record of each child's activity.

The blank tickets (a different colour each day), were carried by the 'curator' as she moved round the building, watching the children, talking perhaps to visitors to the Centre, or to adult members; and the children would have to find her in order to obtain one. For this reason the ticket system encouraged the circulation of the children round the building, in the process of which they would be reminded of the various opportunities for activity that were available to them. And they would have the opportunity to observe, and perhaps later emulate, the social and other skills displayed by their elders.

Our records showed that most of the children under twelve when they joined the Centre began by making almost daily use of the gymnasium for a few weeks; after that they usually began to make use also of the small bicycles, scooters or roller-skates, such things as parlour games and jigsaw puzzles or the swimming-baths. Most boys, particularly between the ages of eight or nine and twelve – and some girls – taught themselves to swim very quickly, adopting a stroke straight away that bore some resemblance to the crawl. Some of the girls resorted to the help of the part-time swimming instructress who held classes for the women.

Later still, many children become enthusiastic table-tennis, billiards, badminton or chess players – activities that required and promoted more specialized or finer sensory-motor co-ordinations, or a more abstract form of judgment. As adolescence approached, the boys and girls would form fluid groups based on a common interest, at first sometimes single-sexed, later usually mixed, and would take some trouble to arrange to meet at definite times in order to be able to practise a chosen activity together. Although, especially in the case of the boys, it seemed to be mainly a common interest that held the group together, it was evident that they were satisfying a need to become socially competent.

There came a time for some children when they could make no further progress in some favourite activity without obtaining advice or instruction. We knew about this because often a small group of them would succeed in persuading an older and more competent enthusiast to give them a few lessons or words of advice in such techniques as ballroom or tap dancing, playing a dance-band instrument, badminton, diving or gymnastics; but this development did not come about until the children concerned had been members of the Centre for several months and had spent some time acquiring basic sensory-motor and social judgment through free play in the gym and the swimming-bath, on the diving-boards and roller-skates; and then had watched others practising, and had themselves practised, the more specialized skill on their own.

The children at the Centre were never the focus of attention; they moved on the fringe of the adult society, and this left them free to learn from observation and in their own time; and it left them free to know what their learning needs were at any moment. We were able to get to know the children well, and to watch them, not only while they were playing, but also as they moved around the building among their friends, mixing with their friends' families and meeting their parents' friends; and we were able to observe how they changed and developed.

Visitors to the Centre often remarked upon the poise of the 'Centre children' and upon the forthright and mannerly way in which they would deal with strangers' questions. This was thought to be due to the fact that from the age of four or five onwards the children were able to mix in the society of whole families enjoying their leisure and acquiring new skills, including the art and grace of human fellowship. But the children's serenity and dignity were also in part the result of the self-respect that the possession of bodily skills of all kinds gave them.

The relaxed and yet purposive behaviour of the children did not arise overnight and sometimes the children of newly-joined member families stood out in sharp contrast. I came to the Centre eighteen months after it opened and I have described it as I saw it. In the early months, when all the families were new together, it frequently happened that the children rushed hysterically from one activity to another in reaction to the unaccustomed freedom, and order emerged only gradually as parents and children and young couples found occupations to their taste. But the really extraordinary perseverance in learning that became a general characteristic of the children was judged to be due to the fact that they were able to find the kinds of functional food – the mental and emotional food – that they most needed, and were able to select for themselves the particular morsels that they were at any moment ready to digest.

CHAPTER THREE

Choice of Play in a Pre-school Playgroup

I started my own playgroup for under-fives in 1952 in order to provide regular companionship and the larger and more expensive play equipment for two of our children, one a four-year-old and the other twenty months. In our old-fashioned suburban house we had a room 15 ft × 16 ft, already used as a playroom by our own children, which contained little besides a table, cupboards, a carpenter's bench and linoleum on the floor. We also had a garden of adequate size, the whole being visible from any part of it, and we were only moderately keen gardeners. Apart from flower-beds at the margins, a chicken-run and rabbit-hutches, a shed and an asphalted path, it consisted of a rather rough lawn. The lawn area included several short banks and a long gradual slope. These proved to provide interesting hazards for children learning to balance either on their feet or on scooters and bicycles, and led to the invention of a variety of games and acrobatic 'tricks' – to use the children's word. In the centre of the lawn stood another useful piece of equipment – an apple tree with low branches.

The first item of equipment that I bought was a large, strong metal climbing frame; then sand and sand tools, two planks of smoothly sanded hardwood, paint, paper, plasticine, one small table and six small chairs – and very little else. I made wooden jigsaw puzzles and inset shapes, a simple 'first' abacus, four makeshift easels for painting, and a rope ladder. We already had a swing, a small rocking-horse, a very small bicycle, a scooter and a doll's pram and cradle.

We began with a nucleus of neighbouring children whose parents agreed to bring them regularly and to pay 2s. 6d. per morning or £5 for a term of about twelve weeks. I obtained the permission of the local authority to take in twelve children, and the approval of my immediate neighbours. To make the number up, I put an advertisement in the windows of the local newsagents.

Later, as the news spread, some of the children came from farther afield. Some were brought by car, but some mothers pushed prams or pushchairs for up to three-quarters of a mile each way.

Most, but not all, of the families from which the children came would, I think, have called themselves middle class, but 80 per cent of the parents sent their children to state primary schools. However, as one would expect from the fact that they were willing to pay 12s. 6d. per week and to trundle their children some distance every morning only to be back again in 2½ hours to fetch them, *all* the mothers took great trouble to give their children what they considered to be good for them. At home, the children had plenty of toys of the smaller kind, some had gardens in which they could play; many had already enjoyed the company of other children in their homes and all were talked to and listened to sufficiently to allow them to learn to speak. Therefore, they did not have to be taught to speak, nor did they need mothering. I was able to concentrate on giving them the opportunities that I guessed many of them lacked for nourishing their faculties. These were (a) the opportunity to play freely in the company of other children without consciousness of the need to please adults, and (b) the opportunity to climb and become physically well co-ordinated and agile.

I knew from my experience at the Peckham Health Centre that the children would, on the whole and in the long run, prefer toys and equipment that gave them the opportunity to acquire skill to those that provided entertainment only. For example, they would prefer a scooter with a single wheel at the back to one with two.

Most of the equipment I provided was in fact used very thoroughly, and the items that were less popular I brought out only occasionally or on request. For instance, I found that cut-out letters and numbers and – surprisingly – large coloured cardboard shapes with which to make patterns, were not a priority interest for children of this age group.

After three and a half years, when our fourth child entered primary school, I closed the playgroup in order to have more time and energy and house space to devote to our own adolescent children. But in 1961, when our fifth child was three, I re-opened it – this time for only three mornings a week, in order to leave myself time to keep house for a family of seven.

It was in 1961 that Belle Tutaev founded the Pre-school Playgroups Association. Parents of young children were becoming aware of the difficulty of providing adequate play opportunities; the Pre-school Playgroups Association mushroomed, and my waiting list soon grew to an embarrassing length. I helped some of the parents to start another playgroup locally, but I began to realize that the most useful contribution to the playgroup movement I could make would be to work out in detail the application to children's play of the discoveries concerning the healthy development of human beings that were made by Scott Williamson and his team at the Peckham Health Centre.

I became increasingly interested in discovering how to keep all the children free to be aware of their play needs: that is, to know what nourishment they required at any particular moment for the development of their faculties and to be aware of the available nourishment afforded by their surroundings at every moment. I tried to eliminate anything that might interfere with the growth of this awareness, and I tried to ensure that the children would not be inhibited by any kind of self-consciousness or fear. At the beginning I had sometimes made attempts to play with the children, or to organize their play; but slowly I realized that this merely distracted them from learning what they needed to learn. Some of them showed me, without actually being rude, that they had more important things to do. The more amenable ones, I came to see, were precisely those who most needed to develop awareness of their needs and the courage to fulfil them; and also to develop self-reliance, spontaneity, and responsiveness to the other children.

Small children will, on entering an entirely new environment, quickly sense whether the adults in charge expect them to act on their own initiative or to wait to be told what to do. On the whole they will quite easily accept either situation. In my group the children soon became accustomed to acting spontaneously and, after a bit, expected it as their right. They treated me more and more like a piece of equipment – there only to be made use of when necessary; and they ignored me for much of the time. Sometimes, when in sole charge of ten or twelve children, I would keep a piece of very simple knitting handy in order to give the impression that I too was busy, and also to keep my hands occupied while my eyes and ears and mind were alive to everything that was going on around me, for it is easy to become involved in an activity with a few children instead of keeping oneself free to observe what is going on in the whole group.

When making notes for this book, I tried to find a means of providing a clear and true picture of the over-all scene in the group from moment to moment, as well as of the nature of the sequence of activity pursued by each child. I tried noting the occupation of each child every two or three minutes throughout the morning in a specially devised private shorthand and on a page divided into columns – one for each child. But the information provided by the resulting tables, besides being too brief to be accurate, gives no idea of the spontaneous manner in which the children move from one activity to another, of the highly individual

29

behaviour of each child, nor of the relationship and interaction of the children with each other and the group as a whole from moment to moment.

No records can show adequately the inventiveness of the children, the varied uses to which the apparatus and materials are put, and the manner in which these uses, though they may have been invented in the first place by individual children, or may have been suggested by me, have been taken up and passed on from the older to the younger children over a period of years, in the same way that children's street games become traditional.

On a few occasions I made brief on-the-spot records of the activity of one individual child for an hour or so, and I find that these records give a better impression of the behaviour and activity of the children as a whole.

I chose Tony as a subject for observation for two reasons. First, he had grown up in the group: his sister had been a member of it for a year before she started school, Tony had often accompanied her and his mother to the house, returning home himself rather unwillingly, and had himself joined the group at two and a half. Secondly, he was capable of making good use of the opportunity to be himself and to develop his powers that play in the group offered, because he did not suffer from temperamentally, or environmentally, caused impediments to his response to and awareness of his surroundings.

I have included a record of a morning's activity of Tony's neighbour, Mark, aged two and three-quarters, who had recently joined the group on Tony's mother's recommendation, and also the notes I made of the activity of Christopher on one occasion when he was only two and a quarter but had already been a member of the group for four months, and of Dylan at about the same age. These two were the younger brothers of children already in the group; both joined before their second birthdays and proved to be quite capable of enjoying and taking care of themselves.

When making these notes I did not try to describe the behaviour of the children in any detail, but did seek to be sure to note any change of occupation. Later, I was able on a few occasions to take more detailed notes of the behaviour of individual children and of their play with other children. (See chapter 4.)

Record No. 1
18 October 1966. *Tony, aged 3 years 5 months. A member of the group for nearly a year (2½ terms).*

09 45   Kneeling on floor by small table and putting pegs carefully into

30

the holes in the peg board. First, all yellow ones round the edge of the board, then a row of red, then two rows of blue.

09 52   Goes up to Andrew. Watches him rocking Janet on the rocking-horse.

09 55   Starts to paint. Uses black paint – very rhythmical vertical or horizontal movements of the brush.

09 57   Leaves his big black splodge and goes to the 'slides'. Walks up one plank and slides down the other in a sitting position, feet together, without holding on with his hands, steering and keeping himself on the slide by controlling the muscles of his trunk and thighs. Is joined by Kathy and they run up with big strides and leap and bounce down (wearing plimsolls).

10 00   On the rocking-horse, making it slide forwards as it rocks.

10 02   Hides in the narrow space between the two cupboards, pulling the door of one back across the opening so that he is shut in. Three children come and play with him. It develops into a 'feeding the cows' game. Much 'food' in the shape of small wooden blocks is posted over the door. Tony is the 'cow' being fed.

10 09   Tony is left alone in his cubby hole; the others have gone away.

10 22   He is still sitting there, covered with blocks.

10 25   Out now, trying to do the small 'village' puzzle.

10 27   Playing with Jane among the blocks.

10 29   Returning to the puzzle, succeeds in doing it partially.

10 33   Threading beads.

10 35   'Pastry' (dough). Carefully cutting out 'buns'.

10 55   Still playing with dough.

Our originally makeshift slide (Pl. 1) has turned out to have many advantages over the ready-made kind; above all, its simplicity and adaptability mean that there is more scope for invention on the part of the children. Its salient features are:

1. The planks are narrow (8 inches wide) and have no raised edges. This means that the child can go down them in any position – even sideways – and he can control his speed by holding on to the edges of the plank with his hands. If, however, he prefers not to hold on, he must balance on the narrow plank and this requires considerable control and skill, especially in a sitting position. (The speed with which most children acquire this skill – almost immediately, it seems, though they have in fact been up and down the slide at least a hundred times in half a dozen mornings – blinds one to the degree of skill that is involved.) The planks are lodged against the top of the 2 ft 9 in. high bench by means of a small block of wood that is screwed under one end of the plank. A heavy

tool chest is kept below the bench and protrudes slightly so that, when the plank very occasionally slips, it falls only a few inches.

2. There are two slides, and going up is as much fun as going down. The children go up in many different ways, crouching, walking, on their stomachs pulling with their hands and pushing with their toes, on their knees pulling with their hands. If there are several children playing on the 'slides' at the same time, there is usually one-way traffic; indeed one of the planks has become, by tradition, the 'up-plank'.

3. The 2-ft-wide top of the carpenter's bench makes a good platform upon which to arrange one's body in a chosen position before beginning one's descent.

4. Although the planks are only 7 ft long, their ends rest upon the lino-covered floor so that the children can continue to slide for another four or five feet.

5. When the planks are supported upon the tool-chest, they form a very low slide (only 22 inches from the ground at the top). Like this, the youngest toddler can use it unaided. Even so, it may be terrifying to a small child if his would-be helpful mother places him on the top of it. Left to themselves, the children begin by climbing up a foot or two of the slide on hands and feet, or even, at first, they may simply lower themselves stomach first on to the bottom of the slide and let themselves slip down on to the linoleum. Gradually they climb higher, but for some time they hold the side of the plank with their hands as they descend in order to control their speed. Later, they turn round at the top and go down face first and increase their speed by letting go with their hands earlier, until in the end they are pushing with their feet against the wall to see how far the extra speed will carry them across the floor. They also enjoy stopping and starting again once or twice on the way down. Then they may progress to going down in a sitting position, facing forwards or backwards, or to going down on their backs head foremost, or to the invention or reproduction of other 'tricks' such as running up and down or bouncing down as on a springboard.

One day an interesting thing happened, and I made a note of it. 'Today I suddenly realized that Caroline and her devoted admirer Sandra (aged $4\frac{1}{4}$ and 4 years respectively) had spent the whole of the morning except for three roughly ten-minute intervals – one for elevenses, one to paint a picture and one to do a jigsaw puzzle – playing on the slides, and in the course of their play had devised a new "trick". They had placed the two planks close together supported upon the tool-chest and had discovered how to slide, first

1 Part of the playroom showing the 'slides' (see p. 31).

(see p. 31)

2 Part of the garden.

3 The ski-ing 'trick'. The planks are supported on the toolchest this time and pushed close together.

4 Diana is bouncing, as can be seen from the shape of her cheeks and the way the plank is bent; Mike is carrying on an animated conversation with Debbie in spite of the juddering of the board under his feet.

Evidently somersaults come more easily to Dave, aged 2, than does the use of scissors to the 3-year-old girl on the left of the table.

6 The climbing frame: 4-year-old Tony is about to slide down the central pole.

7 Not everyone becomes as skilled on the trapeze – but innumerable other achievements give equal satisfaction.

8 The simple E.S.A. tent frame offers opportunities for enterprise and invention and a satisfying feeling of competence. Note the ease with which a 3-year-old can swing from her hands and raise her legs horizontally.

crouching low and finally standing upright on their stockinged feet – neither shoes nor bare feet being slippery enough – in exactly the same manner as a skier descends a snow slope.' In the days that followed, as one or two of the other children imitated them, the new 'trick' became one of the traditional skills of the group. It still is at the time of writing, one and a half years later, though the inventors left the group to go to school twelve months ago. (Pl. 3).

Most children find the slides irresistible from the beginning. If they have already had plenty of climbing experience and have therefore learned balance and motor judgment, they will use them enthusiastically on the first day in the group. If not, they may watch the other children using them while ostensibly playing at the dough table for a day or two, and choose moments when no one else is using them for their first trials. In either case they will probably spend a large proportion of their time on them for the next month or two. Then, having attained a satisfying degree of skill in their use, they will proceed to divide their time more evenly between the various kinds of activity available.

Sometimes, however, there are children who, though casting interested and indeed longing glances at the slides, steer clear of them for several weeks; and in fourteen years there have been a few – and they have quite as often been four-year-olds as two-year-olds – who have taken as much as three or four months to begin to make use of them; and one or two of the four-year-olds have left the group to go to school before becoming skilled enough to have fun on them.

In order to ensure that children such as these will have opportunities to use this piece of apparatus when the more skilled or boisterous ones are otherwise occupied, I keep the slides in position most of the time; all the time, in fact, except when some activity such as 'Moving to Music', roller-skates or building with the large Adventure Playthings building blocks requires the whole of the room space.

The need for this was brought home to me very forcibly by the following event. I had taken the children into the garden and noticed that a certain quiet and 'intellectual' child, who had so far made no use of the slides, was missing. I returned and found him, alone in the room, quietly climbing up the plank a little way and letting himself slide slowly down.

The planks are also used sometimes to make 'bridges' with a stool supporting each end. The children 'swim' under them, bounce on them and play trains along or under them (Pl. 4).

The bench, the planks, some box-shaped stools, a mattress and the tool-chest and the Adventure Playthings building blocks are used to make a variety of balancing and agility apparatus. One arrangement that never fails to be greeted with joy and a renewal of energy and which is often requested towards the end of a wet morning, is known as 'somersaults' (Pl. 5). When the supervisor has built it the children climb on to the bench, slither along the plank that is placed with one end on the bench and the other on the tool-chest, until their heads and arms are hanging over the end of the latter, and then let themselves go, making a somersault on to their backs on the mattress. Most of them cannot reach the ground with their hands when lying on the top of the tool-chest and so, after wriggling as far as possible, at a certain point they have to let themselves fall on to their hands – heads well tucked in – and shoulders. They enjoy seizing the heavy iron handle that hangs at the side of the chest and letting it fall with a loud bang against the side of the chest before they somersault. Some prefer not to somersault – the idea of somersaulting originally came from me – but to stand up and jump from the tool-chest high into the air, or as far out from it as they can, sometimes turning in the air, and landing on the mattress in various, sometimes intentionally, odd positions. If a queue tends to build up one can make the circular circus act longer by, for instance, placing 'stepping stones' leading round from the further end of the bench, so that more children are occupied at any one moment.

Record No. 2
9 May 1967. *Tony, aged just 4, has been in the group for four terms.*

09 45   A quick greeting to the supervisor. Puts lunch packet on the mantelpiece. Waves goodbye to mother from window.

09 48   Painting.

09 53   Takes painting off. Runs up slide and down again.

09 55   New painting.

09 59   Sitting on the carpenter's bench and watching.

09 59   At the dough table and talking to Joanna about his birthday party.

10 05   Putting all the pastry into a box.

10 07   Playing 'fire-engines' with Andrew on the slides. Lots of fire-engine noises.

10 10   Takes the telephone to the top of the bench. Rings up for the fire-engine. Fetches some pieces of Connector to make 'hoses'. 'There is water in this.' 'That is what you put the water in.' (Connector is a building toy consisting of 4-cm. cubes and 9-cm. wheel shapes with holes in them, into which split-ended rods of various lengths

can be pushed. Very ingenious, large and complicated structures are sometimes made with it.)

10 11   On top of bench again, 'I am going to jump.' Jumps to the ground (nearly 3 ft down).

10 15   Playing with the cash register and the toy money.

10 19   Ditto.

10 21   Andrew joins him and they play 'shops'. More children join the game.

10 24   Tony leaves the game to draw round cardboard shapes.

10 26   Building with blocks. Carefully building a 'bird-table'. Selects blocks carefully, seems interested in the comparative sizes of the blocks.

10 34   'Carpentry'. Hammering real nails into wood. (We keep a box containing small hammers; large nails and oddments of softwood. The children also make use of the vice that is fixed to the carpenter's bench for sawing with a junior hacksaw.)

10 40   Hurt finger.

10 43   Takes his shoes off.

10 44   Sliding down the slides very fast on his stomach.

10 48   Sliding upright on his stockinged feet. Usually bumps down on to his bottom halfway down, so that he finishes his slide sitting down. (See Caroline's trick, p. 32.)

10 50   Still sliding standing up. Anna and Andrew join him on the slides.

10 51   At the pastry table.

10 53   Ditto.

'Elevenses'

In the garden (Pl. 2).

11 20   Up the climbing frame. Down the central pole. The same several times.

11 23   Up to the highest point possible in the apple tree.

11 25   Gymnast's rings. Can nearly place his feet into the rings from which he is swinging by his hands (Pl. 7).

11 27   'I done it, I got my feet in.' Very pleased.

11 31   Rings again.

11 32   Back to climbing frame. Down the central pole from the very top.

11 40   On the Tent Frame (Pl. 6). Doing 'tricks'.

11 44   Tug-of-war of sorts with other children.

11 45   Sandpit.

11 47   Making pies in sand.

11 48   Rings again.

11 49   Climbing frame.

Most of the 'fees' given me in advance by the parents before the playgroup opened I spent on the climbing frame since, from my experience at the Peckham Health Centre, I knew it to be more essential than anything else – even tables and chairs. I selected it after consulting several catalogues and after having seen it in use in the Coram's Fields Playground in London. I think it is still the best design available. The varied spacing of the horizontal bars on the different sides is good, because the very youngest children can climb up the side on which the bars are closest together. At sixteen months my own youngest climbed up till she was standing on the top bar but one, and stood holding on to the top bar with one hand while she shooed me away with the other (Pl. 9). Bigger children enjoy climbing on the opposite side where the spacing is wider and allows for greater variety of movement. Eventually most of the children progress to climbing all over the top, or they swing from two of the diagonal bars at the top, wind their legs round the central pole, move their hands to the central pole and slide down it to the ground. In dry weather we make slides by hooking our planks on to one of the lower bars and place a length of vinyl floor covering under the lower edge of the plank so that the children are able to slide on their stomachs as they do indoors. One of the discoveries the children have made for themselves is that it is easier to learn how to slide down the central pole if one practises first from a standing position on a platform – formed by laying a plank across the bars – gradually increasing the height of the platform from the ground. Our frame has been standing in the garden for nineteen years and has been used by children of all ages, even at one period by young teenagers as a forum: half-a-dozen of them would sit perched around the top of it, chatting – secure in the knowledge that they were unlikely to be overheard by any outsiders, or interrupted.

Record No. 3
24 May 1967. *Tony, aged 4, and Mark, aged 2 years 8 months, who is Tony's neighbour and friend; Mark has been in the group for four weeks.*

TONY	MARK
09 45 Painting	Climbing up slide on hands and *knees*, pulling himself up by his hands. Slides down on stomach, feet first. Up again, down on back. Watching others cutting little pieces of coloured gummed

		paper and sticking them on to a piece of white paper. Up the slide again, down on hands and knees.
09 47	Ditto.	Talks to the supervisor about his friend Tony who is painting. Climbs onto the carpenter's bench by way of the tool-chest and sits watching the others.
09 49	Ditto.	Standing at the bottom of the slide with his legs apart to make a 'bridge' for some other children to slide through.
09 50	Ditto.	Watching Peter and Michael slide.
09 52	Ditto.	Sitting on the rocking-horse and watching some children sliding as he rocks.
09 55	Taking his shoes off.	As above.
09 58	Sliding.	Making patterns with sticky shapes.
09 59	As above.	Watching the sliding.
10 00	Pastry.	As above.
10·01	As above.	Watching the 'pastry' play.
10 05	Sliding.	Sticky shapes.
10 07	Sliding head first on his back.	Filling a cup with pastry.
10 08	Sliding standing up on the low slide.	Climbs on to the bench which is now empty of children, goes down the slide (sitting) slowly.
10 10	Rocking on the horse and watching.	Taking turns with others on the slides.
10 13	Watching others.	As above.
10 14	Building with Connector.	Walks up and down the slides whenever they are left free. Down slide sitting.
10 17	Ditto.	Connector with Tony.
10 18	Ditto.	Pulling small trolley up low slide.
10 19	Ditto.	Watching a game that is going on under the carpenter's bench.
10 20	Up and down the slides.	Sliding with Tony.

	TONY	MARK
10 21	Doing the 'village' puzzle.	Playing with the hammer-peg toy near Tony.
10 22	Sticky shapes.	Sliding again.
10 24	Rocking-horse.	Sliding.
10 25	'To toilet'.	Ditto.
10 26	'Carpentry'.	'To toilet'.
10 30	Hammering nails into bits of wood.	Walking up and *running* down the slide (very pleased!).
10 33	Ditto.	Crawling up and running down.
10 37	Ditto.	Still on slides.
10 45	Ditto.	Sliding alternately with watching other children slide.

One of the most popular activities is painting. We have two home-made double easels, consisting of two pieces of hardboard joined at the top with Tuftape and standing in a shallow box (Pl. 12). Powder paint is mixed in about eight colours in small pots that stand in a box between the easels with a long-handled brush in each pot. No washing of brushes is therefore necessary, but if a child wants a colour that is already in use he must wait until it is free or make do with another. The colours sometimes become mixed in the pots but this is more often due to the brush having picked up other colours from the paint that the child has already put on his paper than to the fact that the brush has been returned to the wrong pot. When this does happen there is usually mild consternation on the part of the offending child's painting companions and most children, even two-year-olds, soon learn.

All the children have, I think, painted at some time or other, and most of them paint every day. Painting seems to be, on the whole, an activity that is to them quite unconnected with drawing. At first it consists of rapid to-and-fro or vaguely circular movements of the brush upon the paper. Sometimes colour after colour is used until there is a brownish, formless splodge in the middle of the paper; sometimes one colour alone is used. This kind of 'painting' may go on for days, weeks or months. Then there frequently comes a stage during which the child does painstaking, carefully executed painting *of* the paper as if painting a door or a wall; the paper, however large, being eventually completely covered with paint. Often it seems to be important to the child that the paper is entirely covered in a single colour and he will retain the use of the brush and therefore of the colour of his choice in spite of protests from the other children; or, if he has to relinquish it, he will sit and wait until it is free again. Some children have a favourite colour over a period of days or weeks. I have heard of a child who did thirty blue paintings in succession.

Whether or not the 'house painting' stage has been gone through, there is sometimes a time when a child likes to keep the colours very distinct and makes separate blobs or patches of many different colours. He also becomes interested in the various kinds of mark that can be made with a brush; for instance, spots or wavy lines.

Some time before the children leave the group (one, who had already spent a year in the group, at as early an age as three and a half) they usually – but not always – begin to make carefully executed shapes and patterns. Sometimes irregularly shaped patches of colour are placed contiguously until the whole of the paper is covered; sometimes boldly contrasting and separate shapes and colours are placed with a good sense of balance on the paper. Sometimes a rough ring of one colour is made and filled in with another colour or with a few dots and dashes, and perhaps some horizontal, vertical or radiating lines are attached to it; and sometimes the resulting shape has a marked resemblance to the shape of a human face or figure, but frequently the children themselves appear not to be aware of it or are not interested enough to remark on the fact even when they are questioned as to the subject of their painting. At other times a completely amorphous mass of colour represents – they will tell you – a monkey or a motor car. The supervisor noted that one child would not say what he was painting until he had finished the picture; if questioned before, he would say, 'I don't know; it's not finished yet.'

One four-year-old painted, for about six weeks, rhythmically designed and brilliantly coloured patterns, no two the same, but all obviously inspired by the shapes of houses with their windows and other openings.

There is one thing with regard to painting that all the children have in common: they know very definitely when they have finished painting on one piece of paper and want to begin on a fresh one. Another quality that they share in common is that each has an individual style. At the end of the morning one can usually tell which painting has been done by which child, although one has not watched their execution. A child may change his style at any moment so that one can sometimes be caught out; but the children's paintings are as consistently individual as is all their activity in the group.

Record No. 4

19 May 1967. *Christopher, aged 2 years 3 months, has been in the group for four months.*

09 38 Wandering around, watching and listening. Is interested in a new child.

09 42 Playing with 'pastry' – picking bits from a big lump.

09 50 Fetches his teddy bear. Strokes his neighbour's hair. Patting the pastry.

09 55 Wants to paint but all places occupied. Joanna talks to him: 'Want to go on the slides?'

09 57 Walks up one slide and slides down the other.

09 58 Holding Teddy and watching the other children.

10 00 Painting – up and down strokes, one colour on top of another, but always putting the brush back into the right pot.

10 09 New painting.

10 10 Climbs up the slide with Teddy.

10 11 Slowly slides down and walks up again. Down slowly on his stomach. (Christopher is already skilled on the slides. He is short and sturdy in build and was a great climber at home from the moment he could move around at all. He began to become familiar with our slides some time before he joined the group at twenty-three months because he seized every opportunity to do so when he came with his mother to call for his elder sister.)

10 12 Listening to the fire-engine game going on all around him. Sitting on the top of the carpenter's bench with Teddy, watching the game. (I notice that when using the slides with other children he is careful to keep on the wall side of the bench so that there is no danger of his being pushed off it by larger children.)

10 15 Drops Teddy. Slides down. Starts to climb up the slide but someone snatches Teddy from his grasp. At my suggestion he props Teddy up on the piano.

Takes a Connector rod and pokes the 'pastry'. Picks up a small lump of pastry and sticks it on the end of the rod. Watches others drawing round cardboard geometrical shapes.

10 19 Sitting on the floor doing the big Abbatts' Farmyard jigsaw puzzle.

10 21 Still doing the puzzle with concentration and assurance, lifting the removable pieces out by the attached knob and replacing them over and over again. His movements are deft and swift.

10 30 Sitting with Philippa under the bench and behind the tool-chest and banging with a stick on the supports of the bench.

10 32 Is interested in Peter who is crying.

10 34 Pastry – patting and pulling at it.

10 35 Walks up the slide on all fours. His legs are so short in proportion to his body owing to his age that he looks completely at home and comfortable in that position. Slides down on 'tum'.

10 36 Goes upstairs to the toilet. Bumps downstairs on his bottom.

10 40 Tries to draw round the cardboard shapes, but like all the younger children finds it impossible to hold the shape still, and so soon gives up. (It is in any case not a very popular activity. But just occasionally there is an older child who finds it a very satisfying occupation and will ask for it day after day, carefully filling in the shapes he has drawn with coloured pencils.)

10 43 Watching the others playing.

10 45 Fetches the Seven-Little-Men trolley from the cupboard. Shuts the cupboard door carefully. Empties the men out. Michael says 'Can I help you?' They play together with the trolley and another toy.

10 50 Playing with the wooden train.

10 52 Defends the train from Peter. Obviously Peter had hoped that he would give it up willingly.

10 54 Makes two-storey trains by placing one truck on top of another.

'Elevenses'

In the garden

11 20 In the sand-pit.

11 24 Exploring the shed.

11 25 Watching the guinea-pig.

11 30 Wandering about.

11 31 Walking round the garden pushing a scooter.

11 32 In the shed.

Record No. 5

13 November 1967. *Dylan, aged 2 years 1 month, the youngest of a family of four. Has been in the group for half a term; his elder brother has been there longer.*

10 00 Hammering nails into wood. Great concentration. Tries to put nails back in tin and the lid on. Puts everything away with great care.

10 15 Down slide. . . . Goes to pram. Philippa takes it away from him. He is not worried. Gets on the rocking-horse.

10 20 Plays with 'pastry'. Uses the knife. Cuts small pieces carefully. Tracey tries to take the knife. Dylan won't let it go.

10 25 Plays with pegs and pegboard, watching the pastry table while he does it. Goes to cash register and puts money in it. Mark tells

him to go away, then tries to play shops with him. Dylan takes the bus puzzle. Goes back to play with Mark. Keeps trying to get the cash register for himself, but Mark won't let him.

10 30   Gives up and gets the hammer-peg toy. Carries it out to the hall. Watches Philippa and Alice playing on the stairs. Philippa pushes him away. He goes into the 'house' still carrying the hammer-peg toy.

10 40   Comes back and gets astride the rocking-horse still clutching the hammer-peg toy. Back to the pastry table. Puts the toy down on table and starts hammering it. Leaves table to go to the pram. Jennifer pushes him away. Back to the pastry. Plays with it but watches the others all the time. Puts pastry into a large hollow building block. Jennifer takes it out again and puts it back on the table.

10 50   Back to Mark with his shop. While Mark has gone off to fetch something he gets the cash register. Mark dashes back and retrieves it. Dylan gives up and goes up the slide. He sits at the top watching. Comes down to watch Tracey sawing. Up the slide again. More hammering with Eran.

Record No. 6
18 June 1967. *Tony, aged 4, in the garden.*

09 40   Playing in the sand-pit.

09 48   Climbing up to the top of the rope ladder and down again.

09 49   As above.

09 50   Playing on the plank that is hooked on to a bar of the climbing frame.

09 51   In the sand-pit digging a hole and building a smooth wall. He stops from time to time to watch and listen to the children playing on the lawn nearby.

09 59   Knocking his wall down carefully with a rake.

10 08   Playing a game of make-believe called 'monsters' which involves much sliding and jumping – with three others. (A plank has been placed from the top of a steep little bank across a grassy path. The children are sliding on and jumping from this.)

10 14   In the sand-pit again.

10 15   Playing 'Ring o' Roses' with six others. The game was initiated by Andrew.

10 23   On a scooter, pushing it over the plank bridge.

10 25   Swinging on the rope ladder.

10 28   Doing 'tricks' on the tent frame.

10 30   Having a tug-of-war with Joanna.

10 39   Trying to make knots with the rope.

10 45   'Fishing' from the apple tree with the rope.

10 49   Jumps from the tree 'into the sea'.

10 50   Up the tree again with the rope.

10 51   Dangling the rope from the tree.

One notes that Tony's morning is spent mostly in practising a variety of skills. If one watches closely one notices that, although he is engaged in a large number of different activities during the morning, he does not wander aimlessly from one thing to another. He usually seems to know as soon as he has finished one thing what he wants to do next; and he spends quite a long time on each activity. A few minutes is a long time at this age.

For instance, on 18 October (see Record 1 above) I noticed that he spent seven minutes making a pattern on the pegboard and I think he had already been doing this for a few minutes before I began to take notes. All the time, late arrivals were coming in and there was the usual noisy activity going on all around him. He then made a 'painting' to his own satisfaction which took him two minutes. From painting he moved to the slides and spent five minutes perfecting his power to balance and guide himself as he slid down, and in improving his skill at placing his feet and balancing as he ran at speed up the narrow plank and bounced down again. And then he practised the art of making the rocking-horse slide across the floor as he rocked.

One wonders why he sat in the cubby hole between two cupboards covered with wooden blocks for fully fifteen minutes. Knowing Tony, I am sure it was not out of fear or dislike of the other children. I think it very possible that he was doing it for the sake of the experience; perhaps he was savouring the sensation of being able to hear the other children without seeing them; perhaps he was curious to know how a cow feels when it is shut up in a stall. He was not sleepy or sulking, for he looked as bright-eyed and alert as usual when I peeped at him over the door.

Then he spent about five minutes doing or trying to do a rather difficult jigsaw puzzle with a short interval of building with blocks with another child. Then he practised the skill requiring precise hand-eye co-ordination of bead threading for about two minutes, and then made 'buns' with dough for twenty.

On 9 May (Record 2) he spends his time acquiring many physical or, rather, sensory-motor skills, but he also practises putting his ideas and feelings into words and co-operating in dramatic make-believe games with others. Often he combines the two, as when in the 'fire-engine' game he slides and jumps from the carpenter's bench and makes 'hoses' from Connector.

Later he leaves the 'shop' game in which he has been co-operating with others, to spend fifteen minutes practising various skills requiring precise hand-eye co-ordination and judgment. Then after a short interval he spends five minutes practising sliding down the slide in his stockinged feet – Caroline's ski-ing 'trick' – an activity requiring a high degree of sensory-motor judgment in the field of balance and movement through the air.

Out of doors he spends more than half the time in concentrated gymnastic activity of a degree of skill that a boy five years older might be proud of.

On 24 May he paints for ten minutes, plays on the slides for ten minutes with an interval of five minutes at the dough table. After watching the other children while he rocks for five minutes, he builds with Connector for six or seven. After making patterns with sticky shapes for a little, he hammers nails into wood and saws for twenty minutes.

On 18 June I noticed that he frequently but momentarily interrupted his building in the sand-pit to watch the children playing near him on the lawn and a grassy bank against which they had placed a plank as a slide; and later he joined them in a vigorous and dramatic make-believe game called 'monsters'. It was evident that Tony was aware of what the other children were doing and interested in it all the time that he was occupied in digging a hole and building a wall; yet he carried on with his building and then carefully pushed the whole length of wall down with a rake before joining in the game. This tendency to be executing some enterprise that requires sustained attention and at the same time being aware of what is going on around them is very characteristic of the children's behaviour. One is made aware of it by the remarks that they make to themselves or each other from time to time, and by the sporadic conversations that are carried on across the room.

Tony's 'fishing' from the apple tree and jumping from it 'into the sea' was a game that was at the same time make-believe and an activity that required and promoted skill in climbing, balancing, jumping, managing a rope and tying knots, and also exercised his ingenuity and ability to set himself problems and to solve them. The 'monsters' game, as I noted, involved 'much sliding and jumping' as well as running, chasing and dodging. As in the 'fire-engine' game the children were learning basic sensory-motor judgment and agility at the same time as they exercised their powers of communication by word and gesture, and learned how to co-operate harmoniously with others in a spontaneous dramatic creation. They chose to learn a diversity of skills not only consecutively but simultaneously and therefore crammed a great deal of learning into a short space of time. And yet I have known parents who, having been present at the playgroup for a whole morning, say: 'They don't learn anything there.'

Another remarkable thing that happened on the morning of 18 June was the game of Ring o' Roses that was played for five minutes. As anyone who has given a children's party for very little ones will know, it usually takes the undivided attention of at least one older person to organize a game such as this and keep a group of three- and four-year-olds playing it for five minutes; and yet the suggestion of one far from bossy four-year-old was taken up by a small group and carried out successfully for what to children of this age is quite a long period of time.

Small children usually have good powers of concentration and the extent to which this was manifested in the playgroup was most wonderful because of the potentially distracting noise and bustle all around and over them. I have a note of an outstanding example. An energetic, sociable, adventurous, merry and voluble three-and-a-quarter-year-old spent the whole of one morning before 'elevenses' – that is, at least 1¼ hours – playing with the Escor Aeroplane. The wooden aeroplane comes apart into eight pieces and is put together by means of wooden nuts and bolts. The little boy did not find it very easy and took a long time to put it together to his satisfaction, changing his mind several times about the correct position of the various pieces. He then took it apart and remade it, again taking the greatest pains to get it right.

Another example is to be found in the 'minute-to-minute records' in chapter 4. That morning Dawn built an abstract creation with Connector, altering it and improving it uninterruptedly for forty minutes. Also in Record No. 1, Michael takes twenty-five minutes of concentrated work to produce a painting.

An interesting point about Dawn's activity on this occasion is that, after forty minutes of concentrated work, she suddenly hands her work of art to Christopher who had been watching her with interest and, when it immediately falls to pieces, she is quite un-concerned. Dawn's loss of interest in her handiwork after she has finished it to her satisfaction is typical of the children. For six years no child ever wanted to take his or her 'painting' home at the end of the morning. I did not write the children's names on the paintings they had done, and destroyed them after they had gone home. Then a helper who stood in for me for a few days suggested that they might like to take them home and, by the time I returned, it had become an inviolable tradition to do so.

The reader may have noticed that Mark, who is new to the group and younger than Tony by a year and four months, changes his occupation more frequently and spends more time simply watching the other children. He is a lightly-built, quiet, shy and gentle child, but the records of his activity on 24 May show how, after only four weeks in the group, he already fits his activity into the general pattern of activity formed by all the children:

1. He watches some children using the slide and, biding his time, uses it himself the minute it is left free, and then takes turns with one or two others.

2. He joins in with the others by making himself into a 'bridge' (a very small one) at the bottom of the slide.

3. Having earlier in the morning watched others playing with gummed coloured paper and scissors, he tries it himself when there is space at the table; and the same with 'pastry'.

He spends a large proportion of his time (about forty-three minutes) on the slides, or watching others using them. This interest in activities that require and promote good physical co-ordination and judgment is typical of the healthily self-confident child during his first weeks in the group.

It is typical of most of the children most of the time when they are playing in the garden. In summery weather we spend the whole morning in the garden. Things such as jigsaws and books are placed on a rug on the lawn; the dolls and their bedding and furniture are brought out; a 'house' of some sort is usually constructed; water play is provided and tools put into the sand-pit. In spite of this opportunity for other kinds of activity, the children as a whole spend more than half the time in occupations such as climbing and 'tricks' on the two climbing frames, the apple tree and anything else that it is possible to climb, balance upon and do acrobatic 'tricks' upon, although they may be, at the same time, engaged in make-believe play.

For instance, on 18 June Tony climbs up the rope ladder and uses it as a swing, plays on the climbing frame and on a plank hooked on to it for a slide; does 'tricks' on the tent frame and climbs in the apple tree and jumps and swings from its branches. And on 9 May he spends almost all the time that he is in the garden climbing on various things and swinging from his hands on the gymnast's rings, and trying to place his feet in the rings at the same time as his hands. (The gymnast's rings had at this date not long been available to the children. Later, Tony and many others discovered how to somersault on them.)

Incidentally, Tony, like many of the children, can balance beautifully on a small scooter. I had to search quite widely before I found a really small scooter (with one wheel rather than two at the back) (Pl. 16). I now have three and they are constantly in use. I also have two very small bicycles; they are without stabilizers and are sturdily and simply made, without mudguards or, as it happens, brakes, or any unnecessary trimmings. Some three-year-olds are already fascinated by bicycles. At present a little boy of three and a quarter spends almost all his time out of doors playing either with a bicycle or a scooter. At first, the bicycle may simply be wheeled round and round the garden; then for weeks the child may practice balancing on the seat, with his legs held straight out at a wide angle on each side in order to clear the pedals, while the bicycle rolls down a slight incline and is of course carefully steered, and if necessary braked by using the feet. (Learning at this age would be impossible if the child were not able to reach the ground with both feet while sitting on the saddle. I had to have the frame of one second-hand bicycle cut down to make the saddle low enough.) Part of our garden is on a slight slope, and the children make use of this in order to learn to balance and steer without having, at the same time, to master the art of using the pedals. Pedalling is usually practised at first on the level part of the lawn. This small area must be shared with children using the two climbing frames, and probably a see-saw, and with the apple tree that is used for climbing, yet several children have learned to ride well before their fifth birthdays, quite unaided, and many more have clearly derived an enormous amount of pleasure from riding without pedalling as described above (Pl. 17).

Three out of my own five children learned to ride without any assistance at the age of four, and one before he was five and a half, but they had the advantage of being able to use the pavement outside our house, as the road was at that time comparatively quiet and traffic-free.

Learning to ride a bicycle is something that is particularly well suited to the stage of mental development of a four-year-old because it is a skill that one can only learn with one's body or, rather, to borrow Piaget's term, with the sensory-motor intelligence.

As was discovered at the Peckham Health Centre, roller-skating is also a skill that some children aged four can learn surprisingly well. We have four pairs and they are very popular but we can allow them to be used only infrequently because the only suitable surface for roller-skating is indoors where space is limited.

The Adventure Playthings Triangle Set, consisting of five 'separates' that can be combined in a variety of ways, is good. We usually use them to make a low, but perfectly adequate – and also apparently safe (the children do not even pinch their fingers between the plank and its support) – see-saw, plus a heavy but steerable trolley that can be ridden by one to three children and pushed by another, or one child can ride it alone, lying on it on his stomach and propelling himself with one foot on the ground.

The lawn in our garden slopes in a variety of ways and the steepest bank is sometimes made into a slide by laying a length of 36-in.-wide vinyl flooring on it (keeping it in position with a heavy weight at the top corners). This makes a slide that is wide enough for a child to be able to throw himself down in any position, even head-over-heels, and for two or three children to slide down at the same moment ending up in a heap, with much laughter.

Most of the indoor activities have already been described or mentioned in the records. When I ran the group single-handed and used only one room, there was not space enough to have a permanent 'mothers and fathers' corner or Home Corner. Since there have regularly been two adults present and we have used the hall as a second room, we have made a 'house' from towel horses and old curtains in a corner between the staircase and a wall. It is used daily for different make-believe games, as is also a cash register, imitation money, a telephone, old-fashioned kitchen scales and dolls.

Simple wooden jigsaw puzzles are popular; two are home-made and are unusual in being painted all over in one colour. As in the best jigsaws for young children, the outer part of the rectangle of plywood is fixed to a hardboard base forming a tray, the inner part cut into nine very distinctive and sometimes interlocking shapes. The emphasis is on the shapes. I made these because I noticed that small children pay more attention to the shape of the pieces of jigsaw and to the shape of the space into which they fit than to the 'picture' painted on the puzzle; they seem rarely to use the colours of the pieces as a guide (Pl. 20).

Among our other toys are inset shape boards, pegboards, hammer pegs, beads for threading on laces and perforated cards for pushing laces in and out of. Escor and other constructional toys, including plastic ones, and wooden trains and trucks are used every day. I have been surprised at the amount of time that large and intelligent four-year-olds will sometimes spend pushing

'Keep away. I can look after myself, thank you!' (see p. 40).

to On the left is one way to use the swing without help if the seat is too high, and (centre) this is a child, not a puppet. 'How do you get along the plank?' a visitor asked 2½-year-old Iain (right), 'Do you walk along it?' – 'No, we sit along it.'

11 With satisfaction Michael (4½) watches his friend James (3½) who has at last
learned to slide down the pole (see p. 40).

12 Four can paint at one time without occupying much precious floor space. Easels are made of two pieces of hardboard joined at the top with tape and standing in shallow boxes or trays.

13 Nicola, aged 2½, swings herself on the rope ladder.

14 Some of the children engaged in spontaneous activity of various kinds: one of the tables is usually reserved for playing with dough.

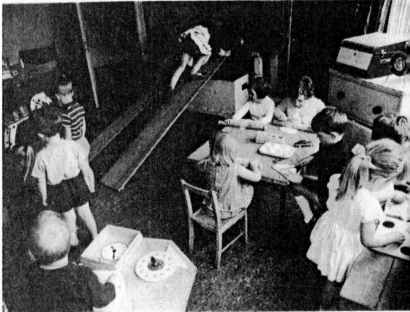

the simplest toy trains about the floor, and in loading and unloading the trucks.

The big hollow 11 in. × 11 in. × 5½ in. and 11 in. × 22 in. × 5½ in. Adventure Playthings building blocks are used during at least the first half of the morning as a set of shelves or, rather, cubby holes, in which to keep and display the jigsaws, peg boards and boxes of small constructional toys, since we have room for only two small tables and six stools. Some of the children put the things back in their cubby holes when they have finished with them. After a general clearing up at eleven the blocks are sometimes used for building, and this takes up most of the room, and certainly more space than can be spared when the 'slides' are in position. Other activities that require considerable space, such as 'dressing up' and moving to music, take place at this time of the morning; or the Adventure Playthings blocks are spread at intervals over the floor for a game of 'stepping stones'. A game of 'somersaults' or 'bridges' is sometimes demanded. There is often a request for a story towards the end of the morning and the second room is used for this so that we are not disturbed by those who prefer a noisy occupation. I find it difficult to foretell which children will enjoy stories; the type of home and background is no guide at all. It is possible that many children choose to listen because they feel in need of a rest from the hard work of learning and of constant decision-making that play in the playgroup entails. When some are listening to the story, the four pairs of rollerskates can be used in the other room.

Only some enjoy moving to music; others prefer to watch. At one time about fifteen years ago the whole group would join in enthusiastically with the BBC's 'Movement to Music'. At that time the programme was superbly directed and seemed to be as good for the under-fives as for schoolchildren. One playgroup supervisor I know tapes the programmes and selects the few that are suitable. She finds that the children like them to be repeated frequently until they know them really well.

The staircase is also used as a piece of gymnastic apparatus. There is no carpet on it; instead it is covered with vinyl flooring and the children enjoy sliding down it on their stomachs or bumping from step to step on their bottoms.

The children seem to find their morning's play very satisfying; and this is not surprising because what they are in fact engaged in doing is bringing into being their unique individual personalities and potential powers and talents. They are, firstly, spontaneously

57

being themselves and, secondly, developing the responsive and receptive relationship with the environment that will enable them to gain an awareness of things and people as they really are.

What strikes one most about the activity of the group as a whole is the individuality of each child; and also the characteristic that is common to almost all of them, of being constantly aware of the total situation. Each child goes about his own business in his own characteristic manner, but not regardless of the others and what they are doing. This is shown by the way in which a child will suddenly contribute to a conversation that is being carried on by others across the room, while apparently engrossed in his own activity, or will leave that activity like a flash for another as soon as a piece of apparatus, that he has evidently had his eye on, is vacated. But it is most vividly manifested by the fact that the children can be engaged in activities involving high-speed, spontaneous movement in a small room, without getting very much in each other's way. If they were not continually aware of the total situation from moment to moment in the room, the effect of twelve two-, three- and four-year-olds playing freely and absolutely without organization in the small space of my room, would be chaos. As it is, there is a kind of interweaving of the strands of diverse, spontaneous activity that results in a harmonious whole.

I think the fact that in bad weather the twelve children have often been confined all morning in one room has made me aware of this phenomenon. It is remarkable that, in a room 15 ft × 16 ft containing two large cupboards, a small piano, two small tables and six small chairs, small painting easels, the large carpenter's bench and the inevitable 'slides', some children will be sliding, jumping or running, some playing with constructional toys, blocks or trains on the floor, and all moving freely from one thing to another, and yet there are few collisions, obstructions of each other or squabbles. Each child moves according to his own purpose, but most of them are aware of what the other children are doing and therefore move according to the opportunity and the space available at the moment, and according to what they judge will be available in the next moment. A child takes the other children's activity into account; he shapes his purpose according to what is realistically possible. He does not, I think, say to himself: 'I must not bump into John, because if I do he will get hurt or his game will be spoiled.' Although John is right in front of him, he may not be thinking about him particularly – indeed, if he were, he might quite possibly bump into him on purpose. John and what John is doing may or may not be included in his immediate sphere of interest at that moment; but in spite of that, he is sufficiently aware of the nature of John's activity and of that of the other children in his immediate vicinity to be able to anticipate the situation during the next second or two.

In this connection, a report on experiments with rhesus monkeys made by Dr Harry Harlow and published in *Scientific American* (November 1962) is interesting. A group of monkeys were reared from birth to six months, each completely isolated in his own cage from other monkeys. For the same period another group were kept equally isolated except that each was with its own mother. Later, when they should have been old enough to fend successfully for themselves, both groups were set free on an island with some monkeys who had been reared in natural conditions. The monkeys who had been brought up with their mothers were able to find food for themselves while the first group were not, but both of the artificially reared groups of monkeys were socially quite incompetent; they were unable to mate successfully and were abnormally aggressive.

A third group were brought up with their mothers but were allowed from the first month, for a short period each day, into a playroom, fitted with gymnastic apparatus to simulate the terrain in which the young monkey would naturally play, in the company of other young monkeys. A fourth group were kept in cages, in groups of four, without their mothers from birth. They also had use of the playroom. Both the last two groups grew up to be normal in all respects, except that those who received no mothering proved to be bad mothers themselves.

Dr Harlow describes the behaviour of the young monkeys in the playroom as follows: 'They developed a . . . *complex pattern of violent activity performed with lightning speed and integrating all objects animate and inanimate in the room.*'

In the case of the children there is a much greater variety of activity and less speed of movement, but in both cases (as was observed to happen in the gymnasium at the Peckham Health Centre) the entirely spontaneous movement of several individuals results in an integrated whole.

Perhaps opportunity for the acquisition of this kind of sensory-motor judgment and for spontaneous activity in mutual awareness is as necessary for the future mental health of human children as it is for that of young monkeys.

We can be quite certain, however, of one thing: we are not fostering egotism in a child if we make it possible for him to be himself in a group of others who are also being themselves. On the contrary, we are enabling him to exercise his capacity to be aware of and responsive to the activity of the others and, while following his own purpose, to fit his activity into the whole that is composed of the activity of all the other individuals.

On the other hand, if we were to control the activity of the children or direct them to activities of our choice or constantly stimulate them and distract their attention, we would prevent this from happening. We would be preventing them from being themselves and from exercising their ability to be aware of others' purposes and needs – from learning the technique of altruism. The will to be altruistic is another matter; but what good does it do to want to serve and help people if one is incapable of being aware of their needs and desires?

Admittedly the altruism displayed by these children is mainly in a limited sphere of experience and response. This comprises the position and movement of objects and bodies, including their own, in space and time. It does not, in the case of most two- and three-year-olds, extend to other activities, even to other physical ones. For instance, I remember that for a few months, between the ages of three and three and a half, one very intelligent, sociable, peaceable and happy, and hitherto gentle, little boy, worried his mother and me by his habit of occasionally biting another child really hard. During this period he said to me one day in the garden as he sat on the swing, apropos of nothing and just as a matter of fact: 'I got strong teeth. I can bite hard.' I believe that he did not yet fully appreciate that it hurts to be bitten.

I heard of one mother who was at her wits' end to know what to do to prevent two of her daughters from being seriously wounded by the biting of the third. She steeled herself, and herself bit the offending child hard enough to hurt her on a single occasion as soon as the latter had bitten one of her sisters. And it worked: this action achieved what scolding and verbal explanation had failed to do. To express righteous indignation and distress does not help the child who is ignorant of the effects of his actions on others. It may, in fact, by making him puzzled and upset, postpone his learning.

It would hardly be possible for a playgroup supervisor to help a child to understand by biting him. And the problem of the child who bites may not infrequently occur in a free-choice playgroup where the children feel unrestrained by the opinions and wishes of their elders.

My friend Pat Thurston had a little girl of three and a half in her playgroup, who was extremely energetic and capable; although very petite in build, she was effectively aggressive towards the other children if they stood in her way. At the time she first joined the group she would frequently bite another child in order to get her way. Pat was forced to concentrate on watching this child, leaving her assistants to attend to the other chores and to watch the group as a whole. She tried time after time, without being angry with the little girl, to make her understand that biting another child was painful to that child, and was something that the children in the playgroup did not do to each other. Several weeks passed and Pat had almost despaired. In fact the thought had crossed her mind to tell the parents that their daughter was too young for a playgroup (which in every other respect she patently was not). Suddenly the child's behaviour changed; she stopped biting and moreover became able to enjoy herself and satisfy her very healthy appetite for activity without clashes with the other children. But on two occasions during the period when Pat had been trying to stop the biting, she had noticed that immediately after an attempt had been made to explain to the child that biting was painful, she had bitten herself. It may have been that she was, after all, interested in Pat's attempts to explain, and wanted to find out what it was like to be bitten.

In contrast to this, I remember witnessing a most helpful and considerate action by a little boy of only twenty-five months. Dylan had been in the group for two months. He never spoke to himself or anyone else, but quietly got on with a variety of activities on his own, moving purposefully from one thing to another, but very sensibly giving way to the others when necessary, since they were so much bigger than he. Then one day a mother-helper brought her daughter Carolyn, aged twenty-one months. Dylan, being un-used to children younger than himself, found Carolyn fascinating and followed her about. At one point, Carolyn, having no shoes on at the time, decided to go into the hall and put on her wellington boots. She stood in the middle of the room and by luck got one foot into a boot, but could not succeed with the other. Dylan had followed her into the hall and had been watching her efforts, and he now came and stood close by her and bent over, presenting his shoulder for her to lean on. I do not know whether Carolyn would have taken advantage of his silent offer because Dylan's brother, aged four and a half, came up and said: 'I'll do it, Dylan,' and held Carolyn up while she put on the other boot.

Later, however, when Carolyn came regularly to the group, we noticed many battles of wills between her and Dylan. They re-mained the youngest in the group for some time. Carolyn had not yet learned that patience is often the best policy and often tried to take things away from Dylan; while Dylan – although, being the youngest of four, he had learned the wisdom of giving in when his desires clashed with those of older children – was not going to give way to someone considerably smaller and younger than himself, and he stubbornly and silently resisted her, however much fuss she made.

I think that Dylan's ability to anticipate Carolyn's needs when she was trying to stand on one foot and get the other into her boot, was due to the fact that he knew very well how it feels to try to balance in a variety of situations, probably including this very same one, for like all children of his age, one of his chief interests was – and had been for many months – learning the art of balance.

Regarding the marked individuality of the children's behaviour, they are, as we have seen, stimulated by each other and often learn from each other, but rarely imitate each other *exactly*. Everything a child does has an individual flavour: new games and 'tricks' are continually being invented by individuals and are sometimes taken up by others, in which case they may become established as traditional, but are always liable to elaboration or adaptation.

They also appear to expect the other children to be originals. The older children are very conscious of each other as personalities: although a new child is never formally introduced to the group, his name is very soon generally known and a child will often remark on the absence of another child before the supervisor has noticed it herself – if she has not marked up the register. Yet the children do not comment upon the strangest and most eccentric behaviour, or appear to be distracted by it, unless it interferes with their own or others' activity. At one time we had a child in the group who liked to fill a small box with miscellaneous objects and to spend much of his time walking around with it in his hands, humming or talking to himself. At another time there was a child who, from time to time, spilled the whole box of small building blocks onto the floor and lay among them thrashing with his legs, and who never spoke intelligibly, but occasionally emitted a baboon-like shriek. None of the other children appeared to find this behaviour at all remarkable; the supervisor was the only person who was surprised or worried by it. I suppose that, because all life is new and strange to children of this age, and they have practically no habits or conventions against which to measure things, they are almost unshockable. (In the same way most children take the fact that a child is physically handicapped for granted, as well as the fact that different children may have quite different-coloured skins.)

Another general characteristic of the children is that they know definitely what they want to do from moment to moment, even if it is to do nothing.

The fact that one very rarely, if ever, sees that blank and absent look on the faces of the children that is common in a certain regimented type of nursery or infant school, does not mean that every child is continuously busy and physically occupied. Some children, particularly new ones, spend much of the time watching the others. But they are not doing nothing. Watching is an important *activity*; the child's need to watch should be respected and he should *not* be distracted from his absorption in watching the others, or 'stimulated'. Some children are extremely interested in other children and their doings; some like to see others do things before they try to do them themselves; they like to ponder and consider what they will do before they do it, and I sometimes wonder if these children learn more quickly than those who rush in and therefore begin by making a lot of mistakes. The reason for this may be that in the latter case the wrong actions have to be subsequently unlearned (Pls. 24, 25).

On the other hand, the incessantly active child can also learn well. One little boy who was with us for over a year and a half, seemed to move and shout all morning without a moment's pause. He was an only child and, luckily for him, his parents possessed a true sense of humour and were amazingly patient and understanding. His physical energy seemed inexhaustible, but he was also mentally active and very interested in language, and his ability developed enormously in every way during the time he was in the group. At that time the group consisted largely of boys, and Mark's noisy enthusiasm was catching. The noise was often deafening; and it was fortunate that there were no children in the group at this time who found noise upsetting, and that I have a good 'head' for noise when I do not have to concentrate on anything.

I remember an outstanding example of the physically *in*active child. A certain little girl was so silent and unresponsive that we were a little worried. However, we left her alone; there was nothing else to be done since, when one spoke to her or even looked at her, she turned away and hung her head. Her elder brother had been in the group for some time when her mother began to leave her as well, so that she was already familiar with the playgroup. But in spite of this she sometimes demanded to be taken home again immediately. More and more often she was willing to stay – and yet she did nothing all morning but watch the other children. Then very gradually she began to occupy herself a little, but still she played on her own and seemed to be trying to avoid drawing attention to herself. We noticed, however, that what little she did, she did with great care and with surprising skill considering how little she had practised. She still rarely spoke to anyone, although at home, we were told, she was quite a chatterbox and also rather mischievous. One day, when she and two other children were washing their hands together, I overheard a child say to her: 'Why don't you talk? Can't you?' Then almost suddenly, it seemed, she became really lively; her gymnastic exploits and her paintings were outstandingly good, the latter brightly coloured, well balanced and well observed. By the time she left the group to go to school she had become one of the leading lights of the group – that is to say, an inventor and initiator of 'tricks' and make-believe games.

This little girl possessed, I believe, a very strong will, a potentially powerful brain and artistic talent. But there was a danger that these tools might never be fully and effectively used, or might be misdirected because of the difficulty that she had in learning how to interact with others happily and successfully. Perhaps it will always take her a long time to become sufficiently at home with new people and in new situations to come out of herself. But I think the fact that she eventually succeeded in doing so in the playgroup, of her own volition, will have made it easier for her to do so in future.

In the end the other children gained from her inventiveness and originality. Some children take much longer than others to begin to make a positive contribution to the total activity of the group, but it sometimes happens that the slow starter who, for weeks – or even occasionally (as in the above case) for months on end – stands and stares for much of the time, turns out to be exceptionally original and creative towards the end of his time in the group.

One mother removed her little boy from our group after a few months and sent him to a group in which the children were organized, stimulated by the adults and entertained. She told us that she was of the opinion that in our group her son 'felt lost'. Personally I think she was mistaken as to the reason for the little boy's frequent and lengthy pauses for thoughtful consideration of the activities of the other children. He was, I feel sure, an exceptionally thoughtful child and the manifold activity going on all around provided him with plenty of food for thought. He was not

15 The narrow handlebars of this small bicycle made it unnecessarily difficult to learn to ride, but Bill made it before he was 5.

16 Joanna is concentrating on balancing on the scooter as it rolls down the slight incline.

17 Although Mike has not yet learnt to ride, he propels himself down this slight slope at record speed; Debbie follows a little more cautiously.

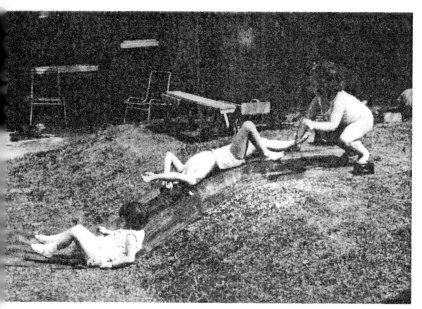

8 Three at a time go down the length of vinyl floor covering on the bank.

9 Polly and a friend arrive at the bottom of the bank slide together.

20 The home-made jigsaws (see p. 58).

21 This pivoting 'Aunt Sally' was constructed for another playgroup by a father.

22 More 'tricks'.

23 Christopher
knows more than
one way of getting
on to the slide from
the tent frame.

24 Watching. Diana looks funny upside down.

25 Is it Dawn's activity that intrigues Peter, or is it the phenomenon of h shadow?

26 Lucy's first day at the seaside, aged 14½ months (see p. 153).

27 Lucy, two months later, on her second visit to the seaside.

28, 29 Billy, aged 10, beginning and finishing a climb in the park before he was informed that tree-climbing was not allowed (see p. 218).

one of those children who are inhibited by fear; on the contrary, he was a determined character who knew very well what he wanted to do and he was enjoying the mental activity.

In the playgroup there is a simultaneous and continuous two-way action of the child on the environment and the environment on the child; the environment providing the nourishment and the child choosing what he will pay attention to and what he will – through his activity – digest. The product of this digestive process is new and original because it is specific to the unique personality of the child. Therefore, each child's activity is adding to the newness and the diversity in the environment; each child contributes to the total amount of nourishment available to all.

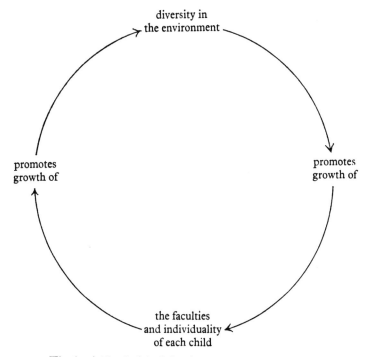

diversity in
the environment

promotes
growth of

promotes
growth of

the faculties
and individuality
of each child

The 'amiable circle' of development in the playgroup

In a *free-choice* playgroup nothing spoils this two-way action or flow, this mutual growth of child and environment. No organizing child-minder, be he adult or older child, comes between the child and the environment that the other children are creating.

For the above reasons there is a minimum useful size for a playgroup. I would put it at ten children.

By now it must be apparent that the children in a free-choice playgroup such as mine are learning. In later chapters I shall describe in detail what it is that they are learning. It falls mainly under two headings – sensory-motor judgment and skills, and social judgment and skills. But the most important thing of all that they are learning is the faculty to be members of a harmoniously active group while, at the same time, retaining and developing their individuality and integrity. Each child is realizing his potentiality. He is engaged in becoming as much of a lively, spontaneous, receptive, responsive, characterful, effectively intelligent and creative person as he has it in him to be.

In present-day living conditions, adults have to plan and provide a setting where this can happen – and then stand back. As we have seen, a group of healthy, aware and self-confident children create between them a rich and functionally nourishing environment. The organizers of the group and the people appointed to supervise the children provide the foundations – that is, the equipment and apparatus for learning – and they maintain the free atmosphere, but the children build on this.

A single child, provided with the same material opportunities – the slides, the climbing frame, the paints etc. – would make very much less use of them. In this situation a child possessing a fertile imagination, and who was in the habit of making do with his own company, might invent games to satisfy himself for a considerable time, but the environment would be a dead and sterile one compared with the ever-changing and developing one that I have described. The 'amiable circle' of development would not operate; the complete educative experience would be lacking.

In the case of a group of only two or three children using the premises (as also in the case of an organized and 'directed' playgroup), there would be no continuously changing scene to which to accommodate himself, no large chunk of reality to get his teeth into, and therefore less opportunity to exercise choice. Indeed the activity of choosing might be a very unsatisfying one, since his environment would be far less likely to afford him the particular opportunity for the nourishment of his faculties that, at a particular moment, he needed.

We know the range of activities needed by children of this age, but we do not know exactly what each child needs to do at any particular moment. No one but he himself knows which are the pieces of nourishment he is capable of digesting. And if we did know what he needed to do, we would not direct him to do it, because choosing is part of this educative experience. To be precise, 'choosing' is not entirely the right word to use if it implies weighing one thing against another. What happens is something more spontaneous: if the nourishment which any of the 'growing points' of his body-of-knowledge needs is present in his environ- ment, he will recognize it, respond to it and digest it.

In a free-choice playgroup, the children have the opportunity to digest their experience because the environment: (*a*) offers a variety of appropriate nourishment; (*b*) is familiar; and (*c*) allows them the freedom to select, as and when it suits them, the nourish- ment that their faculties need. A properly equipped and planned free-choice playgroup is a place in which what the children want to do is also what they need to do.

The casual visitor to the playgroup may not easily become aware of the 'amiable circle' of development that is in operation before his eyes, each child adding his individual and original con- tribution to the environment and also taking from the environ- ment created by all, the particular educational nourishment he needs. He may not even notice the dynamic order that prevails, apparently in spite of, but in reality *because of* the real freedom and spontaneity of the children. Instead, he is likely to notice any excep- tions to the rule that there may be, such as the occasional child who is a slave to compulsive habits and who is therefore more or less blind and deaf to his surroundings. Or there may be a child in the group who has joined the group too late and had insufficient opportunity to be a spontaneous self-governing individual, and whose behaviour is therefore, for the time being at least, neither consistently spontaneous nor purposeful. Or there may be a child who has been upset and put out of gear on that particular morning, by some effect of his home circumstances. The behaviour of such children would jar, and would stick out from the harmoniously dynamic group and attract the attention of the observer.

The behaviour of the majority of the children is healthy and, as Scott Williamson and Pearse say in *Science, Synthesis and Sanity*, one of the main characteristics of healthy activity is that 'it is so natural, so easy, that it goes unnoticed'.

CHAPTER FOUR

Some Minute-to-minute Records of Children's Play in a Pre-School Playgroup during the Summer of 1968

This chapter is in the nature of a series of illustrations of the text of the book. If read straight through it will give a realistic impression of the kind of activity and social intercourse that takes place every day in the playgroup. However, the recordings give the reader no opportunity to appraise the quality of the children's movements. Only a film could do that.

My method of recording was to focus on one child for a whole morning, following him about closely enough to be able to overhear most of his conversation. I tried to describe his behaviour and activity from moment to moment and his interactions with the other children. I also devoted as much time as the speed of my scribbled longhand allowed to recording what was going on in his vicinity.

These records are not edited at all, nor are they chosen to illustrate any particular point, nor as being the most full of incident out of a number. In fact, they are the only records of the kind that I made. I was selective only in choosing the children upon whom to focus. In fact, at this time any of the children in the group would have been equally interesting, if some perhaps a little less active or talkative. Certainly a record of the activity of any of them would have demonstrated that each is constantly learning.

Very occasionally since the formation of the group there has been a child in it who did not learn. His activity may have had for him a healing effect, but as long as he was compulsively working off his feeling of frustration or trying to compensate for his feelings of inferiority, failure, incompetence or impotence, he was closed to the greatest part of his environment and therefore not learning; there was no pregnant interaction between him and the other children or between him and his material environment. The behaviour of these particular children would have been quite untypical of the group. Luckily there were no such children in the group at the time these records were made.

I had previously been trying for many months to record the activity of the children, but in a manner that proved to be useless.

However, my time had by no means been wasted because the children had become accustomed to my scribbling, with the result that they were not inhibited by it nor in the least self-conscious. They were even no longer curious to know what I was doing. Mrs Audrey Boyle had been helping me for some time, and for several weeks before starting the new method of recording I left her in charge of the children and absented myself altogether. As a result the children had become accustomed to going to her for assistance. This meant that I was able to concentrate entirely on taking notes and was hardly ever obliged to interrupt myself.

Record No. 1
27 March 1968. *The activity of Michael, aged 4 years 4 months. A member of the group for four terms.*

09 35 At the 'pastry' (dough) table. Rolls a big lump of pastry a little with the rolling pin. Shoves two biscuit-cutting shapes into dough, banging them in hard with rolling pin. Pulls them out, pastry and all. Movements very quick and deft.
Repeats the process with the rest of the dough.
Singing to himself and talking about what he is doing. James is watching him.
Makes a 'path' with his dough and follows it with his finger – 'Bou-u-m-m-m bong'.
Telling James what he is doing.
James banging with rolling pin.
James 'helps' him.
Michael: 'Don't break my shape. Now-now.' He speaks quietly and gently.
Together they squeeze a big lump of pastry.
Michael: 'Get it all out.' They empty the shapes, pushing out the pastry with their thumbs, and squeeze it all up together. Between them they take out several shapes full of pastry and a hole right through to the table appears in the lump of dough.
Michael: 'There is a big hole in pastry.'
James puts a knob of dough in the middle of the hole.
Michael: 'Put in the boat.' Then he puts shapes filled with dough round the edge of the table: 'This is a train.'

09 45 Michael: 'Let's get all the pastry out.' They push the pastry out of the shapes with gusto.
James: 'Bang-bang-bang.'
Michael: 'Stop.' All the pastry is collected into a lump.
Michael bangs and rolls it out very expertly and quickly.
Michael (singing): 'One shape for me.'
Dawn: 'Come and play in the house.'

Michael: 'Yes, but first I'll get all these out.'
Philippa: 'You like *me* best, don't you?' (to Michael). No reply.
Dawn (to Michael): 'Will you come and be *my* friend – not Philippa's – be Daddy.' No reply.
Michael collects all the pastry in a ball and hands it to James.
Says: 'Want to wipe my hands.' Wipes his hands very thoroughly.

09 52 Goes over to the house and watches the girls playing in and out of it. (They are now 'tigers'.) Returns and climbs up the slide onto the bench. Jumps off the bench: 'I jumped down.' Makes a fighting attitude to a 'tiger'. Pushes her gently but firmly backwards.

09 53 Then retires behind the tool-chest and under the bench making 'sssss-ing' noises. Shouts: 'Please don't get me' several times, quite seriously.

09 57 Is still there making 'sssss-ing' noises from time to time.

09 58 Up low slide on feet. Lies down face first at the top of high slide, hooking his feet over the top edge of slide. 'I can't go.' Dawn unhooks his feet and he slides down.

09 59 Repeats the sequence. Philippa unhooks his feet this time. Up again. Two boys slide down while Michael waits at top. One lies still at the bottom on his back.
Michael: 'He's dead.'
When the boy has moved he slides down very fast with his hands on the slide in front of him.
Repeats.
Up again. Throws himself down the slide as fast as possible, saying: 'You won't catch me.'
Up again, but stops himself halfway down by holding on to the sides of the slide with his hands. 'I can't go. I'm going slowly.'

10 01 Walks up low slide but Susan is sitting halfway up the slide.
Susan: 'You go round. I'm going down.'
Michael: 'I'm going up.'
Susan: 'Look, there is a chair there.'
Michael: 'I'm going up.'
In the end gets off and goes round her, climbing up by means of the chair on to the bench. Slides down high slide.
Up low slide. This time getting on to low slide in front of (above) Susan, who is still sitting there. At the top of slide stops and says: 'Now I'll slide down.' And slides on feet and hands on top of her.
Quickly up again and down high slide.
Jumps up and down singing: 'Round and round and roundy, up I go again.'
Up and down slide again. 'I shot you down,' as he ran into the child in front on the slide and made him descend faster.
Michael: 'Hello, hello,' to Peter.
Up again.
Gets into a tangle with two others who are sliding.
Michael: 'I get doggy.' Goes into the hall.
Comes back: 'I got him.'

10 06   Goes over to painting easels. To James: 'I'm going to paint – red spots.'
Michael: 'Now I'm painting.' Quiet while he makes a red shape. 'Look, I'm making . . .'
'Come and look, I'm making', as he paints with green paint on side of red patch.
'I wet myself.' Has to have pants removed and clean ones lent, and goes upstairs to toilet.

10 12   Returns. 'I'm going to paint.'
Paints a red patch adjoining the green.
Takes blue: 'Mixed it, mixed it.' Makes blue spot in middle of red patch.
'Going to have white now.'
'That's white. Want to wipe hands.' Wipes blue paint off hands. Adds green bit to the top of his patchwork pattern.
His 'painting' grows outward; each patch of colour is carefully made contiguous to a part of the main shape.

10 15   'Get some more colour.' Still using green. Stops to watch the children on the slide. Continues along the top of the paper, painting all round the peg very thoroughly.
'Look what I'm doing.'
Doesn't mind if no one answers.

10 20   He is alone at the easels. The others have finished their paintings. Blue paint now at the top of the shape, and in the right hand bottom corner.
Then green.
'Green paint's finished.' Takes the blue brush and puts on some more blue paint.

10 24   Using new green paint. 'More green' (to me). 'I was looking for this colour.' Paints a big green patch adjoining the blue and down the top left side.
Still using green. Three other children painting.

10 27   Blue line in the shape of an inverted 'V'.
Fills in blue 'V' with green.
Fills in corner of paper, holding corner of paper with left hand to make sure that every bit of the paper is covered.
Fills in lower part of 'V' shape with black and round the peg. (The whole paper is covered with colour now.)
Removes peg and is helped to remove wet limp paper from board. (The result is quite a pleasant pattern.)
'Want to write my name now.'
I: 'There is no room on it.'
Michael (with a big smile): I'll have to write my name on the back.'
I: 'Yes, when it's dry.'

10 34   Michael goes over to the shelves and takes out the Abbatt 'Horse' jigsaw puzzle. He has often done this puzzle before. (It is not easy – twenty-four pieces.)
Empties the tray on the floor. Then puts all the pieces the right

way up on the floor. (This is unusually methodical for a child of this age.) Builds the puzzle from the bottom and the top edges. Working silently and very concentratedly.

Dawn has made a necklace of plasticine (a thing that no one has previously thought of doing, to my knowledge) and has fixed it round the neck of another child.

Two children are doing 'carpentry' and two others are watching. One (Christopher, aged 3 years 2 months) is sawing (supervisor watching him.

10 40   Michael still doing the puzzle. Sometimes tries several wrong pieces before finding the right one. Towards the end chooses the right piece at once.

Michael: 'One piece not there.' He finds it. Follows the outline of the horse slowly with his forefinger.

Empties the puzzle on to the floor again. Begins to remake it, but leaves it and goes up to the supervisor. Another child immediately takes it over.

10 44   Michael (to supervisor): 'I want hammer nails.'

Michael stands at the table hammering a nail into a piece of wood. Looks in the box for more wood. Finds broken hammer: 'Can't hammer with this one. . . . I found a saw.'

10 46   Standing watching Christopher sawing. When Christopher has finished Michael puts a bit of wood into the vice. As he does up the vice he counts: 'One, two, three, six.'

10 51   Michael sawing.

10 52   To Dawn (who is waiting her turn to saw): 'Can you help me?'

Dawn saws, Michael watching.

Michael (to Dawn): 'It takes a long time

10 55   Dawn sawing and telling Michael how it should be done. James watching too. Michael interested in another piece of (grown-up) carpentry equipment that stands on the bench: 'It goes up and down. It's not sharp here.'

10 59   Dawn still sawing rather effectively. Michael watching. Says something in her ear and smiles.

Dawn: 'Now you do it. Tip the saw this way.'

Michael saws for half a minute.

Dawn: 'Now me.' She takes over again and Michael stands behind her again, watching her and the other children.

Michael looking at the morning's paintings that are hanging from clips on the wall beside him, lifting them up by the corners to see the one underneath.

Dawn lets him have a short turn, but he prefers to let her work while he watches.

Michael: 'Where's my painting?'

11 05   Michael: 'Drink time' (as the supervisor brings in the tray).

Dawn: 'We don't want to tidy up, do we?' She then starts to wipe the tables. Michael watches a child doing a puzzle.

11 07   'Elevenses'

11.15   Michael (dancing around and jumping with both feet together and singing): 'Humpty dumpty biscuit. Humpty dumpty biscuit.'
James comes up to him: 'Where's your home?'
Michael hesitates, then says: 'South Croydon,' putting both arms round James' neck.
Michael: 'Let's play Little Red Riding Hood.'
James: 'I'm Hood – Lickle Red.'
Michael: 'I'll be your grandmother. Look at that wolf.'
Michael: 'I'm a wolf.'
James: 'We are both wolves.'
Feint fighting. Chasing each other and wrestling and laughing.
Michael: 'Did I kill you?'
Chasing up on to the bench via the tool-chest and jumping down.
James: 'I'm winning.'
Michael: 'No, you're not.'
James: 'I'm the wolf.'

11 24   Still chasing and playing.
James (to supervisor): 'We're the referee.'

Outside

11 27   Michael up the climbing frame. Hanging inside by the top bar. Balancing on second to top bar without holding on with his hands. 'I'm going to climb out of the window.' Climbs through to outside of frame and down.

11 31   Asks supervisor to put plank (slide) across from one frame to the other.
Walks across plank to small frame. Swings from the top bar of small frame. Drops to the ground: 'Now I'm down.'
Swings on swing seat on stomach.
Then climbs up onto the seat, stands up and asks, 'Can you push me?'
No response from me. Goes back to climbing frame.

11 34   The plank is now a platform on the big frame. Michael stands on it. 'Look, I can go down the pole.' Puts both hands on the pole. Puts weight on to hands, curls leg round pole and slides to the ground.
Dawn does the same.
Michael again.
Dawn: 'Watch me, Mrs Stallibrass – I can hang.'
Hangs by hands from two of the top bars across the corner, swinging her legs.

11 38   Dawn and Michael climb up to platform and slide down the pole several times.
They are both on the platform when Dawn says suddenly and fiercely: 'Get *down*, Michael. Down at *once*.'
Michael: 'Why?'
Dawn: ''Cos I *say* so.' Sings to herself several times, 'You're not so big as me.'

11 40   Peter climbs up the frame. Michael climbs down and goes to the trolley that Peter has left.

Peter (sternly and loudly): 'Don't touch that.'
Michael: 'All *right*' (fiercely) and leaves it. Climbs up frame and stands on platform beside Peter, looking down at the trolley. Peter is looking the other way.
Michael: '*Look*, Peter.' James has taken the trolley. Peter descends hurriedly and with determination. James leaves the trolley and goes to supervisor, complaining that Peter won't let him play with the trolley. She says: 'Perhaps you can use it with him.'
Peter (in a lordly way): 'You can have it.'
Peter back to climbing frame with Michael and Dawn.
All three: 'We're magic, we're magic.'

11 49   Still climbing.

11 50   Michael: 'Let's play another game,' and goes off, but returns to frame.
Sits on the top bar and watches the others.

11 55   Michael and Dawn climbing apple tree.

11 56   Sitting in a fork of tree watching the other children playing. Gets down and climbs up again. Sits in the fork again – 'Look at me.' Climbs to the other side of the tree. Grasps branch and swings out from the tree. Hangs there a little, draws himself up and drops to the ground, landing neatly.
Michael: 'Watch me do it again.' Repeats the sequence.

12 00   Spies a bucket lying on the grass. Fetches it and goes to the sand-pit.
Plays alone in the sand-pit.

Dawn is 4 years 6 months. Has been in the group two terms. Oldest and biggest in the group. James is 3 years 4 months. Two terms in group. Very big for his age. Is quite a lot taller than Michael, though a year younger. Peter is 3 years 9 months. Three terms in the group.

Record No. 2.
28 March 1968. *The activity of Tracey, aged 3 years 5 months. A member of the group for ten weeks.*

09 35   Watching Peter and Susan who are playing with small toys on the slides.
Talks to Philippa about hair styles. (I cannot hear exactly what they are saying.)

09 40   Playing the piano with Philippa and Michael and looking around. Then watching the paint being mixed and talking to Jennifer.
Tracey: 'What's the matter, Jennifer?'
Jennifer just smiles and smiles.
Tracey: 'Put your teeth *in*, Jennifer.'

09 45   Kneeling at the bottom of the slide with Dawn.
Dawn: 'I don't like her' (indicating Jennifer). 'Do you like her?'

82

Tracey: 'Yes.' Gets up and goes up to Jennifer. 'You don't like Dawn, do you?'

Tracey (going back to Dawn): 'Jennifer doesn't like you. *See!*'

Tracey goes up to Philippa and pats her gently. Then she sees Christopher's mother leaving with the baby in the pram, and waves to her.

09 47 Playing with the toy money with Philippa: 'I like some pennies and a shilling.' Philippa ladles out pennies.

Tracey: 'All these pennies!'

They are playing at the window and Tracey is looking at something outside.

09 49 Philippa gets down and Tracey jumps down from the large stool on which they were standing. Tracey asks the supervisor if she may paint but all the easels are occupied.

Dawn and Peter are being 'lions' on and around the slides and 'roaring'.

Tracey stands by the slide as Dawn comes slowly down, opens her mouth as wide as she can and then slowly bends down and presses her open mouth against Dawn's well-clad back. Tracey climbs up on to the bench and on all fours with mouth wide open goes: 'Hagh-hagh,' and moves her head up and down and from side to side. She is also watching the children painting.

Philippa: 'We are lions, aren't we?'

Tracey: 'I'm a mice.'

Philippa: 'You be lions and I'll be doggy.'

Tracey: 'Yes.'

Tracey goes to the rocking-horse and rocks it with her hands. Then back on to the bench. Slides down the high slide, fast. Philippa has smacked Jennifer. Tracey gives Jennifer's back a very gentle little smack.

Tracey: 'Peter, you be doggy and I'll be pig.'

Tracey up the slide yapping and down very fast. Now on all fours, yapping.

10 00 Tracey joins Jennifer at the dough table. She presses a biscuit-cutting shape into her dough while she watches the other children. Asks supervisor for a knife. Is given an old table knife. Digs out the 'cake' she has made with the shape, using the knife. Presses another shape in so that she cuts out a 'cake' and lifts it out with the knife. Presses the cakes back into the hole in the dough.

10 04 Presses another shape into the dough and takes out the cake with the knife. Presses the dough back again and fills up the hollow in her dough with small bits of dough which she picks up from the edge. Sits watching the children who are painting.

Sits watching Jennifer who is busily rolling out her dough and swiftly cutting off bits with the knife and piling them into cake tins.

Tracey wants the knife. Jennifer won't let her have it.

Tracey tells the supervisor that Jennifer won't let her have the knife. The supervisor tells her that she can have it when Jennifer has finished with it.

83

10 09   Tracey rolls out her pastry and presses several shapes into it. She has made a big hole in her pastry and tries to make the hole join up, then squeezes it all up together, rolls it out and cuts out more cakes.

Jennifer gives her the cake tin of pastry and goes over to the slides.

Tracey takes the knife and digs out her cakes. Presses them back in. Takes handfuls of dough and squeezes it.

To supervisor: 'Mrs Boyle, can I do painting?'

Supervisor: 'Yes, there is room now.'

Tracey takes the brown paint brush and pushes it around on the paper quite carefully. Then green paint in all directions. Tracey watches Christopher painting.

She puts pink paint on top of the green.

Then blue paint.

10 15   Then rather dry black, watching and listening to the others in the room. Then brown paint and then yellow, making most of the paint already on her paper into a grey splodge. She carefully paints the corners of her paper yellow.

Tracey: 'Mrs Boyle, I have finished.'

Supervisor: 'Those are nice colours.'

Tracey: 'I don't know what to call it.'

Supervisor: 'You don't know what to call it?' She smiles, 'What is it?'

Tracey: 'A television.'

Wipes her hands thoroughly.

Watches Michael who is trying to thread beads. Dawn is threading beads very fast. Michael is worried: 'I can't win, I can't win.' Goes to supervisor for help.

Dawn (to James): 'If you win, you can be my friend.'

Tracey goes to get a handkerchief.

10 25   Tracey threading beads.

Kevin is pushing the beads around in the box and letting them fall through his fingers.

Dawn is on her fourth necklace.

Peter comes for beads for Michael's necklace. Michael has retired to the hall to do his and Peter is helping him.

10 31   Tracey is threading quietly. 'I got all the mauve ones.' She has to find the beads that have fallen on the floor, as the box is empty.

Michael comes back with his necklace finished, from the hall.

Michael: 'I'm the winner, I'm the winner.'

All the others have gone and Tracey is left alone to finish hers.

Dawn and James have hung their necklaces round the supervisor's neck.

10 38   Tracey puts the last bead onto the thread and gives it the supervisor to tie into a ring and to add it to the others round her neck.

Tracey goes up slide and down.

Tracey pinches Jennifer's leg because Jennifer has kicked Philippa, and says: 'You mustn't kick.'

84

10 40   Jennifer is bouncing on the low slide.
Tracey (from the top of the bench): 'Jennifer can bounce while we are up here.'
Tracey talking to Philippa on the bench.

10 43   Tracey lies on her stomach, head downwards, at the top of the high slide, with her trunk on the slide and her legs on the bench.
Tracey: 'I'm stucked. I'm stucked. Mrs Boyle, I'm stucked.'
Supervisor: 'How are you stuck? By your knees?'

10 45   Tracey climbs down from bench. Goes into the 'house' with others. They are all animals of some sort, rushing in and out with great excitement.
Philippa is afraid to go in. She peeps through the banisters.
Tracey: 'Come in, come in.' Philippa goes in.
James sticks his head out of the house. (The house is an arrangement of rugs and towel horses in a corner between a wall and the banisters.)
James: 'I'm a good man.' Makes a gun with his fist: 'Pow . . . pow.'
Peter fetches some bits of Connector and makes a very realistic gun. Puts his back to the wall and threatens: 'Piow . . . piow. Don't come near.'
Dawn gets a crack on the head with a Connector stick.
There are heaps of children inside the house. They come out: 'We're robots.'
Meanwhile, Christopher is painting all by himself and talking to himself inaudibly.

10 55   Tracey walks up low slide. Jennifer slides down into her and she falls off. Picks herself up and goes to the house.
Tracey: 'Can I come in?'
'No,' from inside. Tracey goes in.
James is lying on the floor outside the house: 'I'm dead.'
Peter: 'I'll kill you.'
James: 'No, don't kill me,' quite calmly, getting up.
Tracey hugging a doll and watching.

10 59   Some children are tidying up.
Tracey watches them. Puts shapes into their box. Puts it in the drawer. Watches others.

11 05   'Elevenses'

Outside

11 23   Tracey holds a scooter and watches Michael on the swing.

11 27   As she comes near the swing, James leaves it; she drops her scooter and runs for the swing, grabs it and climbs on.

11 29   Back to the scooter. She tries to balance on it as she comes downhill along the path.
Philippa is throwing a stick for the dog. Dawn is on the rope ladder. Michael is on the climbing frame. Peter is pushing the heavy wooden trolley around. Jennifer and Mark are in the sandpit. Susan has a scooter.

85

Tracey puts scooter away in the shed. Goes to the sand-pit. Finds a spade.

Dog spits a stick into the sand-pit. Tracey throws it for him.

Tracey digs with Mark who has found a small solid pram wheel. They cover it with sand.

Peter takes their wheel away: 'No, it's the spare wheel.'

Peter gets sand in his eyes.

Dawn is pushing Chris on the swing, James and Michael are on the frame.

Dawn is going down central pole of climbing frame.

Chris is bending down and smelling a hyacinth.

Peter is still crying. Chris puts an arm round his neck.

Michael is trying to teach James how to go down the central pole of the frame. Asks for the plank to be put across the bars to make a platform. Tries to fetch it himself from the shed.

Tracey gets a good heap of sand thrown on to her smart skirt. She cries for a few seconds.

James is still trying to summon up enough courage to try to go down the central pole (but he is trying from too high up).

Dawn is on rope ladder.

Peter and Tracey in the sand-pit.

Peter: 'I'm going to Sarah's school – not with *you*. You shouldn't throw sand in my eyes . . .'

Sitting down beside Tracey on the edge of the sand-pit: 'Mummy bought these new socks.'

Tracey: 'Did she really?'

Peter 'And she didn't ask you to put sand on them, *so*!'

Tracey quickly leaves the sand-pit. Up climbing frame.

Sits on the top bar, swinging her legs and holding with one hand on to one of the bars that slope up slightly to the top of the central pole.

Tracey (to Michael who is on the rope ladder close by): 'I go to Sunday School. Do you, Michael?'

Michael hails supervisor: 'Look at me, Mrs Boyle.'

Tracey: 'I bet you can't do your alphabet.'

Michael: 'I don't know what's alabet . . . You can't swing this swing.'

Tracey (to Susan, who comes by with dolls' pram): 'I bet you can't do your alphabet.'

Susan: 'Hallo! who put you up there?'

Tracey: 'I got there all by myself.' Meanwhile, she has begun to climb around and hang by her hands from the top bar, resting her feet on a lower bar at intervals.

Climbs down and makes for the scooter, but Dawn beats her to it.

Tracey talking to Philippa through the open door of the toilet.

Dawn, Mike and Chris on scooters.

Mark climbs apple tree. Peter still has trolley, Susan pram.

Tracey comes up garden path, says to supervisor: 'We have been in the toilet, we have.'

She finds a scooter, but stops to let Chris 'mend' it.

Tracey says 'Bye-bye' to Chris. Walks up the hill with scooter, runs down holding it.

Tracey climbs apple tree.
Peter has got stuck at the top of the climbing frame.
He insists that he cannot get down.

Philippa is 3 years 5 months. Three terms in group. Susan is 4 years 2 months. Four terms in group. Christopher is 3 years 1 month. Three-and-a-half terms in group. Jennifer is 3 years 7 months. Ten weeks in group. Is Tracey's neighbour. Kevin is 2 years 11 months. Half a term in group.

Record No. 3

9 May 1968. *The activity of Christopher, aged 3 years 3 months. A member of the group for four-and-a-half terms.*

09 54   On slides, running up and down. Stops at the bottom to play with the wooden aeroplane.
Runs up slide. Michael 'stucks' him, as he says. Slides down. Throws a little wooden 'man' gently a little way up the slide and catches it as it rolls down several times.
Runs up low slide. Slides down high slide.
Runs up low slide carelessly, overbalances and jumps off sideways. Up again and down again.
'Swims' on back under the slides (others are 'swimming').

09 57   Goes over to the window and plays with the number-matching tray. With Tracey's occasional assistance, puts the cards with numbers one to ten in the numbered spaces matching the figures correctly. Two are upside-down.

09 59   Turns round and starts rolling out a big lump of 'pastry' (dough). The dough is stiff and he rolls a bit absentmindedly.

10 01   Still rolling. To Tracey: 'Must be very quick,' and rolls very hard.
Cutting slices with knife (an old table knife) and making lines on the pastry with it.
To me: 'Look, that's poisonous,' indicating two children who are being robots with the plastic 'Pipes' toy.
Daryl: 'I spray you.'
Christopher cuts out a heart-shaped 'cake' very efficiently.
Runs up the slide. Jennifer taps him and he nearly overbalances.
Christopher to Jennifer (good-naturedly): 'I kill you.'

10 06   Screws four nuts quickly onto the screw toy.

10 08   Wanders round.

10 10   Painting – red dots, then black lines in all directions. Wild movements and bangs with the brush. (This is not his usual purposeful style.)
Removes his paper and carefully pegs on a new piece on while I help by holding the paper.

10 12	Plays with the pedal of the piano while two others are 'playing'.
10 13	Over to cupboard. Squeezes himself into the space between the two cupboards, holding one of the doors open.
10 15	Adds another piece to Dawn's creation with Connector.
10 16	Is animal of some sort – rearing up and pretend clawing. Then on all fours, yapping. Seizes Connector pieces from Daryl with great show of ferocity and then hands them to Dawn. Yapping.
10 18	Building with Connector. Hits someone with stick. I remonstrate.
10 20	Connector. Engrossed in building. Enjoying the round wheels which slide up and down a long stick, which he has stopped at both ends with a cube.
10 21	Watching Dawn building her very complicated creation. Sometimes yaps, is kneeling on the floor, sometimes trying to help Dawn. Peter seizes a stick off Dawn's 'building' and 'posts' it through a convenient hole in the side of a stool. I ask him not to spoil Dawn's building.
10 23	Christopher is yapping at Dawn and clawing the air in front of her. Dawn: 'Stop it . . . Put this on it . . . No, get that off . . . Thanks.'
10 25	Christopher aiming and shooting: 'chr . . . chr,' with Connector stick.
10 25½	Hammer-peg toy.
10 27	Still hammering the pegs quickly and surely right through and then turns it over and hammers them all back again. All his movements are quick and deft. Dawn still building with Connector.
10 28	Christopher in the hall mock-fighting with Michael and James, and chasing up and down the first flight of the stairs. Now following them round with a galloping step, stopping to pretend to box.
10 30	Sits at table with plastic toy.
10 31	Back to the boys. Michael: 'We're cowboys.' James: 'We friendly cowboys.' Christopher rocks on the rocking-horse. Leaps off and wrestles with James. Michael seizes him from behind. Christopher jumps on to horse: 'On my horse.' Leaps off again. Runs after boys. Very controlled and amiable play. Back on horse.
10 34	Sits at table with plastic toy again.
10 36	To toilet.
10 40	Dawn has been playing with the Connector all this time. Christopher is crying. I did not see why.
10 41	Lying on his back, in a corner, dreamily.
10 42	Turned over on to his stomach. Is singing very quietly to himself and holding a small brick in his hands.

10 43 Gets up with a glimmer of a smile and walks around. Back to corner and lies down and sings and talks to himself again. (He seems to be more restless than usual. Perhaps he is more affected by the fact that I am following him around and writing than the others were when I made notes of their activities.)

10 44 Up, and over to pastry. Cuts and bangs with knife and scrapes lumps of pastry with the knife on to the floor.

10 45 Runs around. Then back to pastry, cutting off bits.

10 46 Dawn still at Connector – with John now.
Christopher gets on John's knees. John: 'Stop it, Christopher.'
Christopher over to Peter. Mock fighting.
Christopher climbs on to chair singing. . . . Runs into hall. Mock-fighting.

10 48 Daryl and Peter are carrying a big cardboard box full of bricks between them, Peter walking backwards. They go up the low slide, Peter walking backwards quite quickly, put the box down on the bench and sit making car-noises.
Daryl: 'No, I'm driving.'
Christopher is sulking. He wanted some of the bits of Connector from Dawn's creation. (She is *still* building.)

10 50 Christopher sitting on the floor and watching the others. Peter and Daryl are now playing pretend 'fire-engines'. Michael banging on the stool with a Connector 'hammer'.
Jennifer has a large cake of dough on the floor. She lies on it and squashes it flat with her stomach. Her jersey makes a pattern on it. Then she stands on it with both feet and pauses to study the effect. She picks it up and rolls it into a ball.

10 55 Dawn gives her spiky construction to Christopher. He is pleased and smiles broadly.
Christopher: 'It's a robot.' It is very tall and waves about and sways, falls and breaks. Christopher: 'Dawn!' He leaves it and joins Daryl, Dawn and Peter on the carpenter's bench.
Daryl: 'We must go to the station park.'
Christopher goes up and down the slides two or three times.

10 58 Christopher is sitting on bench beside the car drivers. (Argument between Daryl and Peter about who is to be the driver.)
Christopher on all fours yapping and squeaking alternately.
I ask him is he an animal? 'No, I'm a doggy.'

11 00 Christopher slides down the slide, slowly.
Collects up the dough and puts it away in a polythene bag.
'Elevenses'

11 10 Jumping to the floor from the bench, over and over again.

11 12 'Plays' the piano quietly for two minutes. Likes making his hands move in opposite directions.

11 15 Joins others in the hall for a story.
Dawn, John and Daryl are building with the Adventure Playthings

hollow blocks which serve as a set of shelves to hold the jigsaws and other toys and boxes for most of the time.

11 20   These children are now playing 'shops' inside their building. They have got the kitchen scales and weights and paper bags and the toy money and bricks to put in a bag.

11 30   Peter comes out of the hall. He and Daryl climb out of the window, which is open. They climb in again – quite a feat – but because it gives on to the road I regretfully shut the window.

11 45   There are still five children listening to the story, including Christopher.

Daryl is 4 years 2 months. Has been in group for just over one term.

Record No. 4
20 May 1968. The activity of Susan, aged 4 years 4 months. A member of the group for four-and-a-half terms.

09 40   Susan standing by the window. Philippa comes up: 'Shall we go on the slides?'
Susan: 'No.' Goes to the dough table. Philippa goes once or twice up and down the slides and then joins her.

09 41   Susan asks for the knife. I go to fetch it but get waylaid.

09 44   I give Susan the knife and she digs a hole in the flattened ball of pastry.

09 45   Susan asks for the box of 'candle sticks'. I fetch the box of small coloured wooden counting rods (usually used for making patterns) and she sticks one in the hole and fills up the hole with small bits of pastry that she picks off the edge of the piece of dough, so that the rod stands up straight.

09 47   Repeats process with several rods.
John and Nicola are on the slides as they have been since they arrived five minutes ago, running up and sliding down.

09 50   John sits at dough table and imitates Susan, sticking a few rods quickly into a flat piece of dough, then jumps up and asks the supervisor if he can paint. She says, yes, when there is space.

09 53   John on the slides again.
Susan has stuck about twenty-five rods into her dough.
Nicola is now sticking rods into dough.
Susan is fixing small pieces of dough on to the tops of her rods.

09 55   Susan pulls the rods out, makes her dough into a smooth ball and rolls it out a little. She fills a hole that appears with a lump of dough. To me: 'Will you roll it out for me?' I roll it a little for her.
Nicola is trying to roll hers out, but is also watching and listening to the other children.
Christopher comes and sticks some rods into a piece of dough while muttering to himself something about a birthday cake.

09 58   John is now painting.

Nicola and Susan go over to the easels. They ask the supervisor if they may paint.

09 59½   Supervisor: 'There is a space for you now, Nicola. You are next, Susan. I'll tell you when there is a space.' Susan stands watching the others painting.

10 01   Susan still watching the others painting with interest and amusement.

10 04   At last there is a space free. Susan does green shapes like a thick inverted 'L'. 'This is a hammer.'

Mark is watching her. 'That's a hammer,' pointing to a small green roundish splodge.

Susan: 'No, this is a hammer, that's nothing.'

10 06   She does a yellow splodge, then a brown hammer shape above the green one: 'This is a little hammer on top of the big one. I want to do another picture.'

She is given a clean sheet of paper and pegs it on herself while I hold the paper. (This was my suggestion because the pegs, having been thoroughly painted by the previous child, are covered with thick wet paint.)

10 09   Susan does a blue shape very carefully on her clean paper.

Susan: 'That's Garry.'

I: 'Is it a picture of Garry?' (Her elder brother.)

Susan: 'No, it's Garry's number.' I look carefully and notice that it is a perfect 'G' but very thickly drawn because the brush and the paint are both thick.

Susan: 'Now I'll do Susan.' Tries to make an 'S'. Is not satisfied. 'You do one for me.' I hold her hand and guide it. She goes over my 'S' carefully, making it thicker and clearer. Then another 'G'. Then fills in the 'G's. Asks for more paper.

10 16   Does 'S'-like snaky shapes on new paper, in yellow. Wants another piece. I turn the paper over and she does splashy spots all over it, banging with the brush.

James comes up. 'Hallo Mr Susie.'

Susan: 'I'm not Mr – I'm Susie.'

James: 'You're *Mr* Susie.'

Susan: 'I'm Susie.'

(ditto – ditto)

James: 'I'm a girl. You're a boy.'

Susan: 'I'm a girl. You're a boy.'

James (laughing): 'I'm a girl. You're a boy.'

Susan (getting a little cross): 'I'll tell Garry. He'll hit you.'

James: 'I'll hit you.' He punches her, not hard, on the back and goes into the hall.

Susan runs after him. She gets pushed backwards on to a seat, but falls off the seat, sits down hard and goes to the supervisor for comfort.

10 25   Plays with the vice. Fetches a stool to stand on. Asks for the saw, finds a piece of wood and puts it into the vice. Saws a small end

off it carefully, keeping her left hand well away from the saw. (With a happy smile): 'I got a bit off.'

10 30 Saws the wood in another place. Gets a third of the way through the wood quite quickly but gives up and wants another piece of wood. Chooses a smaller piece but it is hardwood and she won't get very far with that, I fear.

10 31 Absentmindedly sawing and watching the others on the slide. Dawn is face downwards on the top of the slide, stopping herself from sliding down by holding the plank with her hands. James is on the bench behind her.
Dawn: 'Hold on to my legs ... not my socks ... Hold on to my *skin. Hard.* Come on.'
James: 'I'm holding on.' She lets go with her hands and James follows, holding on to her calves. They are both very pleased.
James (to me): 'We went down together with no falling off.'
Susan leaves her sawing, puts the wood back into the box and goes up the slide and down again, once or twice.

10 40 Susan is watching Dawn and James inventing new ways of going down together. Susan is amused.
James: 'Wasn't that super?' They had slid down kneeling, facing each other.
Susan is hugging little Kevin, who is standing beside her.
After a bit Kevin pushes her away. It becomes a game of 'pat-a-cake'.

10 45 Someone asks for a 'house' to be made. The supervisor builds a house in the hall with rugs and towel horses. Susan asks to play houses, but goes into the front hall and rocks on the rocking-horse. Philippa calls: 'Come in the house, Susan.' She makes the horse slide along the floor as she rocks towards the 'house'.
Susan: 'Can I come in the house?' Parks the horse outside the house and joins Philippa, Tracey and Michael in the house.
Philippa: 'I want to be the baby. Will you be Mummy?'
Susan: 'I don't want to be Mummy.'
Michael: 'I'll be Daddy.'
Philippa: 'You be Auntie.' No response from Susan.
Philippa: 'You can be a big girl. Mummy's gone out. You have to look after us and make our beds.'
Peter gets on to the rocking-horse.
Susan: 'He's my horse. I want to go on the horse.'

10 49 Philippa (to Tracey): 'I'll make our beds.'
Susan (to me): 'It's my horse.'
I: 'But you left it and went in the house.'
Michael: 'I'll punch you, Peter.'
Susan: 'No, leave him.' She makes a gesture to defend Peter.
Tracey and Philippa are lying on the floor in the corner of the house: 'We're babies, aren't we?'
Susan: 'I suppose I'll have to tuck you in. [to Peter] Get some more blankets, will you?'
Peter: 'There are no more blankets.' But he goes and finds one.
Susan covers the 'babies' up and goes off.

92

Peter: 'Shut up, babies, shut up.' The babies are babbling and talking baby talk. 'We're ill, aren't we?'
Peter: 'You both get out of the house.'
Tracey: 'We're babies. That made my hiccoughs come.'
Susan comes back with another cover.
Peter: 'Would you like to come and see the ducks on the pond?'
Susan (to Michael who has been standing quietly in a corner of the house): 'Look after them, will you?' Goes with Peter into the playroom, where some children are 'swimming' on the floor.
Susan: 'They are ducks . . . shall we go home?'
Back in the house (to Peter, indicating John): 'He wants to come in. He can't, these babies are ill.'
Peter at the door, threatening John.
Susan: 'He can't come in, he might get germs. [to Peter] Go and ring up the doctor. [to the 'babies'] Do you like doctors?'
Philippa: 'No, we only like nurses.'
Peter: 'Doctor is coming.'
Susan: 'No, nurses please.'
Mark: 'I am the doctor.'
Susan: 'Go away, doctor, we want nurses.'
Peter: 'Go *away*.'
Philippa: 'We'll have doctor, then.'
Peter: 'You babies, stop it.'
Philippa (to Tracey): 'Shall we have doctor or nurses? Do you want doctors and nurses? . . . Say yes. Susan, get the doctor, only the doctor, Susie.'
Susan: 'Doctors and nurses. You have got to go to sleep. That's what the doctor said.'

11 00   Philippa and Tracey are still lying on the floor covered up.
Peter: 'Go and ring the doctor.'
The 'babies' kick off their covers.
Susan: 'What are you doing, babies?'
Philippa: 'We don't want to play.'
Susan goes into the playroom and plays with the telephone with Mark for a moment. Then sits on the tool-chest and gives John an extra bit of speed down the slide, which pleases him. Then goes back to the house, saying: 'I want two doctors and nurses.' Peter has had an argument and is crying. Susan tries to comfort him.

John, 4 years 9 months, and his sister Nicola, 2 years 10 months, have both been four weeks in the group.

Record No. 5
25 June 1968. *The activity of John, aged 4 years 10 months. A member of the group for eight weeks (less two weeks' holiday).*

09 30   Sucks his toy car and looks around him.
Up the slides and slides down holding his car in his hand. Sits on the slide talking to Mrs Boyle about his sister Nicola.

09 32	Sits down to paint.
09 33	Takes black brush. Pushes the brush slowly up and down on the paper while he listens to James talking to the supervisor about his little purse.
09 41	Continues using black paint, but stops every now and then to watch and listen to the others.
09 42	Has painted what looks like a creature with three black legs. He stands up to see what Susan is painting.
09 45	Fills in the spaces between the legs of his figure so that it is simply a solid black mass. 'Look what Nicky is doing.' She is making a little pool of grey paint in one corner of the box in which the easel stands.
09 47	Makes another vertical leg (?): 'Look what I've done.' 'Got to paint all this.' Fills in the space between the legs. (Jennifer has painted a very obvious face, a thing she has never done before in the playgroup and which has not been done, Mrs Boyle says, by anyone for a term and a half. Jennifer does not remark on what she has done. Afterwards she does a lot of wavy lines all over the paper and over the face.)
09 50	John (to Mrs Boyle): 'Look what Kevin's done.' Kevin has splashed a little paint over on to John's paper. John: 'Kevin! Stop it. . . . I'm using all the black up.'
09 55	'I'm using all the black up . . . Jennifer!' She has finished her picture and removed the peg so that his picture falls down. I suggest that he puts his brush into the pot so that he can use both hands to peg his paper up again. He does so, but a minute later says: 'Teacher, I've finished.' Stands up and runs his finger through Nicola's hair and says (indicating her painting): 'What's all that?'
09 57	Up and down the slides twice. Fetches his car, walks up slide backwards (the steep one) and slides down holding his car, in a sitting position, beating rapidly with his feet on the slide as he goes. Then, still in the same position, pushes himself backwards up the slide by means of his rubber-shod feet. Slides down. All the time interested, it seems, in what the others are doing.
10 00	Pushes his car into the end of Mark's wooden train. Crashes it to pieces; Mark laughs but leaves the train. John up the slide again, and down. Plays a moment with the wooden tractor. Then accompanies Nicola into the hall, where she shows Peter their new umbrellas.
10 04	On to the bench, climbing up by way of the tool-chest. Lies face downwards on top of slide and waits while someone slides down in front of him, then slides down, car in hand.
10 05	Fetches 'village tray'. Begins to do it, but leaves it to sit at the dough table. Rolls out dough. Holds it in his hand and presses

biscuit cutter (a star shape) into it. Squeezes it together and rolls it out a little. Is sticking his fingers into the dough. Then squeezes it together and rolls it out a little. Nicola and Jennifer are with him at the dough table. Mark and Tracey are painting and talking; Kevin threading beads; Susan telephoning. John bangs dough with end of rolling pin, rolls it out, presses a point of the star shape into it, making marks all over it. Knocks the star shape into the dough, takes shape out, then lifts the 'pastry' from around the star he has cut out so that it is left on the table; laughs with pleasure at this.

10 15   Squeezes dough into ball again.
Mrs Boyle holds up Mark's painting for me to see. We agree it is a good one. John says: 'Mark has covered it all over.'
He stamps out another star and puts it in the baking tin. Asks Nicola for some of her pastry. (She has acquired most of it, and the knife.) John rolls his dough out again a little, knocks star cutter into it with the rolling pin again. Puts the star-shaped cake into the six-bun baking tin where he has already put two others, and says: 'I've got three more to do.'

10 21   Obtains some more dough from his sister, asking her for it politely. Cuts out three more star shapes.
Jennifer wants the knife that Nicola has.
John: 'You can have it when she's finished.'
Nicola takes one of his cakes out of the baking tin.
John: 'No! Put it back!' Insists on her putting it back.
He holds up the baking tin full, smiling, and says, 'Look!'
I: 'How many cakes have you got?'
John: 'All these.'

10 25   Watching and listening to the other children.
Takes his cakes and lays them in two layers in the narrow cardboard box in which the cutters are kept.

10 26   I am called away.

10 30   When I came back, John was having a fight with James, which became quite serious on John's part. He hurt James, who retired for a moment and then returned to the attack and got pushed over and bumped himself.
I: 'Why are you fighting?'
John: 'He hit me, so I hit him.'
I: 'James only plays at fighting; he doesn't fight hard.'
John: 'I do.'
Now he is fighting with Peter; they are wrestling.
Peter: 'You don't hurt me.' It seems to me that John is controlling himself more and being a little more gentle.
They stop and run up the slide and jump down from the bench, one after the other, several times. Mark joins in.

10 34   Still jumping.

10 35   John goes back to the pastry table.

10 36   James comes up and punches him (not at all hard but with much

95

bravado.) John jumps up. They spar, jumping around. John is holding back, but repeats: 'I'll do it again to you, I'll do it again to you.'

James is panting loudly and looking very worried.

He eventually retires, boohoos for a moment or two, and then sits disgruntled in a big chair.

John plays with the 'village' toy.

Peter (to James): 'You are a baby.' To John: 'I told him he's a baby.'

James: 'I'm not playing with you lot.'

John goes up to the toilet. He has set up most of the 'village'.

James (looking out of the window from his chair): 'It's raining very hard.'

Mark (from the slide): 'It's raining, it's pouring, the old man's snoring.'

Peter and James are shouting 'baby' cheerfully at each other.

John starts to thread beads.

Susan has made a 'slide' – a slope down and a slope up with the 3-ft long building planks for the truck to run on, out in the hall. John goes into the hall and fetches his car, and then pushes it up and down the slide several times, making car noises.

James is talking about his new coat with a hood on it.

John (to me): 'Nicola has got a coat and a hood and I've got a coat and an umbrella.'

James is banging John, Peter and Mark in turn with his little plastic purse, swinging it by its handle. It does not hurt them and they take no notice.

James (to me): 'That serves *them* right.' He is slightly truculent, but cheerful.

Record No. 6

26 June 1968. *The activity of Mark, aged 3 years 9 months. A member of the group for three terms.*

09 33   Mark comes in, smiles to me and the supervisor. His mother goes to put his lunch packet on the mantelpiece, but he wants to do it himself. He can just reach. His mother is surprised, but says: 'He *is* growing. He can reach the latch of the front door now if he stands on tiptoe, and I have to watch him.' Mark goes to the window and plays with the toy money; his mother kisses him and then stops to talk to the supervisor. Susan comes up and plays with Mark. Mark waves to his mother through the window.

Susan: 'How much money do you want?'

Mark: 'Sevenpence.' Susan starts pouring it into his hand.

Susan: 'I'll put money in the bowl. .... Tell me when to stop.' Pours it from tin to bowl.

Mark: 'Stop.'

09 35   Susan goes to greet Dawn who has been away on holiday for a fortnight, and they talk and then climb up the slides, still talking. Mark has two marbles in his hand, and puts them carefully in a

crack on the shelf at which he is playing. Pours the money from tin to bowl and back again, turning round now and then to watch the others who are accumulating in the room.

Puts the bowl upside down on top of the tin: 'Look what I've done.'

I: 'What is it?'

Mark: 'A box.' He goes over to Tracey at the dough table and shows her his two marbles. Then walks up the slide backwards. 'I can go backwards.' Runs down and leaps off at the end.

Our kitten is in the room and there is talk about kittens between three or four children.

Mark: 'I got a real cat at home.'

Mark (to Dawn): 'I've got two marbles.' Then (to Peter): 'I *did* come to your party. . . . My Daddy's in Scotland.'

Mark walks up slide backwards and slides down watching and listening to Dawn and Susan, who are trying to rock on the rocking-horse standing opposite each other on the ends of the rockers and holding hands. The operation is directed by Dawn. Considerable balancing skill is involved. Mark is smiling with appreciation as he walks backwards up the narrower 'high slide'. Still watching, he comes slowly down the wider slide.

Dawn: 'Can we have the house up, Mrs Boyle?'

Mark: 'And can I go in?'

Peter: 'Can I be Daddy?'

Dawn: 'No, Mark is Daddy.' Takes Mark by the hand and goes towards the house. Somebody says: 'You can be doggy, Peter.' More talk about dogs and cats.

Dawn and Susan agree to have no children, but Dawn pushes Susan and Mark closer together, finds that Susan is half a head taller than Mark and says to him: 'Susan is bigger than you, so you can't be Daddy.'

Susan (to Mark): 'You can be baby.'

Peter: 'I going to be kitten.' Lollops on hands and feet into the house. Susan, Dawn and Mark follow.

Susan (to Mark): 'Come in, baby . . . You go to sleep.' He lies down in the corner.

Dawn: 'Let's shut the door . . . it's all dark.'

Susan: 'Be quiet. We've got babies in here.' (Whispering): 'You go and get the doctor and nurses.'

Dawn whispers inaudibly in reply.

Susan: 'Baby, go to sleep.' Mark is lying down.

Peter leaves the house on all fours: 'I'm running away.'

Dawn and Susan go to get 'doctors and nurses'.

Dawn (to supervisor): 'Is Michael coming?'

Mrs Boyle: 'No, Michael is away on holiday.' They return to the house. They tell the baby to go to sleep. There is an argument between them about who is 'mummy'.

Susan: 'We're both mummys. But I sleep with the baby, I always do.' Lies beside Mark.

Dawn: 'You two can be two babies.'

Susan: 'No.'

Dawn: 'Come out then, Susan, *out*.' Susan gets up.

Dawn (to me): 'We are going to make it all dark in here.' I am required to mend the house.

I: 'Now it's dark, isn't it?'

Mark (looking at me through the banisters): 'No, it's not dark, I can see.'

Dawn and Susan have gone out.

Susan comes back with some plastic toys: 'The doctor sent these for you.' No response from Mark.

Susan: 'Do something. When I do things to you, you cry. . . . Pretend you don't do what I want. . . . You all hot. Yes . . . go to sleep.'

Dawn returns.

Susan: 'Are you a nurse?'

Dawn: 'Yes. How is baby?'

Susan: 'Not all right. Have you got a cup and a pencil?' (To Mark): 'Do you like doctors?'

Mark: 'Yes.'

Susan: 'You don't like nurses, do you? You cry.'

Dawn (to Mrs Boyle): 'Can we have a pen to make the medicine?' She is given a large thick pencil. They mix medicines.

Peter and John come to the house. Peter stops John from coming in: 'I'm daddy.'

Dawn: 'Mrs Stallibrass! Peter is knocking our house down.'

Peter: 'I'm looking out of the window. This baby is ill.'

10 05 John still fails to get Peter to let him in and Dawn and Susan are arguing about how to treat the baby.

Susan is trying to persuade Mark to cry: 'All babies cry.'

10 10 Peter is sitting in the 'house' with the others. He says to Dawn: 'I'm going to doctor's.'

Dawn: 'What's wrong?'

Mark is resisting being turned over.

Susan: 'Shall I smack my baby? . . . Turn over, or I'll smack you.' Pats him gently. 'Shall I smack you?'

John and Nicola want to play in the house and keep coming to see if the present occupants are willing to vacate it.

10 14 Mark leaves the house and asks to paint.

Susan asks Nicola if she would like to be a baby. Nicola agrees.

Mark is using red paint. Makes a long thick strip of red in a rough rectangle, slowly, carefully making the strip a regular ¼-inch wide. Then makes a red square in the middle. Then fills in the whole of the red rectangle.

He is alone at the easels; Tracey and Dawn and Jennifer are on the slides.

10 18 Mark now does a strip of red all round between the rectangle and the edge of the paper; then makes a big black spot in the space between the lower edge of the rectangle and the outer red ring. (There is more space here than above or at the sides.) Then three green spots beside the black and then two smaller orange ones above them.

10 22   Mark, having finished his picture, wipes his hands. Susan comes past, taking her 'baby' (Nicola) for a walk, holding her by the hand and talking to her.
Mark watching others. Goes up slide. Points his picture out to Dawn. Runs down the steep slide.
He is playing with John's car.
Peter snatches it. Mark appeals to John. John takes it from Peter and gives it back to Mark.
Mark up the slide with the car.
Tracey and Mark are sitting on the bench. Tracey to Mark: 'Look, Kevin is in the river. That is the river.'
Mark makes the car go up and down the slide several times, holding it in his hand. Then tries to make it run down by itself, racing the wheels first. 'Missed!' (as it falls off). Gets down, picks it up, goes out to the 'house'.

10 33   Back on the bench, races the car wheels, turns the car over to watch them going round several times.

10 37   Gives car back to John.
Crawling on the floor; (to Mrs Boyle): 'I'm doggy.'

10 38   Up to toilet.

10 39   Down again.
Peter hides behind the door.
Mark joins him: 'You keep behind my back and I pull the door back, see.' Peter comes out. Kevin and Mark hide and whisper together. Kevin comes out and pulls the door to. Mark holds on to the other handle and resists. Kevin gradually wins and shuts the door. Mark manages to get it open, but fails to keep it so. Mrs Boyle stops them from playing with the door.

10 43   Mark watches Dawn, who is playing very expertly with the Escor roundabout.
Fetches posting truck. Asks Mrs Boyle for the sliding door that belongs to it. Fills up the truck with blocks and small toys and slides the door in at the back to shut them in.
Mark seizes the 'policeman' doll, that belongs to the Escor toys and is usually used as the pilot of the Escor aeroplane, from Dawn who is using it unnecessarily with the roundabout, and gives it to James who is looking for it for the aeroplane. Mark rolls the truck down the slide, but John is coming up backwards, and he pushes the truck up again. Rolls it down again. John is sitting absentmindedly at the bottom of the slide. Mark jogs him gently with the truck till he gets up and goes away. Mark empties the truck and fills it up again. The roof of the truck is forced off because he has overfilled it. He takes it to Mrs Boyle and she fixes it. Tracey comes up and tries unsuccessfully to slide the door into place. Mrs Boyle shows her how to do it. Tracey seizes it before she has finished and does it herself. Mark and Tracey play with the truck together.
Tracey leaves. Mark says: 'Watch, Mrs Boyle.' He has stuck a hollow wooden piece of the Scandinavian building toy 'Actiplay'

into one of the posting holes, like a chimney, and he drops a little rod down it.

10 51 Gets the wooden tractor and pulls it by its string up the slide behind him. Stays at the top of the slide, letting the tractor down on the string. Kevin seizes the tractor and after a tug of war pulls it from Mark. Mark gets down and retrieves it. Slides down very slowly, letting tractor down in front of him. Up again, sits on the top of the bench, winding the string round his legs.

10 55 Slides down, letting tractor down in front of him.
Leaves tractor. While watching the others, slides down a little way in a sitting position, with hand and a foot on each slide.

11 02 Puts some toys away for supervisor.

11 10 'Elevenses'

Outside

11 22 Mark scooting. Going downhill along the path quite skilfully. Has a race with James up the other path, running with the scooter. Gets left behind: 'Wait for me!'
James is very excited because the strawberries are red. Mark joins him dancing round the strawberry bed, pointing at the ripe ones under the net.

11 31 Is sitting on the big trolley between Dawn and Susan. Dawn is steering the trolley down the path. They pick up a little speed at the bottom, and it's a little worrying for Mrs Boyle and me watching because they have to steer between the wall of the house and that of the garage.

11 35 James: 'Here is a pear.' He has found a tiny apple about $\frac{1}{4}$-inch long. Mark and John go to look. John: 'It might be poisonous, don't eat it.'
James: 'I'll tell my Mummy about these poisonous pears.'

11 37 Mark in sand-pit with Susan.
Finds a bit of old clothes-line. Tries to undo the knot, but it is impossible for anyone to do this and I tell him so.
Digs in sand.

11 42 To the toilet.
Sits on the trolley.
Tries to take the bit of clothes-line from Kevin. Fails.

11 46 Someone draws my attention to the fact that James is eating the minute apples that have fallen off the tree. I tell him that it is not a good thing to do, as it might give him a stomach ache, and that the apples on the tree will become ripe and good if they are left there. I try to explain why some are falling off.
James: 'We've got pears growing nicely in our garden and none of them are falling off.'
Mark does a somersault on the gymnast's rings that are hung from the apple tree.
Does it again, a delighted grin on his face.
Again.

11 48   Is pushing the small baby-walker round the garden.
Susan is trying the rings.
Dawn and Nicola are sliding on the long strip of vinyl flooring
placed for that purpose where the lawn slopes down steeply,
forming a bank. They throw themselves down upon it. Nicola
does a somersault to begin her slide. Her own idea, I think,
certainly not Mrs Boyle's.
James and Mark are running round the garden, each holding an
end of a 4-yd piece of clothes-line. They have wrested it from
Kevin after a struggle and he cries a little, then picks up a scooter
and pushes it around.
The lawn is littered with large toys: see-saw, rocking boat, water
bath and scooters, and the tent frame, but James and Mark,
running with the rope taut ˙between them, thread their way
through them and around the apple tree in an extraordinarily
skilful way. The game becomes a tug-of-war, with Dawn and
Susan at one end and the boys at the other. In the end the boys
are pulled over on their faces without hurt, or are at least lying
on the grass – I did not see how they got there – and the girls are
victorious.

11 55   Dawn and Susan on the vinyl slide.   ˙
Dawn: 'There is an ant on it.'   .
James (in his booming voice): 'I saw a hurting ant.'
Mark taking his cardigan off. Does a 'trick' on the tent frame.
Blows bubbles in the water with a piece of rubber tubing.
Back to the tent frame. Kneels on the bar that is 2 ft 3 in. from
the ground, holding the side pole with one hand; stands on the
bar, puts his hands on top bar (4 ft 6 in. from ground) and
swings, resting feet at intervals on the lower bar. Then presses
with his feet on lower bar and throws his head back, arching his
back and forming a curve with his body. Does a somersault on
the rings. 'Watch me, Mrs Boyle.'
Does another one.
Dawn comes over and they each swing on a ring. Then they
swing facing each other and crashing into each other.

12 02   Mark is pouring water. He fills a teapot from a small jug.
'Make a cup of tea.'
'Anybody want a cup of tea?' he calls. He repeats the question
four times.
Pours out his 'tea' into cups.
Blows bubbles very hard through tubing. 'You do it like this'
(to another child).
Pouring again: 'Anybody want juice?'
Tracey: 'Yes.'
Mark: 'Get a cup then.'
Spends some time scooping water up with a plate and tipping it
into a cup.

*Mark is rather small, shy and quiet, and for most of his first year in
the group spent much of his time watching or playing close to the*

supervisor. Now, as can be seen, he has no fear, is active and enjoys himself tremendously. One had formed the impression that he stuttered, especially when he is very anxious to communicate something, but this morning I noticed no stuttering at all. Perhaps he only stutters when talking to grown-ups or when trying to retain the attention of another child in order to explain or describe something to them and at length.

Perhaps this chapter should be re-read on completion of the book, because, if one is aware of all the various kinds of knowledge and skill that the children acquire while playing in a group such as mine, these factual records will mean more.

Among the things that the children are learning are:
general sensory-motor judgment and many particular sensory-motor skills;
social judgment and awareness of and knowledge of themselves and others;
the power to describe events and objects and their feelings in words, and to communicate with their fellows.

Besides exercising – and therefore, developing – their individuality, they are learning adaptability and resourcefulness and even, sometimes, tact. For instance, Philippa quickly suggests alternative parts that Susan might play in the 'mothers and fathers' game, which would both suit Susan and serve her own and Tracey's plan to be 'babies'.

One can watch them acquiring wisdom; making the best of a situation that has not turned out to be all they would have liked it to be, or discovering that patience is the best policy, or that it is not possible to obtain creative co-operation from others if one tries to impose one's will indefinitely upon them; discovering, in short, that you have more fun if everyone is happy.

As they play they become aware of the reality outside themselves, and of their own capabilities, so that on the whole they attempt the possible. They act realistically and with discrimination, and therefore tend to be successful in their undertakings. This fosters in them the courage to respond spontaneously to the environment; in other words, to act in a manner that is true to themselves. They act as integrated, whole personalities. It could be said that they are becoming capable of free-will.

CHAPTER FIVE

The Play of Babies

Picture a six-month-old baby lying in his pram on a summer's day, awake and comfortable, and neither tired nor hungry. He waves his arms and legs in the air and plays with his toes; or arches his back, pushes downwards with his heels and bumps his bottom up and down; or he tries to sit up or to roll over on to his stomach. He feels his rattle with his fingers, sucks and bites it and follows its movements and the movements of his hands with his eyes. He gurgles, coos and babbles; smiles to himself, grimaces and blows bubbles. He is 'playing'. But if one pauses to reflect about his activity, one realizes that this 'play' consists of using his senses, his muscles and his central nervous system.

Now think of the behaviour of a year-old baby. By this time he sits upright and can, *with one smooth, easy movement*, lean forward and reach for a toy – perhaps a favourite doll that is lying at the foot of the pram. In six months he has made a great advance in judgment and skill; he has vastly increased his sensory-motor knowledge of things and of how to do things. For instance, he has learned to judge the distance of a familiar object, or at least he has learned how far he must stretch in order to reach something that is lying at the foot of his pram. He has learned how to pick up the doll – and other familiar objects – without fumbling, and hold it firmly between his fingers and thumb while he carries it close. He has learned how to keep his balance while leaning forward and straightening up again – an action that requires nice sensory-motor judgment as well as muscular strength. A baby's head is a comparatively large and heavy part of him; therefore leaning over is a difficult and hazardous activity for him until he has learned through experience and practice how far and in what direction he may lean and at what speed he must move. Much practice, or, in Groos's phrase, 'playful experimentation' has been necessary for the successful learning of the complex skill of reaching for his doll.

In order to be able to pick up and carry the doll with ease, the baby must also have learned quite a lot about its physical qualities. It is obvious that he is not born with a knowledge of an object such as a doll, and that he cannot gain it simply by becoming older and bigger and stronger. Neither can he acquire it by the use of his eyes alone. (It is not at all unusual to see a baby of a few months try to pick up a piece of the pattern from a plastic tablecloth or other boldly printed material.) He can only obtain a knowledge of the doll by acting on it with several of his senses and with his limbs: by touching, stroking, poking, holding, squeezing, and sucking, licking and chewing it, and by turning it over and over, waving it about and shaking it, while he watches and listens to what happens.

Now a year-old baby has been interested in objects for a few months, and has recently spent much of his time investigating – and experimenting upon – anything he can get hold of; and it is because he has already learned about the doll's three-dimensional form, its weight and consistency and degree of malleability, and because this knowledge has become integrated in his mind with the two-dimensional visual pattern it makes, that he is able to seize it so deftly, and lift it so nonchalantly, neither fumbling nor dropping it unintentionally.

At this stage the baby will probably enjoy a game of hiding and finding things, for he has come to the exciting realization that things exist. It has begun to dawn on him that what he sees or feels may have a continuing existence quite apart from himself and what he may be doing; and that when it disappears he is sometimes able to cause it to reappear again at will.

At every stage a baby wants – and needs – to feel conscious of being an effective agent, and in spite of his intense interest in objects and their specific characteristics and functions, he may suddenly switch to using them purely as something upon which to exercise and develop his sensory and motor powers – anything may, at any moment, be used as a missile, a target, a battering ram or simply as something to be taken apart or broken up into little bits.

All mothers know that at a certain age, babies love to drop things to the ground. At first the baby may simply be practising the skill of voluntarily letting go of things. Later he may try to perfect the art of making things fall just where he wishes them to fall. At some time or other he is sure to become interested in what happens to them when they fall, how they look as they go, and in the noise they make on hitting the ground. He may also, on occasion, simply be enjoying the feeling of power that it gives him to remove everything from his cot – including if possible the mattress – and to spread them around him on the floor.

Very few people have published detailed observations of the entirely spontaneous behaviour of babies and small children. Of these, probably the most enlightening and readable are by Milicent

Washburn Shinn: *The Biography of a Baby* and *Notes on the Development of a Child*, originally published over 90 years ago. Miss Shinn must have spent much of her time watching – with humble wonder and keen observation – every aspect of the behaviour of her baby niece Ruth, and in writing down, in far from boring detail, everything else she had seen and heard. These books teach us more about babies than the kind that tell us what the *average* baby can be expected to do at this or that age. Also, although the author had no such intention, they show us what kind of response from adults it is that encourages healthy, joyous and nourishing activity in babies.

One day when Ruth was two months old, Miss Shinn was holding her up against her shoulder – as she frequently did in order to let the baby look about her – keeping her own cheek close to the baby's head to provide a prop for it whenever Ruth grew momentarily tired of holding her head up. 'But today she was not satisfied with having her head erect: she persistently straightened her back up against the arm that supported her – a new set of muscles thus coming under the control of her will. As often as I pressed her down against my shoulder, she would fret, and straighten up again and set to work diligently looking about her.' After this Ruth was 'possessed by the most insatiate desire to be up where she could see. It was hard to think that her fretting and even wailing when forced to lie down could mean only a formless discontent, and not a clear idea of what she wanted. As soon as she was held erect, or propped up sitting amid cushions, she was content.'

By the middle of the third month, her smiles were fewer, and she looked about her earnestly and soberly; and in the last week I noted, without understanding, the expression of surprise that had come into her face as she gazed this way and that. The wide, surprised eyes must have meant that something new was before them. Were things beginning to separate themselves off to the baby's sight in definitely bounded spaces? . . . the wonder grew day by day, and for weeks the baby was looking about her silently, studying her world. She would inspect the familiar room carefully for many minutes, looking fixedly at object after object till the whole field of vision was reviewed, then she would turn her head eagerly and examine another section; and when she had seen all she could from one place, she would fret till she was carried to another, and there begin anew her inspection of the room in its changed aspect – always with the look of surprise and eagerness, eyes wide and brows raised.

The first occasion on which Miss Shinn plainly saw an expression of surprise on the baby's face was at six-and-a-half weeks.

> She lay making cheerful little sounds and suddenly, by some new combination of the vocal organs, a small, high crow came out – doubtless causing a most novel sensation in the little throat, not to speak of the odd sound. The baby fell silent instantly, and a ludicrous look of astonishment overspread her face.

Another time Ruth showed surprise at an unexpected happening, and then a determination to discover the reason for it. The family came of farming stock and were accustomed to sitting the baby on the floor inside an old – and well-cleaned – horse collar.

> Sitting as usual in her horse collar, she was bending herself back over it, a thing that she had done before, but today she kept it up so persistently and bent herself back with such exertion, that at last the back of her head touched the floor. She righted herself with an expression of great surprise. Evidently she had been experimenting in new muscular sensation only, and (as happens to all experimenters sometimes) she had got an extra result that she had not bargained for and did not understand. She bent back again with her head screwed round to see what had given her the touch. In this position, she did not reach the floor. She sat up again, looked at me with a perplexed face and tried it over a full dozen times till stopped by her mother who was afraid she might hurt herself.

Here is an example of a baby's interest in learning to recognize objects by sight when seen from different angles:

> . . . she sat in my lap, watching with an intent and puzzled face the back and side of her grandmother's head. Grandma turned from her knitting and chirruped to her, and the little one's jaw dropped and her eyebrows went up with an expression of blank surprise. Presently I began to swing her on my foot, and at every pause in the swinging she would sit gazing at the puzzling head till grandma turned, and nodded or chirruped to her; then she would turn away satisfied and want more swinging. . . . At first amazed to see the coil of silver hair and the curve of cheek turn suddenly into grandma's front face, the baby watched for a repetition of the miracle till it came to seem natural, and the two aspects were firmly knit together in her mind.

Millicent Shinn continues:

> She began, too, to watch people's motions carefully for long
> spaces of time – all through the process of setting the table, for
> instance – with a serious little face, and an attention so absorbed
> that it was hardly possible to divert her if one tried (which one
> ought not to do, for power of attention is a precious attainment,
> and people have no business to meddle with its growth for their
> own amusement).

If a baby is the type that likes to lie on his stomach, he will
learn quite early how to roll on to it. Probably he will do it the
first time by chance in his efforts to raise his head and shoulders
from the pillow as he simultaneously squirms and presses his heels
into the mattress; then, through successfully reproducing the
activity, he learns which muscles must be contracted and which
relaxed and by how much and in what sequence. I have noticed
that it may be some time before the baby learns how to roll back
again, and he may cry when he becomes tired of holding up his
head, and have to be rescued and replaced upon his back.

Rolling kept Miss Shinn's Ruth happy 'for six or seven weeks.
It enlarged her world greatly. If by chance she rolled over in the
same direction a number of times in succession, she would drift
halfway across the room, meeting no end of interesting things by
the way.' Then, at eight months, there was a fortnight of rapid
development in movements. Miss Shinn describes how, although
Ruth could not yet crawl, she often got on to her hands and knees,
and from that position discovered two different methods of getting
into a sitting position. During this time she also discovered how
to move while on hands and knees – but only backwards:

> The baby at once tried to utilise it to get to people and things,
> and it was funny to hear her chattering with displeasure as she
> found herself borne off the other way – backing sometimes into
> the wall, and pushing helplessly against it, like a little locomo-
> tive that had accidentally got reversed. She soon gave up trying
> to get anywhere by this 'craw-fishing', however, and then she en-
> joyed it, merely as movement. . . . Next, from hands and knees
> the baby learned to rise to hands and feet; to kneel, and then
> to sit back on her heels; and to make sundry variations on these
> positions, such as kneeling on one knee and one foot, or sitting on
> one heel with the other foot thrust out sideways, propping her.

She was eight and a half months old before she began to creep
forwards and it was another fortnight before she *enjoyed* crawling,

until then only using it in the last resort as a method of getting somewhere. On the other hand she was, at this time, always pulling herself to a standing position,

> ... not to reach anything, but from an overwhelming desire to get to her feet [for when she found herself on them] she rejoiced and triumphed. At this stage she almost invariably used a *low* object to pull up by, so that she could lean over it, propping her weight with her hands – or with one hand, as she grew more confident. ... In kneeling, too, she showed joy. She could not keep her balance on her knees for more than a few seconds, but while she did, she exulted in the exploit, and patted and waved her hands in glee.

For a period when Ruth was about ten months old and had learned to crawl and to pull herself up and stand alone,

> her toys were neglected; she was impatient of being held in arms, and eager only to get to the floor and use her new powers. She crept happily about for hours from chair to chair, from person to person, getting to her feet at each, and setting herself down cleverly again; smiling and crowing at each success. She ran away from us on hands and knees laughing, if she thought we were about to pick her up.

> She did not want to leave the floor for her meals, 'and was reconciled to them only if she might stand at her mother's side and take her milk and porridge in small doses interspersed with play.' She also enjoyed practising standing alone without holding on to anything – including the falling down.

Miss Shinn goes on,

> In these days there was evident an intangible but great increase in the little one's mental alertness, her eager curiosity in following our movements, her look of effort to understand, her growing clearness in grouping associations and interpreting what she saw. Her handling of things had long developed into elaborate investigation, turning an object over and examining every side, poking her fingers into crevices, opening and shutting lids, turning over the leaves of books; and now she was no longer satisfied with investigating such objects as she came across by chance – she began to have a passion (which increased for weeks and months, and made up a great part of her life) to go and find out what there was to see.

Here is one last example of Ruth's pattern of play. One day she managed to climb into her aunt's lap and the next day

spent a long time zealously climbing up a doorstep and letting herself down backward from it. The day after that, she tackled the stairs and climbed two steps. Later in the day, I set her at the bottom of the stairs and moved slowly up before her. The little thing followed after (her mother's arms close behind, of course; no one would be crazy enough to start a baby upstairs without such a precaution), tugging from step to step, grunting with exertion now and then, and exclaiming with satisfaction at each step conquered; slipping back once or twice, but undiscouraged – fifteen steps to the landing, where she pulled to her feet by the stair-post, hesitated, made a motion to creep down head first, then crept, laughing, along the landing, and up five steps more, and shouted with triumph to find herself on the upper floor. She even looked with ambition at the garret stairs, and started towards them; but an open door tempted her aside to explore a room, and she forgot the stairs.

For the rest of the month the baby dropped to hands and knees and scrabbled joyously for the stairs at every chance of open door; she was not satisfied without going up several times daily, and having people who believed in letting her do things, and ensuring her safety by vigilance while she did them, instead of holding her back, she soon became expert and secure in mounting. She made assaults too on everything that towered up and looked in the least climbable.

This was before Ruth had learned to walk and when she was still under a year old.

This baby was a particularly happy, sanguine, alert, enterprising, dogged and adventurous one, but it is impossible to tell to what degree these qualities were due to her inherited nature or the effect of her environment. Her animate and inanimate environments appeared to be particularly favourable to the development of these qualities in a baby, and it is likely that somewhat similar examples of behaviour to those quoted in this chapter could be observed of most babies whose environment was consistently of a similarly high quality.

A baby when playing increases his knowledge by the use of methods that are not dissimilar from those used by scientists; he tests objects that are new to him in one way after another, trying the effect of various actions on them – sometimes going through his whole existing repertory of skills.

His attention is caught by unexpected events, and he tries if possible to understand them – to fit them into his existing scheme of things or, if some particularly intriguing happening stops, he will try to make it recommence by acting in some way that he has already found to be an effective way of making things happen. The Piaget children adopted – as their father put it – 'certain procedures for making interesting phenomena recommence'.* Having caused the toys suspended from the hood of the cradle to sway and dance and jingle by vigorously moving their arms and legs, they would try to make any interesting sight or sound continue by the same method. Head-wagging was another 'procedure' used; and, as Piaget says, since this was a more specific movement and not expressive of general pleasure, one could be relatively sure that the baby was using it in order to make things happen. At eight and a half months, Lucienne knew that she could make the toys hanging from the hood of her cradle swing by wagging her head from side to side, and for several weeks she tried to make all sorts of things continue by the same method – to make her father repeat a cry, and to make a placard hanging in a railway carriage (which had stopped moving because the train was stationary) continue to swing. Laurent did the same thing to try to make his father continue to swing a paper knife, snap his finger against his thumb, and move the newspaper that he had unfolded in order to read. One wonders, however, if these babies might have stopped believing in the efficacy of this magic much sooner if their father had been less understanding of their intentions and slower to comply with their wishes, for they very quickly learned the real causes of some events. Laurent, the youngest of the three children, was particularly precocious in this respect. This was no doubt due partly to his having inherited a particularly observant, questioning, industrious and pertinacious nature, and partly to the amount of opportunity he was given by his father for mental activity and for assimilating just the kind of sensory-motor knowledge for which he was ready.

By three months he had learned to shake the rattles that hung above him, by moving his arm which had been attached at the wrist to the rattles by means of a long string – long enough for Laurent to have to stretch his arm right back over his head in

* Professor Piaget observed and recorded the behaviour of his own three children from birth, and quoted from these records in his books. The quotations here are from *The Origin of Intelligence in the Child* and *Play, Dreams and Imitation in Childhood*.

order to make the rattles swing and sound. By three and a half months, he could take hold of an object on sight of it. His father then decided to make another experiment: he attached a chain to the rattles, and placed the chain in the baby's hand. At first, when by chance Laurent made the rattles sound, he waved his hand to and fro but let go of the chain. However, he played with the chain from time to time during the day, and finally learned that it was the chain that made the rattles move. For in the evening when he was sucking his fingers, he was observed to touch the chain accidentally with the back of his hand; and at once he removed his right hand from his mouth, grasped the chain and pulled it very slowly, while watching the rattles. 'After a few seconds, during which he still pulls the chain very gently, he pulls much harder and succeeds. He then bursts into peals of laughter, babbles and swings the chain as much as possible.' On another occasion, Piaget notes that Laurent made the rattles sound by pulling the chain backwards and forwards for a quarter of an hour, with much laughter.

If any baby at all has a rattle of some kind suspended above him at the right height, he will often hit it accidentally as his arms wave about; he will be amused by the visual pattern it makes when it swings and the noise when it is hit; then at some time or other he will want these things to continue after they have stopped, and after a lot of ineffectual effort he will eventually learn how it is done. Then he will set himself to learn how to hit that rattle every time, and he will rejoice exceedingly in his increasing expertise in hitting it and, later, in seizing and shaking it. As Millicent Shinn says, 'It is an epoch of tremendous importance when the baby first with real attention brings sight and touch and muscle freely to bear together on an object.'

Babies learn a variety of new skills through their efforts to make interesting happenings continue. For instance, an infant may be lying in his cot, doing nothing much, perhaps exploring his lips and gums with his tongue, perhaps playing at smacking his lips together, sucking in his cheeks or blowing bubbles with his saliva. Suddenly, by chance, he makes a sound that captures his attention for some reason – perhaps because it is new to him – and if he happens to make the same sound again from time to time, he may then try to make it intentionally – and succeed. This may take some time but eventually he sorts out the right movements of his throat, tongue, lips etc. from the ineffectual ones. Success may cause him to become rather boringly attached to this particular sound, but sooner or later he will realize that variations can be made on it. As Groos says, 'the child that attains to the voluntary production of tone is fairly launched in experimentation, and without this playful practice, he could not become master of his voice.'

A baby imitates himself, but also enjoys being imitated, as many mothers know. If someone will play with him he will enjoy a game of mutual imitation, for he relishes his power to obtain a response from his environment.

> At 0:6(25) [6 months, 25 days] Jacqueline invented a new sound by putting her tongue between her teeth. It was something like 'pfs'. Her mother then made the sound. Jacqueline was delighted and laughed as she repeated it in her turn. Then came a long period of mutual imitation: Jacqueline said 'pfs', her mother imitated her, and Jacqueline watched her without moving her lips. Then, when her mother stopped, Jacqueline began again, and so it went on . . .*

When one reads these descriptions of learning-activity in infants, one notices that, whenever the baby succeeds in extending his ability or skill in some way or another, he manifests satisfaction, joy, excitement or intense interest, and he usually proceeds to repeat the new activity – whether it originated through imitation or invention – several times.

Here are some examples (from C. W. Valentine's *The Psychology of Early Childhood*) of the way babies repeat a newly acquired skill over and over again.

> B. at 0:4½ [4½ months]. Yesterday he discovered the trick of sucking his lower lip and today has practised it constantly. Often practises singing by starting on a high note and running down a kind of scale.

> Also Y. is noted, at 0:6, as constantly practising for a week or more two new noises: (a) a kind of trilling, and (b) a sound like 'tch'.

> B. at 0:6½. We noticed for the first time a new movement: he took a spoon by the handle and then gyrated his fist so that the spoon described a semi-circle in the air. He repeated this five or six times, watching it meanwhile.

> B. at 0:7½ struck notes on the piano 100 times – with great signs of pleasure.

* This is one of many similar obsevations that Piaget made, and later quoted in *Play, Dreams and Imitation in Childhood*.

At 0:8, B. had a period of a few days when he particularly enjoyed waving things about wildly, handkerchiefs, bibs, pieces of clothing etc. This is typical of the way in which a particular kind of play would begin, occupy a lot of time for a few days or weeks or even months, and then disappear.

R. W. White of Harvard is a psychologist who understands the significance of the activity of babies. He writes that 'the more closely we analyse the behaviour of the human infant, the more clearly do we realize that infancy is not simply a time when the nervous system matures and the muscles grow stronger. It is a time of active and continuous learning.'

For the first few months of his life, a baby's play is usually fairly fruitful. Unless he is kept in pitch-dark soundproofed solitary confinement, he will spend his waking hours exercising his limbs and his voice, and using his senses and his mind – in an elementary manner – on the sights, sounds and objects in his immediate vicinity. His powers are nourished by the activity and begin to grow. But as they grow, they will need more varied and less easily provided nourishment. He will continue to know exactly what he wants to learn to do, and we also need to have some idea of the sort of knowledge and experience he needs, or we may find, for example, that, no longer satisfied with being able to throw all his toys out of his pram, he may want to see if he can throw them out of the window, over the fireguard or into the washing machine.

He will become capable of forming personal relationships and will become particularly attached to one or sometimes two people. Later he will need to become familiar with a number of people if his mental and emotional potentiality is to be realized.

Some of the descriptions included in this chapter of the activity of babies – learning to judge distances, speeds and angles, for instance, or finding out which muscles must be contracted and by how much and so on – may have made it appear as if I supposed them to be engaging in cerebral activity beyond their ability. But this is so only because I have necessarily used words. Although a baby neither uses words nor mentally manipulates symbols of any kind, his activity is nevertheless mental activity; for the assimilation and co-ordination of the visual, tactile, kinetic and other sensory-motor knowledge that he acquires takes place somewhere in his brain. The baby is using and developing his intelligence, although at this stage his intelligence is mainly sensory-motor intelligence. Through his voluntary activity – his play – he learns about three-dimensional space, about the effects of the force of gravity upon himself and objects, about other causal relations of things, and about the physical qualities and the characteristic behaviour of an increasingly large number of objects and creatures. Through his play also, the infant develops his potential ability to see and hear and grasp, to distinguish and recognize objects, scenes and sounds, and to control and direct the movements of his limbs. As well as this, he learns which sights, sounds, sensations, objects, people and activities he prefers to others, and works out how to get more of what he likes. In short, *he learns to act and feel and think and choose.*

PART II

The Nature of Nurtural Play

Introduction

So far I have merely described the play of babies and children who are in a position to choose what they will do from moment to moment in a suitable environment. But now, since it is evident that in these circumstances their play is learning-activity, I shall study it with a view to discovering exactly what sort of knowledge children choose to acquire. For it is time that we knew not only that children learn through play, but also *what* they need to learn if their human potentiality is to be realized and they are to grow into men and women mature and healthy in every sense.

It is possible to find this out because the *spontaneous* play of children is – circumstances permitting – the means by which they develop their basic human powers. I base this assumption on the following hypotheses:

1. Every young creature has an inherent urge to play.
2. His powers develop when they are exercised in and on an appropriate environment.
3. A healthily growing creature knows exactly what experience his powers currently need when he is in the presence of opportunities for this experience.

My own observations have confirmed this, but I would not consider myself justified in attempting to base what amounts to a technique of child-nurture upon it, if it were not for the fact that certain eminent students of animal and human behaviour have independently developed theories – or produced pieces of evidence – that support it.

In the 1930s Professor Jean Piaget of Geneva was discovering and formulating a theory of how a human being *knows* and how he becomes capable of effective and appropriate activity and of rational and creative thought. Professor Piaget had extraordinarily wide scientific interests and experience, being a philosopher, a mathematician and – most important – a biologist; moreover, he considered it necessary to spend a great deal of time over a period of several years studying the play of babies in their home surroundings. Unfortunately his theory of learning has been couched in terms which caused many educationalists to ignore it or to apply it only to a narrow field such as the teaching of mathematics. Therefore, in spite of the fact that Piaget's name is a household word in the educational world, insufficient practical use has been made of his – to my mind – most important discoveries of all.

It is understandable that people seeking to know what Piaget had to say about *play*, and looking up his references to it, would not find much to help them. This is because he gives the word 'play' a very limited meaning; for instance, he *contrasts* 'play' with imitation, and sometimes – when describing the activity of children over about eighteen months – with learning-activity.

I was fortunate in chancing to begin with *The Origin of Intelligence in the Child*; and, at my first attempt to read it, I realized with excitement that his thought ran on similar lines – as far as the development of mental faculties goes – to that of Scott Williamson. After further study I realized that their two theories of how a child's faculties develop – although expressed in quite dissimilar language – were basically the same.

Piaget holds that intelligence has a predetermined limit – probably very rarely ever reached – in each individual, but that a child's intelligence is *not* predetermined in the sense that it is given at conception and develops inevitably with age, irrespective of the nature of the environment. On the other hand, he also rejects the theory that intelligence is a mechanism that will inevitably operate more and more effectively if it is sufficiently stimulated from the outside, or that it can be likened to a piece of clay that involuntarily receives impressions from the environment which then become accidentally associated.

Instead it is, he says,* 'a relationship, among others, with the environment', and this relationship grows through – and only through – the voluntary activity of the child in response to an appropriate environment. How well it grows depends on the attitude of the child to his environment, and this in turn depends on the nature of the child and on the nature of the environment and, on the effect each has on the other. A child's emotional relationship to his environment becomes more sensitive and appropriate, as well as stronger through active response to it. His power to feel grows through use. For instance, the emotions of fear and anger seem to be undifferentiated at first in a baby.

It seems probable that the laws governing the development of intelligence postulated by Piaget apply equally to the development of all one's relations with the environment – one's awareness, sensibility, judgment, spontaneous responsiveness and free will.

* *The Origin of Intelligence in the Child* (1953), p. 19.

CHAPTER SIX

Why and How Babies Learn

Chicks in the shell have been observed in laboratories to practise the movements of their heads and necks that they will later use in the process of pecking for food; and, as everyone knows, they peck their way out of the shell. Then, as soon as they become hungry and food is present on the ground, they will peck at it, but, at first, inaccurately; it takes them about a day to become able to hit a grain of corn every time.

A number of experiments have been made in which chicks have been put in darkness immediately on hatching, and fed by hand for a varying number of days. It was found by S. G. Padilla that if, after eight or more days in darkness, they were then placed in the light and among scattered corn, they did not peck and were, moreover, quite unable to learn to obtain their food by pecking. This proves beyond a doubt that, if a chick's faculty to peck grain effectively is to flourish, it must be exercised – and at the right time.

It is also certain that chicks do not need to be taught how to feed; they do not even need to be able to imitate the model of a pecking hen. They learn on their own, and quickly, under the right conditions. The latter include light, air, freedom to move, food grains to be found on the ground, and appetite.

Perhaps one may conclude that the chick's faculty to peck grain is present on hatching, but only latent or dormant, in the same way as the plant is present in the seed, or the complete individual creature in the fertilized egg, and that it will only germinate and grow under the conditions described above. In other words, it will develop only if it receives the nourishment of appropriate exercise.

The activity of pecking grain is not a simple one; in fact it requires a variety of knowledge. It requires a sensory knowledge of the nature of a grain of corn, of the nature of solid ground and of the effects on the moving chick of the force of gravity. Furthermore, the chick must know how to balance while moving its head and neck, how to judge distances visually, how to bring its beak to the exact spot on which the grain of corn is lying, using exactly the correct amount of force, and how to seize the food in its beak and swallow it. In fact, it requires the co-ordinated activity of almost all the chick's potential faculties. No wonder a chick takes a day to learn to do it effectively.

The chicks that were deprived of this opportunity to use, and to learn to co-ordinate, their faculties became in effect mentally subnormal. Their intelligence had failed to develop because it had had no chance to exercise itself in this – to chicks – fundamentally important field of activity.

A new-born human being is far more helpless than a newly-hatched chick, but possesses the seeds of an incomparably greater range of powers. Some of a baby's potential or dormant faculties, such as breathing or sucking, can, like a chick's, be quickly realized; others, including the use of his hands and his eyes, grow more slowly but are capable of far greater development and elaboration. A child's faculties, if provided with adequate and timely nourishment, will grow and differentiate, culminating eventually in powers of a completely different order from those of chickens.

If one treats this fact with the wondering respect that it deserves instead of dismissing it as a truism, one comes to realize what an enormous amount and variety of nourishing exercise a child's faculties will require if he is to realize his full potentiality.

His capacity at any moment depends upon the quality and quantity of functional nourishment that he has digested. This, in turn, depends upon his innate characteristics, upon his environment, and upon the effect that each of these has had upon the other.

Among the 'seedling' faculties ready to grow and flower at different stages in a child's growth are the skill of sucking, of moving his hand towards a desired and visible object, of balancing on his feet, of recognizing his mother – or other caretaker – as someone he prefers to other creatures, and of obtaining from her the response that he desires.

A faculty can only digest a certain amount and kind of food at any one moment, but the kind of nourishment it will require next must always be within reach, or its necessarily sequential development will not proceed smoothly and rapidly enough. Both the child as a whole and his individual faculties develop sequentially. The authors of *The Peckham Experiment* write:

> The study of the sequential development of the faculties after birth is in our opinion of as great an interest and importance as is the study of embryology from which is gained a knowledge of the sequential development of the individual's features before birth. Herein lies a rational basis for a future science of education.

They say that, as in all biological processes, the law governing the sequence is inherent in the organism itself.

Let us try to discover more about the process and begin by studying, with Piaget's help, the early development of some of the baby's faculties. A baby can and does make sucking movements at birth – perhaps even before; but as midwives, and some mothers to their chagrin, know, the baby quite definitely needs to learn how to feed from the breast or bottle, and before he is able to use this potential faculty effectively, there is quite a lot for him to learn. He must learn how to keep his lips and tongue curved firmly round the nipple while he contracts his tongue and cheek muscles rhythmically; and he must also learn how to co-ordinate sucking and swallowing with breathing. Some babies learn this so quickly that it appears as if they were born with the knowledge. Others have difficulty in co-ordinating and adapting their movements and in concentrating on the task in hand; they need patient help for a day or two and everything made as easy for them as possible. Of Piaget's children two, Lucienne and Laurent, behaved in the former manner and one, Jacqueline, was rather slow to learn.

No two babies look exactly alike – except for identical twins – nor do they behave in exactly the same manner: each has a different temperament and different tastes, and each has a slightly different environment. (It is impossible for a mother or a nurse, however hard she tries, to respond in exactly the same way to each of the children in her care.) The baby's temperament and tastes, and his environment, affect each other from the start, and both influence his activity, so that even a baby a few hours old has a past history. I do not only mean what happened to him in the womb and during the birth process; I mean that he has a past history of activity. Piaget mentions that '... Lucienne and Laurent at a quarter and a half an hour after birth respectively, had both sucked their hands. ... Lucienne, whose hand had been immobilized due to its position, sucked her fingers for more than ten minutes.' I myself remember that, less than a quarter of an hour after my fourth child was born, loud sucking noises were heard coming from the cot. The midwife glanced at him as she bustled around and said: 'He has found his thumb already.' Certainly that particular baby seemed to know how to suck immediately he was given the opportunity.*

*Many environmental circumstances affect the speed at which a child learns to suck. If the baby is put to the breast within an hour or two of birth, when he is not yet frantic with hunger all he receives as a result of sucking is a few drops of colostrum. This satisfies him at this stage, and is much easier for him to cope with without choking than a jet of milk. Colostrum also helps develop the baby's power of digestion.

The new-born infant is patently inexpert even at sucking his thumb or his fingers; at first it is a hit-and-miss activity, clumsy and noisy. It seems that the baby is not born with a knowledge of how to suck *a particular object*; he simply has a tendency to make sucking movements in response to a touch upon his mouth, and he must adapt these movements to the form and consistency of the object if he is to be able to suck it efficiently.

Piaget is not content merely to describe phenomena. He wonders why and how babies behave as they do. He asks himself questions such as: 'Why did Lucienne suck her fingers, a quarter of an hour after birth, for ten minutes in succession?' And comments: 'It could not be because of hunger because the umbilical cord had just been cut.' That she should begin to suck at her hand was to be expected: it was held closely against her mouth owing to the manner in which she had been wrapped up, and the 'sucking reflex' (or tendency to make sucking movements at a touch on the open mouth) would have come into play automatically. But, Piaget asks, why did she continue to suck for so long when sucking led to no apparent result? The following paragraphs contain what I believe to be Piaget's answer to the question.

The finger- or thumb- or hand-sucking of an infant only a few minutes old is an entirely different kind of activity from the finger- or thumb- or hand-sucking that an older baby undertakes in order to comfort himself, or when sleepy or bored. Nor is it similar to the activity of a nine-month-old baby who puts anything he can get hold of into his mouth and sucks it as well as biting, mumbling and licking it in order to make himself the more familiar with it, or in order to rub the places on his gums where his teeth are emerging. It is also different from the baby's avid sucking of his fingers when he is hungry, for, in this case, the baby quickly rejects them and yells or restlessly moves his head from side to side, seeking for something more satisfying to his stomach. A baby sucks his fingers for different reasons on different occasions, but the latter three examples have one thing in common: in each case the baby knows very well how to suck objects effectively. He has acquired the necessary know-how, whereas the baby that has been in the world for only fifteen minutes has not. For him sucking is a learning-activity.

As soon as it is used upon an object, the automatic sucking 'reflex reaction' begins to become something other than a mechanical and unchanging habit. The 'seed' of the baby's faculty to suck begins to 'sprout' because of the nourishing 'warmth and moisture' it has obtained through being used on an object. The 'reflex' is nature's device for getting the process started. Once growth starts, the faculty requires nourishment in the form of exercise and therefore continues to exercise itself upon the object. This is why a baby only a few minutes old will behave in such an apparently purposeful manner.

Faculties flourish on exercise, and without it stagnate or wither away. Calves can find the cows' teats without help and can immediately suckle competently, but if they are prevented from suckling, the faculty atrophies and their innate know-how is lost. In *Intelligence and Experience*, McV. Hunt says: 'All dairy farmers know that if a calf is fed from a pail for a certain number of days, it is safe to allow it among cows in milk as it will no longer try to suckle.'

As Lucienne lay trying to suck her fingers for ten minutes at a stretch, the power of her sucking faculty to adapt itself to circumstances was growing stronger through exercise. Or, to put it differently, her faculty to suck had, after those ten minutes, made a beginning of growing; it had grown a little shoot from which another bud could easily sprout. This means that when, later, she has the opportunity to suck a different object, such as a nipple, she will not be so clumsy and unskilled at her first attempt as she would have been if she had never before exercised her faculty to suck on any object. There will still be plenty for her to learn, because the new object has a shape and consistency of its own to which the position and movements of her mouth must accommodate themselves if she is to suck it effectively. As her movements become adapted to the new circumstances, the faculty to suck incorporates this know-how into itself, so that henceforth it consists of a body-of-knowledge of how to suck a finger *and* of how to suck a nipple. In the case in question the order of events could have been reversed. If Lucienne had learned how to suck a nipple first, the period of clumsy and inefficient sucking of her fingers would have been shorter. The nipple and the finger both provide the faculty-to-suck with *functional* food.

The gist of all this is that Lucienne was, through her activity, digesting – that is, selecting and absorbing – the knowledge needed by her faculty to suck. Although she had taken her first breath only fifteen minutes earlier and so did not as yet feel hungry for milk, she already felt hungry for experience that would nourish her faculty to suck, and that was the reason why, when the opportunity arose, she continued so long and energetically to suck her fingers. This is, I believe, Piaget's answer to his own question – transcribed into common or garden language.

Before he is many days old, a baby begins to exercise his faculty to see. At first he may simply tend to turn his head towards the window or a lamp, but by the age of two or three weeks, his attention is definitely attracted to *moving* objects and his efforts to keep them in view are increasingly rewarded. Then, from five weeks onwards, Piaget noticed that a baby will also look at an immobile object – after a movement has attracted his attention in its direction – with concentration, apparently trying to keep it in focus. When his son Laurent was one month and seven days old, Piaget moved the hood of the baby's bassinet over to the foot end; Laurent immediately looked at this.

Then he follows roughly the line of a white fringe which edges the hood and he finally fixes his gaze on a particular point of this fringe. At 0:1(8) [one month and eight days] same experiment and same result. But when he looks at the fringe, he sees my motionless face (I stood there in order to observe his eyes). He then gazes alternately at the fringe and at my head, directing his gaze himself since there are no movements to attract his attention from one thing to another.

Piaget asks himself why the child should do this since the things at which he looks have no meaning for him, for he has never sucked or grasped them and so cannot know them as things to suck and grasp; furthermore they have no depth or solidity since the baby has not yet learned to use both eyes together at all consistently. They are therefore only 'spots' which appear and disappear. Why then should he look at them so persistently? Piaget says that it is *because the activity is nourishment for his faculty to see.* This is the reason for the apparent interest of a baby five and a half weeks old in his father's face and in the fringe. At this age the infant's faculty to keep objects in focus so that he can see them clearly, to alter the focusing of his eyes as he looks at objects nearer or farther from himself, to use both eyes together, and to direct and control the movements of his eyeballs, is ready to develop rapidly if it is exercised. An infant's powers are bound by the same biological law as living organisms: they must feed on the environment if they are to grow and not wither away.

Piaget records that at twenty-five days old Laurent

spends nearly an hour in his cradle without crying, his eyes wide open. At 0:0(30) same observation. He stares at a piece of fringe on his cradle with continuous little re-adaptive movements as though his head had difficulty in not changing position, and his gaze brought it to the right place. So long as he gazes thus, his arms are still; at other times when he is awake they tend to wave to and fro.

At that moment the baby's whole being was strongly affected by the fact that he was engaged in developing the mental processes that are involved in seeing. And this was the cause of the temporary inhibition of the almost continuous involuntary movements of his eyes, head and arms that a baby of this age tends to make when he is awake.

In recent years, scientists belonging to different schools of thought, and engaged in studying different aspects of human and other organisms, have come independently to conclusions which parallel those of Piaget. They have become particularly dissatisfied with the hitherto generally accepted theories of motivation, such as the one that attributes activity to the need to reduce the tension caused by somatic 'drives', or to habits formed through tension having been reduced in certain circumstances in the past.

They have discovered through their experiments that creatures have, for example, an 'intrinsic love of learning', or a 'desire to be mentally and physically active', to 'become familiar with their surroundings', to 'investigate novelties', 'acquire new skills', and 'obtain mastery over things and themselves', as they have variously expressed it.

My information on this point has come mainly from Dr R. W. White,* who describes how students of learning in animals have time and again observed that animals do not need the prospect of a reward to push them into investigating new objects, exploring new territory and learning new skills.

He quotes H. F. Harlow, who has shown that monkeys will work for weeks at solving simple mechanical puzzles with no reward other than finding a solution. He tells the story of a female chimpanzee who solved a series of problems, getting a slice of banana for each solution; but instead of eating them, she piled the slices in a neat row on the top of the apparatus. Then she repeated the whole series of problems, putting one slice of banana back into the food dish after each trial.

Even rats enjoy solving problems when all their sensual needs have been purposely sated. One researcher reported that rats would even cross an electrified grill simply for the privilege of

* In his paper, 'Motivation Reconsidered: the Concept of Competence'.

exploring further afield. In fact it has been found that hungry rats will not solve difficult problems, the solution of which is rewarded by food, as effectively as rats that are not particularly hungry, the reason being that in the former case they are in so much of a hurry to reach the food that they do not take into account all the factors necessary to the solution of the problem.

(It occurs to me that perhaps children wishing to please anxious parents or impatient schoolteachers, or ambitious to be 'top' or fearing to be 'bottom' are, like the hungry rats, too intent on finding the answer as quickly as possible to be able to comprehend the nature of the problem, and that this attitude may have a bad effect on their mental development. This thought was inspired by John Holt's *How Children Fail*.)

In *A Textbook of Psychology*, D. O. Hebb tells of an experiment with rats. The rats were put into an apparatus, one at a time, in which there was a choice of routes to a dish of food; one was direct, and one involved going through a simple maze. Going through the maze meant having to make right or wrong decisions – in effect solving a very simple problem. When the maze was changed after each run so that the problem was a new one on each journey, the rats chose to go through the maze rather than to follow the direct route to the food 40 per cent of the time. When, however, the route was unchanged, they preferred to do so only 12 per cent of the time, 'the difference showing up even in the first block of five trials'. It appears that an environment that requires only routine, mechanical, habitual behaviour is uninteresting and unrewarding to well-fed and contented animals. One may suspect that the same applies to children, and infer that such an environment has no nurtural value for either.

Dr White says that 'we are witnessing a significant evolution of ideas' concerning what it is that motivates animals and human beings to act. He is not surprised that this should happen, since 'any biologically sound view of human nature must take into account the fact that man and the higher animals develop a competence in dealing with the environment which they certainly do not have at birth and certainly do not arrive at simply through maturation'; and that, 'in the mammals and man, with their highly plastic nervous systems, fitness to interact with the environment is slowly attained through prolonged feats of learning.' He says: 'Considering the slow rate of learning in infancy and the vast amount that has to be learned before there can be an effective level of interaction with surroundings, young animals and children would simply not learn enough unless they worked pretty steadily at the task between episodes of homeostatic crisis.'*

The child's need for food, cuddling, sleep, and so on, demands immediate satisfaction when it occurs, but it occurs only intermittently. White says that the very strong urges the child feels for these things interrupt from time to time the more gentle but steady and persistent urge he feels to develop his powers and to make himself familiar with his environment.

When considering the play of babies, White observes (and anyone who has watched a toddler purposefully and gleefully trying out his powers and investigating his surroundings will surely agree with him), that their behaviour is not 'random behaviour produced by a general overflow of energy', nor are they at the mercy of any and every stimulus; 'their behaviour is directed, selective and persistent'. The purposeful efforts of children to learn to see, grasp, walk, think, speak – and of all young mammals to discover the nature of the environment and to produce effective changes in it – have a common biological significance: they are the result of the need to become 'competent', that is to say, to become 'capable of interacting effectively with the environment'. But the playing child does not know that he must exercise his faculties in order to become a competent human being; he does so because he enjoys doing it, and he enjoys it because it gives him a sense of power over himself and circumstances. It reinforces his feeling of possessing the ability to respond to his surroundings as he would like to respond to them. Hence learning of this kind is its own reward. White puts it that behaviour which promotes the development of latent ability in any field of activity gives an animal or a human being a satisfying 'feeling of efficacy'.

His thesis can be summed up by the statement that one of the most influential forces – if not the most influential force of all – governing behaviour is the organism's urge 'to realize its capacity to interact effectively with the environment'.

White is concerned with the question of motivation. Piaget asks another question: *how* do a child's faculties develop? In other words, how does the organism become capable of effective and fruitful interaction with the environment?

The presence of the thumb in a baby's mouth triggers off mechanical sucking movements. These are energetic but inept; however, after a few moments, if the thumb remains in his mouth, his lips and tongue begin to shape themselves to the thumb, and

* Compare with the quotation from K. Groos on p. 12 above.

126

his sucking movements begin to accommodate themselves to its form and consistency. Little by little the inborn ability to make sucking movements differentiates into a faculty-to-suck-a-thumb. The baby continues automatically to suck at anything that falls into his mouth, but if it happens to be his thumb, his faculty-to-suck-a-thumb immediately operates; the baby does not have to learn from scratch on each occasion. He begins almost exactly where he left off, and eventually the specific manner of holding his lips, and the specific movements of his cheeks, jaws and tongue that are necessary for the effective sucking of a small thumb will have become co-ordinated in space and time with each other and organized to form a whole that is called into play in its entirety whenever the baby's thumb falls into his mouth – and later, whenever it touches his face, and later still whenever the idea of sucking his thumb occurs to him and he has nothing better to do. The faculty to suck his thumb can and does exactly reproduce itself over and over again in response to exactly similar circumstances. But if the circumstances are slightly different – if, for instance, a baby finds a new object such as a nipple or a dummy or a piece of his clothing in his mouth – he will in the first moment make use of his faculty-to-suck-a-thumb upon the new object. But a nipple or a dummy or the fold of his dress is different in shape and consistency from his thumb, and so the manner of sucking must change, if he is to become skilled at sucking one of these objects. This happens, as we have seen, without causing the knowledge of how to suck his thumb to be erased from his memory. The baby's faculty to suck now consists of several distinct skills, one of which is called into play by the sensation of a thumb in his mouth, another by the nipple, a third by a dummy and a fourth by a fold of material.

This means incidentally that something very interesting has happened: the baby's 'sensory-motor intelligence', as Piaget calls it, has begun to be active – at least as far as the activity of sucking is concerned – for the baby is able to recognize his thumb immediately it falls into his mouth as something that is sucked in a certain manner, and to recognize the nipple as something that requires to be sucked in a different manner, and the dummy in a slightly different manner again. This kind of recognition of objects as things to be acted on in a certain manner is obviously of a quite different order of activity from the power to discriminate objects that will come later when the baby has become aware of objects as such, and of himself as an object, and is capable of distinguishing to some extent between what is and what is not himself. It is nevertheless intelligent activity of a kind – a practical, sensory-motor kind; his sucking activity is definitely not mechanical or random or undiscriminating activity, although much of a baby's activity can, at this very early stage, still be so described. As far as the activity of sucking is concerned the baby has begun to act as a centrally controlled and directed whole.

Piaget has observed that sooner or later the baby plays at sucking his lips or licking them and exploring them with his tongue, and that this develops into other kinds of play such as bubble-blowing or smacking his lips together and thus making a clapping sound, but the faculty to suck has a limited power of development.

The faculty to grasp begins to develop later and grows more slowly, but has a far greater potentiality for growth and differentiation. A person's hands can continue to develop skills to the end of his life.

Babies are continually grasping at things. C. W. Valentine quotes from the diary that he kept of the activity of his children:

B, at 0:5½, was so fond of grasping at things that this constantly made dressing him more difficult. Often when nursing at the breast he would stop to grasp at his mother's dress, a chain, a paper she was trying to read and so on.

Piaget noted of his son Laurent:

At 0:2(7) he scratches the sheet which is folded over the blankets, then grasps it and holds it a moment, lets it go, then scratches it again and grasps it, and so on without interruption. At 0:2(11) this play lasts a quarter of an hour at a time, several times during the day.

As Piaget explains, the baby grasps at his sheet in the first place because of two particular spontaneous movements that all babies make from birth, if they are free to do so. The first of these is to wave his arms jerkily and at random and to stretch and bend his fingers much of the time when he is awake and not feeding. Secondly, a baby automatically closes his fingers over an object that touches the palm of his hand or the inside of his fingers. Because of these two tendencies, a baby's hand will frequently touch his covers and his clothes and he will close his fingers on them. However, before the age of ten weeks or so, the natural tendency of the baby's hand would be to jerk away almost at once and to move in some other direction. Therefore when, on the occasion described above, Laurent's hand remains more or less on one spot, scratching and grasping and momentarily holding the sheet over and over again, Piaget concludes that he is beginning to have a 'tactile interest' in the sheet, and that his faculty to grasp is beginning to develop. During the following week Piaget noticed that Laurent spent less and less time scratching, and often grasped the sheet or other object almost on first touching it, and that he held on for longer.

At this stage the infant's faculty to grasp is exercising itself, but so far in a very primitive and inept manner: he uses his fingers together as a unit and his thumb with them instead of opposite to them. Therefore it is only if he encounters something which fits easily into the palm of his hand (like a finger), or which, like a sheet, moulds itself to his hand, that he can hold it. This primitive form of grasping must have quickly developed into a useful accomplishment when our ancestors lived in trees. Indeed it has been discovered that a new-born baby is able to hang from its hands supporting its own weight if a small rod is placed against its palms and slowly raised. I would not like to try the experiment myself, but I am always surprised afresh by the strength of a tiny baby's grip when I put my finger into his hand. Strength alone, however, does not make a baby capable of holding a *variety* of objects firmly between his fingers and thumb, or of picking them up. He has to learn from experience how to do this. At two and a half months Laurent was still at the beginning of the road; he was grasping at all sorts of things but he was making the same undiscriminating grasping response to all objects, whatever their shape or nature.

However, as the baby occupies himself with grasping, his senses and his brain are active; he is paying attention to what he is doing, and he begins to be responsive to the nature of the object that he grasps. He still grasps automatically at anything that touches the inside of his hand, but now it sometimes happens that, before he relaxes his grip or stretches his fingers again after having closed them upon an object, he has received something from the object. This something is a bit of knowledge of how to grasp that particular object. It is evident that the baby retains and absorbs this bit of sensory-motor know-how, because as he grasps his sheet, or his own hand, or his nose again and again, he begins to adapt the manner in which he holds and moves his fingers and thumb according to which of the objects it is that he is grasping. He begins to shape his hand to the shape of the object and to move his fingers and thumb in a manner that suits its consistency and weight.

Here is the beginning of the interaction – or two-way flow – between the baby and his environment. In Piaget's terms, this interaction consists of the simultaneous assimilation of the environment by the organism and the accommodation of the organism to the environment, resulting in the reorganization and development of the organism – and change in the environment.

As the days go by, it becomes evident to an observer that certain objects are becoming known to the baby as objects to be grasped in a particular manner. He responds to these more and more appropriately, as far as grasping them is concerned; he fumbles and experiments less, until eventually, at the first touch of one of them, he may immediately make the precise movements that are necessary in order to take hold of it effectively.

One of the most noticeable signs of progress in grasping at this time is the baby's increasing use of his thumb. The use of the thumb opposite to the fingers is essential for the skilled manipulation of objects and even for the effective holding of most objects.

Although the faculty to see begins to develop before the faculty to grasp, a baby learns to grasp many objects by touch alone, and it is some time before he learns how to direct his gaze to his hands and what he is holding, or to bring his hands into his field of view, and, finally, to move his hand to an object that he sees in front of him and take hold of it.

As Piaget says – and Millicent Shinn also noticed – for a baby at this stage, there are several separate worlds, among them a visual world and a tactile world. The baby is unaware that the thing he sees is one and the same as the thing he touches, and which he may already recognize, when he touches it, as something that, if it is to be grasped, must be grasped just so.

Faculties develop independently of each other, but two or more may, through being used simultaneously upon the same object, gradually become co-ordinated to form a more complex faculty. Piaget says they 'mutually assimilate' each other. The baby learns how to move what he is looking at and to keep what he is moving in view, usually practising at first on his own hand. Piaget describes how Lucienne at 0:3(13) looks at her right hand for a long time and opens and closes it, and when her hand suddenly moves towards her left cheek her eyes follow it, her head also moving. Her hand then returns to its previous position and Lucienne spies it again, and smiles broadly while wriggling and kicking with pleasure. During the following days she often watches her moving hands or her hand holding an object. Then,

Observation 68. At 0:4(9) Lucienne makes no motion to grasp a rattle she is looking at. But when she subsequently brings to her mouth the rattle she has grasped independently of sight, and sees the hand which holds this object, her visual attention results in immobilising for a moment the movement of her hand, although her mouth was already open to receive the rattle which is 1 cm. away from her. Then Lucienne sucks the rattle, takes it out of her mouth, looks at it, sucks it again, and so on.

The next day, Lucienne is looking at her rattle with an obvious desire to suck it. 'She opens her mouth, makes sucking-like movements, raises her head slightly etc., but she does not stretch out her hands although they make grasping movements.' Then Piaget places the rattle next to her outstretched hand. 'Lucienne looks alternately at her hand and at the rattle, her fingers constantly moving, but she does not move her hand closer. But when the rattle touches her hand, she grasps it immediately.' Five days later, however, Lucienne can seize her rattle if it is close to her hand and if both rattle and hand are in her field of vision at the same moment. If the rattle is near her eyes but far from her hand she still simply stares at the rattle and moves her hand vaguely. Similar behaviour was observed on the part of the other two children.

Miss Shinn noticed an amusing instance of the lack of co-ordination between the different faculties during the baby's fourth month.

One day, as she lay on her back, a rubber ring fell out of her mouth and lay encircling her nose, resting on its bridge and on her upper lip; she made many efforts to reach it with her lips, stretching her mouth ridiculously, but had no idea of using the little hands which fluttered wildly in helpless sympathy.

When the two faculties of looking-at-and-seeing and reaching-for-and-grasping have been co-ordinated in the baby, he quickly becomes able to grasp all the objects that he has already learned to grasp by their feel, immediately on sight of them. He will be less immediately successful with strange objects because he has first to discover their nature and characteristics as three-dimensional objects through handling them. (Even an adult may hit himself on the nose, if he goes to pick up what he believes to be a heavy wooden box, when it is, in fact, made of cardboard.)

It is obvious that for a long time a child's hands – apart from his mouth – will be his only reliable sources of information as to the three-dimensional shape and the consistency and the weight of an object. Therefore 'don't touch' can be one of the most frustrating and inhibiting commands to which a small child can be subjected. Margaret Mead tells how the Australian aborigines make drawings of objects that are in plan – or diagrammatic – and when aborigine children are shown pictures in which perspective is used, they are surprised and intrigued, and say: 'You have painted it the way it looks, not the way it really is.'

Owing to a combination of circumstances, a baby may complete a certain sequence of digestion exceptionally quickly. Laurent began to achieve the co-ordination of hand and eye very early. This happened, according to Piaget, because at a few weeks old he began to enjoy the activity of clasping and unclasping his hands, and this activity would normally take place in front of his eyes. Beginning at 0:2(24) he is observed to watch his hands as they move, very attentively. His interest in the moving pattern made by his hands was certainly a contributory cause of Laurent's very precocious ability to move his hands towards some desired object and take hold of it. As he practised looking at his hands he rapidly became skilled at following their movements with his eyes. At the same time his desire to keep them in view began to affect the movements he made. He became increasingly able to keep his hands where his eyes could see them. Within three weeks of becoming interested in watching his hands, Laurent was able to reach for and grasp any well-known and conveniently shaped object that appeared within his range.

Another circumstance that contributed to this speedy learning was that his father helped the process in the following manner. At 0:3(3) Piaget places his motionless hand about 12 cm. from the baby's face. Laurent looks at it and makes sucking-like movements, but does not try to grasp it. Then Piaget, without moving his hand, extends his little finger and touches the baby's hand very lightly. Laurent immediately grasps this finger without looking at it, and on losing it searches with his hand until he finds it again, and then looks at it most attentively. Later in the day and on following days Laurent clasps his father's hand if it appears close to his own hands but not touching them; at this stage he does not try to grasp any other objects placed similarly, but confines himself to looking at them. Piaget explains that the sight of a hand – albeit a much larger one – set in motion Laurent's habitual activity of clasping and unclasping his hands, and as this hand was in the path of the baby's moving hands they inevitably met it and clasped it instead of each other.

During the next three or four days Laurent is given plenty of opportunity to grasp objects but he does not do so unless he can see either his own hand or his father's and the object at the same moment. By the end of the week, however, the sight of an attractive object immediately causes him to bring his hand – wherever it may be – effectively towards it.

Laurent first grasped objects that he could see close to his hand at 0:3(6); Lucienne at 0:4(15) and Jacqueline not until 0:6(1). Piaget attributed Jacqueline's tardiness not to any natural slowness in learning, but to the fact that she alone of the three children was born in early winter and had spent her first months thoroughly immobilized by shawls and blankets outside on a balcony; the other two had been free to move their arms and use their hands during the time they were out of doors. Certainly it appears, from the recorded observations of the three children's behaviour in Piaget's books, that Jacqueline was as quick as, if not quicker than, the others to respond effectively in other fields of activity; and, in the Piaget household, it is likely that she soon caught up with the others in this field of learning. Presumably, in the days when babies were swaddled, they must have made up for lost time as soon as they were allowed to move their limbs freely. Infant humans, besides learning slowly compared to the young of other species, are usually – but not always – resilient; but people discovered by experience, no doubt, that it was unwise to keep them swaddled for too long.

Every baby will sooner or later become expert at picking up and holding a number of everyday objects on sight as well as touch, the two-dimensional pattern that he sees having become assimilated to the three-dimensional qualities that he experiences when he holds one of these objects, and vice versa.

In the same way, playing with objects – and therefore bringing all his senses and his co-ordinating mind to bear on them – will make him aware eventually that they have a persistent existence, and that he can become better acquainted with them. Then he will respond to them quite differently from the time when they were to him merely temporarily convenient things to suck, or grasp, or look at. Knowledge of the permanence of objects, of what is and what is not himself, and of what is and what is not caused by himself, is a consequence of the progressively more effective exercise of his faculties upon his environment.

A faculty that is exercised in circumstances of a gradually increasing complexity and difficulty will become more and more a precision instrument, and the baby will want to use it in circumstances that require the exercise of precision. For instance, if he has had plenty of opportunity to improve his hand-eye co-ordination by playing with all sorts of objects as it pleases him, he is likely to go through a period of being attracted to the occupation of picking up matchsticks, small crumbs, or beads – or even pins – and dropping them into a receptacle of some kind.

Faculties also become differentiated into more specialized classes – they grow new shoots. Grasping differentiates into holding and letting go, into touching, stroking, poking, pinching, carrying, dropping and throwing, into squeezing when a thing like a sponge responds to squeezing, and into pulling when a thing like a blanket responds to pulling. One skill gives birth – as it were – to others while remaining completely undiminished itself. Certain faculties can develop only when others have already attained a high degree of development; some, such as the faculty to use the thumb opposite to the fingers, form the foundations for many more faculties; and others, like the faculty to balance while moving, are capable of growing in precision and complexity and of adapting to new circumstances for many years.

A baby's ability does not grow in the same way as the pile of coins in his money-box, or as a snowball when it is pushed slowly over the snow. He does not make a mental collection of assorted and unconnected pieces of knowledge in the same way as a man may purposefully collect a heterogeneous selection of quotations and funny stories in case they come in useful in the future. Instead, a baby's ability grows like a tree whose branches multiply by the growth along their twigs of new buds, which themselves grow into twigs, and so on. A child's faculties (1) require regular nourishment if they are not to wither and die; (2) can only grow in due season; (3) are capable, through the digestion of suitable nourishment, of sprouting new shoots; and (4) one bit of growth makes the next bit possible – a bud cannot grow on a non-existent twig. When a baby elects, entirely of his own free-will, to learn something new, he does so because his body (or tree) of knowledge is ready to put out a new shoot in that particular direction.

Where the *nourishment* necessary for growth is concerned, the metaphor is no longer useful, for a tree appears to grow on the same unvarying mixture of water, air and the chemical constituents of soil, whereas each of a baby's faculties requires a different kind of nourishment, and a progressively more complex nourishment. A faculty cannot continue to digest exactly similar pieces of food over and over again; what is more, it needs different kinds of food in a particular sequence.

As we have seen, at the beginning of a baby's life nature takes care of this. A baby has a biological need to nourish his faculties; and his faculties can usually find available the nourishment they need – moving objects to watch, objects to suck and hold. Just as the child's body digests exactly what it needs from among the various constituents of the food that is present in the stomach at any time, so the baby selects exactly the nourishment – not only the amount but the kind – that his faculties need at the moment, *provided* it is available.

The reverse of this is also true. A small child will not voluntarily pay attention to the things in his environment that he is as yet incapable of digesting. If forcibly fed, so to speak, the knowledge will pass straight through him without affecting him – it will be forgotten.

If he has already digested the knowledge of how to hold a rattle by its handle while he waves it about and shakes it in order to make it sound, he will readily learn to hold and wield a spoon when the opportunity to do so occurs; and if he is allowed frequent practice with a spoon, or alternatively to play for as long as he likes with a stick and earth and pebbles, he will jump at the chance to use a paint brush or a fibre-tip pen. Similarly if he is adept at picking up a fold of his blanket or his dress and stuffing it into his mouth, he will have little difficulty in doing the same with a biscuit, when he is first given the opportunity, since a similar kind of pinching movement is required in both cases. Again, the baby who has acquired the art of holding his feeding bottle or beaker with both hands while he drinks will find the action of grasping the table leg in order to pull himself to his feet easier to execute than a baby who has never before tried to clasp a cylindrical object with both hands. As Piaget might say, the baby has in these cases already formed a 'schema' which needs little adaptation in order to serve the new purpose. It follows that the greater the variety of objects the baby has learned to grasp the more likely it is that when he encounters a new object it will be similar to one that he already knows.

It may seem unnecessary to point out that a child learns what is easy for him to learn, but when we are engaged in caring for babies and toddlers we tend to ignore this fact. This is because we do not remember that play is learning-activity, and we are unaware of the extent of a baby's ignorance; so we do not notice that he chooses to attempt to do things that are akin to those which he can already do. As D. O. Hebb has observed, an infant tends to select for investigation things that are different but not too different from those with which it is already familiar, things that have a quality of what he calls 'difference-in-sameness'; the baby's curiosity is aroused by the slightly strange and the mildly frightening, his desire to master by the slightly difficult and the mildly frustrating.

No wholly healthy child will choose to occupy himself indefinitely with things that provide him with no new knowledge or provide no scope at all for innovation. A certain amount of repetition may be necessary for digestion, but what seems to an onlooker to be exact repetition may in fact be a slight variation of what went before. At the same time, babies enjoy recognizing familiar objects, movements, shapes and sounds, and repeating a recently learned activity because of the pleasant feeling of efficacy and power obtained. Here is one of Piaget's examples of the behaviour of an older baby, showing how strong is the desire to make a skill – or the solution of a problem – a permanent part of his mental equipment by repeating it several times over:

> Observation 119. At 1:3(12) Jacqueline is sitting in her playpen with one leg through the bars. When she tries to stand up she does not at first succeed in withdrawing her foot. She moans, almost cries, then tries again. She then painfully succeeds in disengaging herself, but as soon as she has done so, she replaces her leg in the same position and begins all over again. This happens four or five times in succession.

Jacqueline was not an incipient masochist. She simply wanted to extend her powers by using an existing skill in new circumstances. Therefore, although she showed symptoms of distress, the activity was a satisfying one.

Many mothers realize that it is in their own long-term interests to let a child struggle to dress himself when he wants to do so, but one must frequently give a child credit for more sense than he appears to have when he voluntarily persists with what is a patently frustrating activity – and let him carry on. On one occasion in my playgroup a small boy had been playing with an 'Escor' wooden aeroplane for over an hour. He had put it together to his satisfaction once, had taken it to bits again, and had not succeeded in getting the various pieces together exactly to his liking a second time; this angered him but he persevered. We do not know how long he would have continued or whether or not he would finally have been satisfied with his efforts, for a mother-helper took it away from him, because – she said – he was becoming frustrated.

One of the chief characteristics of a healthy small child is, in Groos's phrase, 'his joy in being a cause'. He has a healthy appetite for power. And we must see to it that he has plenty of opportunity to acquire power over his own body and over inanimate matter, and that he is allowed to exercise power over other people up to a point. The 'naughty', 'disobedient' child is usually one who has not been able to satisfy his appetite for power, and finds that one of the few ways of doing so that are open to him is to exercise his power to make his parents angry.

I believe that the most graphic manner of describing the why and how of learning in babies is to use words such as 'appetite – food – digestion – growth', and so on. But it is possible to use less earthy terms. For instance, one can say that the child, through his activity, gives meaning to his environment. He carries this meaning within him and by means of it is able to give meaning to more and more of his environment. Things that have meaning – that ring a bell – are interesting. It is interest that reveals his need (both to him and to us). The baby selects for attention those bits of his environment that bear a relationship of some sort to what he already knows.

This also works the other way round: a baby wanting to solve a practical problem selects from the facts – or 'schemas of activity' or bits of know-how – that he already possesses, those that bear some relation to the problem. He may put into execution schemas of activity that have already been successful in similar situations in turn, one after the other. Alternatively, he may begin by doing this, and then – as in the case of Lucienne in 'Observations 179 and 180' below – try a new kind of behaviour. He pauses and takes a good look at the situation before him and as he does so becomes aware of various, previously unconnected facts in his possession that each bear some relation to it. From the proximity of these several facts in his mind comes inspiration. He has invented the answer.

Piaget says that speed is almost the only difference between the process of mental invention through the combination of two or more ideas, and the process that occurs when a baby, through using his looking-at-and-seeing schema with progressively more effectiveness over a period of days or weeks in combination with his reaching-for-and-grasping schema, eventually solves the problem of how to take hold of the rattle that is hanging in front of him and that he desires to suck. The two processes are similar; both consist of the 'reciprocal assimilation of schemas of activity'. Certain originally unconnected facts, which the child has already at one time or other incorporated into his total body of knowledge, combine, in the presence of opportunity for new activity, to produce new growth.

In his Observation 179 Piaget shows his daughter, aged 1:4(0), a small open box containing a watch-chain 45 cm. long. The box is deep and narrow and the opening measures 34 mm. × 16 mm. Having shown Lucienne the box with the chain in it, he takes it away and returns, placing the box and the chain separately on the floor. Lucienne immediately tries to put the chain back into the box.

She begins by simply putting one end of the chain into the box and trying to make the rest follow progressively. Lucienne finds this procedure successful the first time (the end put into the box stays there fortuitously), but fails completely at the second and third attempts.

At the fourth attempt, Lucienne starts as before but pauses, and after a short interval, herself places the chain on a flat surface nearby (the experiment takes place on a shawl), rolls it up in a ball, takes the ball between three fingers and puts the whole thing into the box.

The fifth attempt begins by a very short resumption of the first procedure. But Lucienne corrects herself at once and returns to the second method.

Sixth attempt: immediate success.

Then (Observation 180) Piaget plays at hiding the chain. He begins by using the same box, and puts the chain into it.

Lucienne, who has often practised filling and emptying her pail and other receptacles, then grasps the box and turns it over without hesitation. Then I put the chain inside an empty matchbox, and close the box, leaving an opening of 10 mm. Lucienne begins by turning the whole thing over, then tries to grasp the chain through the opening. Not succeeding she puts her index finger through the slit and succeeds in getting out a small fragment of chain. She then pulls it until she has completely solved the problem.

I put the chain back into the box and reduce the opening to 3 mm. It is understood that Lucienne is not aware of the functioning of the opening and closing of the matchbox and has not seen me prepare the experiment. She only possesses the two preceding schemata: turning the box over in order to empty it of its contents, and sliding her finger into the slit to make the chain come out. It is this last procedure that she tries first: she puts her finger inside and gropes to reach the chain but fails completely.

A pause follows during which Lucienne manifests an interesting reaction.

She looks at the slit with great attention; then, several times in succession she opens and shuts her mouth, at first slightly, then wider and wider. . . . Then she unhesitatingly puts her finger in the slot and, instead of trying as before to reach the chain, pulls so as to enlarge the opening. She succeeds and grasps the chain.

During the following attempts (the slit always being 3 mm. wide) the same procedure is immediately rediscovered. On the other hand Lucienne is incapable of opening the box when it is completely closed. She gropes, throws the box on the floor, etc. but fails.

It is evident from Piaget's record that Lucienne first tries methods of getting things out of boxes or other receptacles which have proved successful in the past; she turns the box over or tries to catch the object, or a piece of it, between her fingers, and to pull it out. All this activity proving ineffective, she stops and sits back.

She relaxes, stops concentrating so narrowly on that chain, and looks at the problem as a whole. She fishes, as it were, in her pool of experience for recollections of facts that she has discovered for herself during past activity and which bear some kind of relationship to the whole or to a part of the present situation.

Part of her 'catch' on this occasion was certainly the fact – perhaps learned through having tried and failed to pull an awkwardly shaped toy into her play-pen between two of the bars – that it is possible for an object to be on one side of an aperture and to be too large to come through to the further side. Another piece of knowledge that she probably possessed was that it is possible to make a small hole that has appeared in one's blanket into a much bigger hole by pulling the sides of the hole apart with one's fingers.

It was the far from fortuitous arrival in the forefront of her mind of these two previously quite unconnected pieces of knowledge which made the nature of the problem she was trying to solve clear to her and which produced – all at once – the solution.

If she had been using words to herself, they would have been, 'slit too narrow – must be made wider – slits can be made wider by pulling'. She did not, of course, use words, and the fact that she opened and closed her mouth several times, each time a little wider, showed that she did not even clearly visualize the enlargement of the slit. Opening her mouth – a thing she does not normally *see* – was simply a reproduction of the *action* of making wider, and signified that she was in the process of recalling the activity of making an opening wider.

Then she acted. She had solved the problem in her head: Lucienne had invented a method of getting the chain out of the box. But inspiration had not come to her out of the blue: it had grown – if quite suddenly – out of a combination or synthesis of the relevant knowledge that she already possessed, as she attended to the circumstances of the problem. The latter had acted as growth-producing nourishment to her existing body of knowledge.

For practical purposes, there are two important points to grasp. First, the faculty to think, like all a child's faculties, grows from the use of previously developed faculties. Piaget says that thinking is internalized ('intériorisé') and very much speeded-up action. Therefore a child must have plenty of opportunity for action if he is to become capable of thought. As Piaget reminds us, using one's senses and taking in through them is just as much an activity as is using one's muscles. The ability to think also depends upon the amount and quality of the knowledge that one has digested. So, before a child is capable of planning in advance the simplest of operations or of solving the simplest of practical problems, he must have made himself familiar through his spontaneous activity upon them with the nature and the characteristic behaviour of some of the objects, forces and creatures in his environment.

Secondly, a child must be sufficiently free from distraction, interference and worries to be able to be aware of both his external and his internal environment (or body of digested experience), and, through using the former to nourish the latter, to further its growth. For instance he should be free to stand and stare for as long as he likes and then, suddenly, to act. In this manner he will 'grow' the faculty to think creatively.

Piaget's study of imitation in children has thrown light on the process of learning through digestion. The first third of his *Play, Dreams and Imitation in Childhood* is devoted to the study of imitation in infants up to the age of fifteen months.

He found that a baby will readily imitate a sound made by another person or thing if it is very similar to one that he frequently makes himself. Also, a baby of four or five months, who has reached the stage of being able to move his hand at will, will imitate the movements of another person's hands if these movements are similar to those that he frequently watches his own hands making. Babies repeat over and over again the sounds that they can hear themselves make and the movements that they can see themselves make; but if someone else will join in, the activity is transformed into a game of mutual imitation, which appears to be – as one might expect – more interesting for the baby than self-imitation.

Babies also repeat over and over again the movements that they can feel themselves making but cannot see, such as protruding their lips or their tongues, putting a finger in and out of their mouths, or blowing bubbles. Now, if someone makes these movements in front of the baby while he is himself making them, he may or may not be encouraged to continue. If he is, then it seems as if it is a case of imitation; but it may simply be that the baby believes that his own activity is the cause of the movements he can see, and hopes by continuing it to make the interesting spectacle continue, or it may be that he is merely hoping to prolong a pleasant social contact.

Observation 18. L., at 0:5(9), put out her tongue several times. Each time I also did so. She then showed great interest, put out her own as soon as I pulled mine back and so on. Unlike J. at 0:5(2), L. again began putting out her tongue after a moment's interruption, when I resumed my suggestion. The next day, however, and at 0:5(11), 0:5(12), 0:5(14) and 0:5(16) my stimulus produced no reaction whatever.

At 0:5(21) she made a noise with her saliva as she put out her tongue. I imitated the noise and she imitated me in her turn, again putting out her tongue. Her behaviour then became similar to what it was at 0:5(9) but an hour later as well as on the following day nothing remained of the association. At 0:6(2) I made a special effort to make her put out her tongue or merely open her mouth, but without success.

After this Piaget tried at intervals of a week or a fortnight to get her to imitate this and other movements of the mouth, but it was not until after the age of nine months that 'movements of the mouth were consistently imitated'.

Piaget explains her behaviour thus: for Lucienne at five or six months the actions of her father and of herself made no permanent connection in her mind because they *could* have no connection since each belonged to a separate body of experience into which the other could not be incorporated; one belonged to her visual world and the other to her world of tactile and kinaesthetic sensation. The *spectacle* of a person sticking out his tongue had no relation for her to the *sensations* that she felt when she stuck out her own tongue. So, if an association were to be formed it could only be a temporary one.

At this stage – four, five or six months – Lucienne and the other babies were capable of imitating certain hand movements but not the same ones in each case; it depended upon which movements the baby himself had been in the habit of making and therefore watching.

Later, after about nine months, when the knowledge that the baby has acquired separately of the look and the 'feel' of objects has become co-ordinated in his mind so that he is beginning to be aware of objects as wholes having a persisting existence of their own quite apart from himself and his own actions upon them, he will try to imitate gestures that he cannot see himself make, but that he is in the habit of making. The following is an example of the first attempt by an older baby to imitate a facial movement:

> At 0:8(28) I put my face close to that of J. and then alternately opened and closed my eyes. J. showed great interest and touched my eyes with her fingers. The same thing occurred at 0:9(1) and during the following weeks. At 0:11(11) only, I noted a completely negative reaction. At 0:11(14) however, she tried to imitate me, and made a mistake. . . . She watched me, laughed, and then, while continuing to look at my eyes, slowly opened and closed her mouth. She reacted to my stimulus eight times more in the same way.

Jacqueline evidently wanted to imitate her father's movements but she had probably never as yet intentionally opened and closed her eyes, or at least far less frequently than she had intentionally opened and closed her mouth. She knew he was opening and closing part of his face, and so she opened and closed the part of her own face that she knew best how to open and close.

Piaget notes that some previous writers have claimed imitation of movements of the features in babies of only a few months old. He says that it is a fact that babies can be *trained* to put out their tongues or to put their fingers in their mouths on seeing these actions performed by another. For this training, patient repetition of the movement in front of them is necessary, interspersed with many demonstrations of approval. A conditioned association is formed which, if it is to last, needs repeated reinforcement. The latter is what in fact happens where smiling is concerned, for this activity is usually rewarded by increased attention and demonstrations of affection including 'a repetition of the model that is imitated'.

Piaget says that imitation secured by training, which he calls 'pseudo-imitation', is quite different from the spontaneous imitation that is the result of 'assimilation'. The most obvious difference between the two is that in the case of pseudo-imitation the power to imitate is soon lost if the training is interrupted. The knowledge – or rather the know-how – is forgotten because it has not been digested. And this is because the baby does not, at this stage, possess a body-of-knowledge and know-how into which this particular bit of know-how can be incorporated.

Another difference between skills – and other knowledge – acquired by 'training' and those acquired spontaneously through digestion is that the latter are adaptable to new circumstances; in other words they are living and capable of growth. They are a part of the whole growing tree and are not simply pieces of inorganic matter stuck on to it like the decorations on a Christmas tree.

The amount of knowledge that a child can digest at any time depends upon the number of growing shoots that have been put forth by his tree-of-knowledge – in other words it depends upon what he has already, through his activity, digested. It is also a fact that physical maturation – in the sense of the gradual increase in the size and strength of and the change in the proportions of a child's body – plays a part in determining his power of digestion at any particular time.

But the point that it is important to grasp for all practical purposes, is that a healthy child will want to learn to do what he has become *newly capable* of learning to do. For instance, when a baby has learned how to pull himself to his feet with the aid of a table leg or the bars of his play-pen, and then become strong enough and learned enough balance to be able to stand up without aid, and when he has exhausted the interest and fun to be obtained from this occupation, he will begin to have an appetite for learning to walk (though some babies achieve such a useful turn of speed on all fours that they continue to crawl whenever they are in a hurry). Then in no time at all – as it may seem to his mother – he will feel quite capable of learning to climb up the stairs or on to a chair or out of his cot. Or again, at a certain stage a baby becomes interested in the noises he makes involuntarily, and soon he finds he can make them intentionally. Then he becomes interested in the noises made by others, and this offers endless opportunities for new learning *provided that* there are a diversity of *distinguishable* noises to be heard, and eventually – for the more fortunate babies – it leads to the power to make people listen to him and to answer him in some way or other that seems appropriate to *him*.

As we have seen, a baby's tendency to do what he has become newly capable of doing operates within a few minutes of birth.

Having begun to suck at his thumb, he continues, because sucking his thumb has increased his ability to do so effectively. Later, when the baby has begun to develop the skill of grasping, he takes every opportunity to grasp things. It occurs to me incidentally that Piaget received such willing co-operation from his children because he so frequently offered them the chance to do something which they had become – only a few minutes or hours previously – capable of doing.

When a baby is allowed to learn to do something that he is ready to learn to do, it will lead to his becoming capable of learning – and therefore of his wanting to learn – something more difficult in the same field. His appetite for learning is satisfied and increased at the same time.

Healthy development can be visualized in the form of a circle.

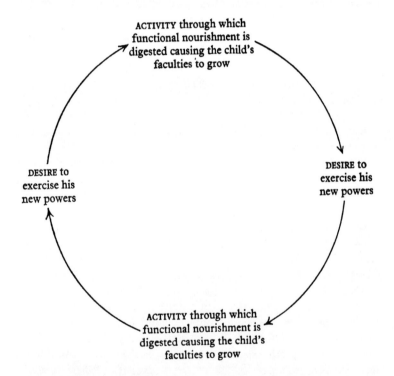

ACTIVITY through which functional nourishment is digested causing the child's faculties to grow

DESIRE to exercise his new powers

DESIRE to exercise his new powers

ACTIVITY through which functional nourishment is digested causing the child's faculties to grow

This upward-spiralling circle operates, if opportunity for the kind of nourishing activity that his faculties need for their growth at the time is regularly and freely available to the child. Activity as such does not increase the baby's ability to be aware of and to respond effectively to his environment. The only kind of activity that does this is activity that he chooses spontaneously for himself from all the present possibilities *because* the growth of his faculties requires it.

Although 'a healthy appetite' is often used to mean a large one, irrespective of the needs of the individual concerned, a truly healthy appetite is one that is appropriate to one's needs. In the latter sense a small baby has a healthy appetite for activity. It is not only quantitatively but also qualitatively appropriate to his needs. At any particular moment in time he knows exactly what he needs to pay attention to, and what he needs to do.

CHAPTER SEVEN

Learning-activity 1 – Sensory-motor

The play of a child in my playgroup consists of learning-activity: he may be laughing or shouting or simply watching the other children with interest and appreciation, but all the time he is selecting and absorbing experience, knowledge and know-how. He is continuing to develop the faculties that he began to develop as a baby. For example, a baby learns to judge the distance between the various pieces of furniture in the room, and how to crawl and then toddle expertly among them: the playgroup child learns to judge the speed, and anticipate the direction, of various kinds of moving objects and creatures, and how to move expertly among them. Or a baby acquires a familiarity with his mother's characteristic behaviour that enables him to engage in mutually enjoyable activity with her: the playgroup child does the same thing with a number of children.

The learning-activity of the children can be conveniently discussed under three main headings: 'sensory-motor', 'social', and 'becoming oneself'. Development in each is dependent upon development in the others. For instance, a child must have acquired a certain amount of sensory-motor judgment if he is to be able to satisfy his need to relate successfully to other children. In particular he must be able to control his limbs and to keep his balance while moving: it stands to reason that if you have a tendency to poke your finger into a person's eye or nearly send him flying when your intention is to give him an affectionate hug, your opportunities to learn social judgment will be few. Conversely, if a child has had no opportunity to learn how to interact with his peers at the 'critical period' for such learning, and therefore clings to mother or dolls or books or the television, he will be unlikely to encounter opportunities for the kind of adventurous activity that causes the growth of agility and the ability to balance while moving.

In fact, as my 'minute-to-minute records' show, the children in my playgroup are usually engaged in activities that develop their potentiality in all three spheres simultaneously. On the 'slides' they are obviously learning balance and agility and physical co-ordination but, when a child is using the apparatus for his own purposes at the same time as others are using it for theirs, he is also nourishing his faculty for social judgment. Each child is learning how children in general tend to behave when playing on the slides and also how particular individuals are likely to behave. He wants to get the greatest possible use of, and pleasure from, the slides, and, given time, he learns that co-operation with the others usually furthers his desires – at least in the long run – while obstructive behaviour beyond a point does not.

Apart from learning this psychological fact, he acquires the physical ability to fit his movements into the general pattern formed by the movements of all the others – so that he does not *involuntarily* obstruct the flow of movement – and he learns that being a creative part of that pattern can enhance his pleasure. As they play on the slides, each child is developing the faculty to *be himself within – and in relation to – a group of equally spontaneous individuals*.

An example of sensory-motor judgment is a person's estimate of the speed of an approaching vehicle. Through experience, one learns how vehicles of different types *look* when approaching at different speeds.

Now, when driving a car and wishing to turn into a side road across the oncoming traffic, one does not say to oneself, 'that car is approaching at x m.p.h., and has y yards to cover before it reaches the patch of roadway that I must cross in order to turn off the road; my speed is z m.p.h., and the gradient of the road is 1 in 20; the power of acceleration of my car at this speed and on this gradient is at the rate of q feet per second,' and then proceed to make a mathematical calculation in order to discover whether there is in fact time to turn into the side road immediately, or whether one must wait first for the approaching car to pass. Instead, one comes to an almost instantaneous decision. This is possible because of the particular sensory-motor judgment one has acquired as a result of the digestion of one's past experience of driving on busy roads.

The sensory-motor and mental activity through which one arrives at one's decision takes only a second or two; it takes very much longer to describe. One compares the look of the approaching car with the way cars have looked on previous occasions – although the word 'compares' suggests a lengthier operation than is actually performed. In reality, one simply *knows*, from the look of the car, how long it will take, at its present rate of travel, to reach the patch of roadway that one wishes to cross. One also knows, from one's physical awareness of the speed of one's own car and of its power of acceleration in the present circumstances, how long

147

one will take to approach and turn across that area of the road oneself. Through the co-ordination of these separate bits of sensory-motor information, one judges whether or not it is safe to continue on one's course, and to save one's time and one's temper and avoid unnecessarily holding up the traffic that is following.

A child is occupied for most of his time in acquiring sensory-motor judgment of one kind or another. When a baby is lying in his cot in the morning, practising his repertory of sounds such as 'dad-dad' or 'mam-mam', he is acquiring sensory-motor judgment – in this case, auditory and vocal judgment. He is listening to and discriminating between the sounds he makes, and he is learning how to vary the movements of his throat, tongue, lips and jaws in order to produce various different sounds. He is, as it were, forming hypotheses and testing them by experiment, and when he feels that he has been successful in producing a certain sound, he repeats it over and over again. It thus becomes established; it is a strong and healthy new growth on his sapling of knowledge of how to make sounds. From this growth will spring new shoots because soon he will become interested in making variations of the sound.

It is well known that little children enjoy activity that promotes visual and manual judgment and hand-eye co-ordination. Children of two, three and sometimes four will choose – from among a wide selection of occupations, and disregarding all distractions – to spend their time placing exactly similar pegs into exactly similar holes until they have entirely filled the 'pegboard', or carefully covering a piece of paper, however large, from top to bottom and side to side with paint of one colour, or threading beads without making any selection according to colour or shape. At this stage they are not at all interested in making patterns or in any sort of 'artistic', expressive or descriptive use of the materials. Later they will be, perhaps a few days or even minutes later – but now, and often for weeks and months on end, their aim seems to be to develop their ability to make various specific movements with precision and speed. Whether speed or precision has priority depends upon the temperament of the child; but all small children, whatever their characteristic constitution, will, given the opportunity, practise these or similar skills of hand and eye.

As the child practises, his visual judgment becomes more reliable and sure, his muscles stronger and under better control, and he becomes familiar with the nature of various tools, objects and materials and of what can be done with them. In the case of painting, he becomes gradually more capable of making the brush do exactly what he wants it to do. All irrelevant or unnecessary movements are gradually eliminated, and his arms, hands and fingers execute his intentions with increasing precision. He is happy in his skill, and continues to practise it, either immediately or the next day. Eventually the knowledge of how to cover a sheet of paper with paint and, later, to make exactly the kind of lines and spots he chooses is thoroughly digested by the child and is therefore permanently available to him – to his great satisfaction.

The child learning to use paints and a brush is acquiring sensory-motor judgment in a particular field, the baby learning to articulate sounds in another, but children also practise acquiring judgment in activities that involve the whole of their bodies. They delight in becoming able to move their bodies and limbs with increasing speed and precision and perfect balance while running, jumping, climbing, swinging, sliding, tumbling. If they have the chance, they will devote a large proportion of their time and energy to imitating or improvising numerous 'tricks', as they call them. In the playgroup, some of these activities are quite spectacularly acrobatic, some so simple that one may easily not recognize them as 'tricks' unless a child informs one of the fact; but they all require some degree of muscular control and strength, and the co-ordination of various movements in time and space. They all require knowledge: knowledge of the effect of the gravitational pull upon the different parts of the body in different positions and at different rates of movement, knowledge of the nature of the objects which the child is using, knowledge of the range and the limits of his own powers, and the knowledge that enables him to judge distance, height, and the speed at which he and other things are moving. Obviously he can only obtain and co-ordinate all this complicated knowledge by means of many hours spent in active experience. Furthermore, whether he is pulling himself gingerly on to the first bar of the climbing frame, or nonchalantly turning a somersault over the top bar, he must be able to sort out, select and co-ordinate the information that his senses are giving him, and, according to his judgment of the circumstances obtaining at every moment, direct the activity of his muscles so that his intention may be achieved. This compound know-how can only be acquired through the spontaneous and regular nourishment of his faculties in this field of activity.

I shall want to refer frequently to sensory-motor ability of this kind and so I must give it a name. For want of a shorter one that conveys my meaning accurately, I shall call it 'general sensory-motor judgment'. Its development is a primary and fundamental need of children at all ages. The children who have been in my playgroup over the years – and in other free-choice playgroups that possess the necessary space and equipment – have conclusively demonstrated that this is so, as far as the under-fives are concerned. The children of school age at the Peckham Health Centre showed by their choice of occupation that older children have the same need.

Learning to ride a bicycle is an occupation that requires and promotes general sensory-motor judgment. People who can remember their efforts to acquire this skill may also remember that there came a point when no amount of 'thinking' was of any use, and they found themselves forced to leave it to their bodies to make the rapid and subtle adjustments of position that were necessary in order to balance in the new circumstances. However, one should not use the word 'body' in opposition to 'mind' – at least in this connection. The activity of the body and its parts is centrally organized and directed, and all learning-activity is intelligent activity. Perhaps one can make a distinction, as Piaget does, between 'reflective intelligence' and 'sensory-motor intelligence'.

Why is it that even three-year-olds are so keen to master the art of cycling? Although bicycles are now comparatively little used on the roads, a small child's father, brother, sister or the 'paper-boy' may still ride one, in which case the child may want to identify with them, or with a speeding motor-cyclist; but I do not think that this alone would cause both boys and girls to spend so much time and effort on this learning-activity. I think they have a further motive, and this is the extension of their general sensory-motor judgment. They want to use their faculty to balance and to control their limbs in a new situation.

It would be interesting to compare the use made of bicycles and tricycles in a playgroup where there is adequate and suitable space for both. Tricycles are useful for various make-believe games and for learning a certain amount of balancing skill, but are not so good for the latter as bicycles. However, they are much more dangerous because it is possible to mount them and make them move at some speed before one has learned how to control them and particularly how to take corners on them. It is impossible to have them in our playgroup because of the very small area of level ground and the number of steep little banks.

Roller-skates are another piece of balancing apparatus that children will queue up for and try very hard to learn to use successfully, although they are less popular than bicycles with the under-fives. At the Peckham Health Centre, small bicycles and roller-skates were very much in demand, the latter by children of all ages. As was noted on one occasion (see p. 22) one very young schoolchild who was 'off school' for a week came every afternoon with the intention of roller-skating, and was not at all put off by the fact that there were no other children skating at the time, or that he might sometimes be quite alone on the playground.

Anyone acquainted with a toddler is able to observe instances of the universal interest of children in acquiring general sensory-motor judgment. No toddler wants to stop short at the achievement of the useful art of walking; he proceeds – often in defiance of authority – to discover how to make increasingly complicated, subtle and gravity-defying movements. Groos noticed this: 'Almost as soon as a child has learned to preserve his equilibrium in ordinary walking, he proceeds to complicate the problem by trying to walk on curbstones, in a rut, on a beam, on a balustrade or narrow wall.'

Valentine also reports:

> Sometimes B. would set himself *difficult tasks*. Thus not long after learning to stand up, he tried to stand up holding his big ball in his mouth. There were repeated failures, the ball dropping, but again he would try until successful. . . .
> B. at 1:8 jumps from the couch repeatedly. Once he fell on his face and cried hard; but almost at once climbed up and jumped again. Hurt himself again but persisted.
> B. at 2:8 climbed up the banisters on the outside.

I have watched a toddler of sixteen months 'dancing' to rhythmic music so energetically, bending both knees and springing up, that she actually lifted both feet clear of the ground simultaneously. Her mother told me that she frequently does this at home, smiling with joy. When there is no music, she often babbles ecstatically while she jumps up and down.

It is difficult to find recorded examples of the spontaneous interest of toddlers in learning the niceties of balance, because few people have thought it worth their while to notice it. Millicent Shinn, however, gives one in *Notes on the Development of a Child*. At the time this particular observation was made, the little girl was fourteen to sixteen months old.

> During all this period a noticeable trait was the child's interest in doing something novel with her body, apparently in mere curiosity and sense of power. In the sixty-first week she found she could walk with her head thrown back, looking at the ceiling, and practised it for a long time. In the sixty-fifth week she

walked about in her father's slippers, lifting her encumbered feet skilfully. At sixteen months she hit upon the feat of walking backwards and practised it all day, much interested and amused. In the seventieth week, her great joy, when indoors, was a shallow box, some $2\frac{1}{2}$ inches high, upon which she would stand, stepping on and off with endless pleasure.

This extract provides us with an especially valuable piece of evidence because the observer was obviously not looking for this kind of behaviour, in fact she seemed to be a little surprised (note the use of the word 'mere'). She simply recorded minutely what the child did, and how and with what kind of emotion she did it. Usually behaviour such as this in a child is held by students of child development to be 'just play' and therefore unimportant; or, when the writer's subject is play, it is excluded on the grounds that it is undertaken by the child in its 'normal process' of gaining control of the muscles of the body; and it is apparently expected that this process will take place inevitably, however limited and restricted the child's opportunities for play may be.

In fact the behaviour recorded by Miss Shinn is typical of children of that age. It shows how much time and concentrated effort children devote to this kind of learning-activity and the delight they take in it. It also demonstrates how a child will repeat the same action over and over again until he is satisfied with his proficiency and will then turn his attention to practising a variation on it.

Because one does not remember how one felt at the age of one or two, one does not realize how much a small child needs to learn if he is to be able to step on and off a box only two-and-a-half inches high with ease and agility. First, he has to learn from experience in what manner his body and its every movement are affected by the force of gravity, and what movements it is necessary to make – and at what speed – in order either to counteract this force or to make use of it in order to achieve his intention. In other words, he has to acquire a sensory-motor knowledge of kinetics as far as is necessary in order to perform this particular activity successfully. Secondly, he must learn by trial and success to judge the distance of the top of the box from the ground, and accurately and exactly how – and by how much – his limbs must be moved to correspond with the visual distance, and how the parts of his body must be angled and his joints flexed from one instant to another during the action. There is probably a great deal more to it than that. The main organs involved are (a) most of the muscles and motor nerves of the body, (b) the senses of sight and balance, (c) the network of nerves and sense organs known as the proprioceptor system (which keeps the co-ordinating intelligence informed of the position of the body and of its parts in relation to the whole), and (d) the kinetic sense organs which perform the same office with regard to the movements of the body.

When a baby tries for the first time to step on to or off a box two or three inches high, he will probably stagger a little and may even fail to keep himself the right way up throughout the operation. In order to be able to perform the apparently simple action successfully, he must have already learned how to make a co-ordinated use of the above-mentioned sense and motor organs in the performance of less exacting but similar activities. He must already have built up a body-of-knowledge concerning his body and its capabilities and concerning the physical forces and the matter in his environment that enables him to walk on the level and to bend and straighten his knees without overbalancing. In other words, he must have acquired a certain amount of general sensory-motor judgment. Then, on this existing sensory-motor body-of-knowledge, he grows – through his activity – a new 'limb', the knowledge of how to step on to and off a box of a certain size.

It will be realized that the child's general sensory-motor body-of-knowledge must have reached just the right stage in its growth if he is to be able to recognize and take advantage of the new opportunity for gowth. The human embryo develops limbs before beginning to develop fingers and toes. The child's body-of-knowledge also develops sequentially but – and in this it is different – only if it is lucky enough in encountering circumstances that are favourable to its growth. The foetus does not run this risk, for its environment is exactly suited to its needs and so, if it is healthy, it progresses inevitably through all the necessary successive stages in the course of time.

One summer, we took our children to the sea-side for the day. We arrived at lunchtime and sat down on a gently sloping concrete sea-wall to eat. The youngest child was aged fourteen months and just able to walk alone, and she proceeded to scramble about on hands and feet on the sea-wall. Later, the older children went a few yards down the beach in order to play on the sand and in the water. We cleared up and joined them with the baby, but after a very short while, she toddled back to the concrete slope and continued to explore the possibilities that it offered for moving up and down, backwards and forwards and sideways on a sloping surface; and there she insisted on staying. I do not think that her preference for playing on the sea-wall to playing with sand and water on that occasion was due to fear of the sea or to a dislike of the feel of the sand and water on her bare feet, for at that time she enjoyed playing barefoot in the sand-pit at home, and the sea was not at all rough or intimidating. Apart from this, when we were again by the sea two months later, she divided her time about equally between playing in the sand, paddling in the water and trying to climb up the rocks. On the first occasion the sea-wall evidently provided her with the opportunity to learn the art of moving about on a sloping surface just at the moment when she was ready to learn this particular skill. What interested her more than everything else at the moment – more than unlimited water and sand, more than little rippling waves, more than rolling balls down sand castles, or demolishing the sand pies that the other children made for her, or filling pails with pebbles – was the knowledge of how to move in a variety of ways on a large, hard but not slippery, gently sloping surface. This was what she wanted to learn on that particular day (Pl. 26).

If children cannot be allowed to wander about, finding for themselves sloping concrete sea-walls and other educative nourishment, adults must provide them with equally nourishing substitutes. We must try to make it possible for them to find things to do which they are at the time capable of doing. We must provide the opportunities and then sit back, for we cannot digest experience for them, and in any case we do not know exactly which bit of knowledge they are at any moment ready to digest. Only the child himself knows this. We can trust a child to recognize what experiences will nourish his general sensory-motor judgment at any time, if the latter is already well-nourished and therefore healthy and capable of digestion.

At the Peckham Health Centre, the babies in the 'nursery' began climbing on the very short wooden slide and flight of steps, enclosed by railings (called Russian steps), even before they could walk. Soon afterwards they progressed to the longer and steeper slide; and almost all the schoolchildren who were under the age of twelve or thirteen when they joined, hastened to make use of the opportunities for developing their general sensory-motor judgment that were available.

More recently I have observed children of this age obeying their instinct to acquire general sensory-motor judgment, uninfluenced for the time being by any other consideration. At one time, I took one of my children regularly to a recently built swimming pool in the centre of a large housing estate, and sat watching in the gallery. There were always a number of children – mostly boys of all sizes – playing continuously in and out of the water. Although at the time there was no instruction given, the children were quickly learning to swim and dive, for I noticed a marked increase in skill over a period of three or four months.

As I watched, I noticed that the children never organized races among themselves; sometimes they chased each other, but there was no hysteria. Indeed they were highly serious and completely engrossed in what they were doing. They reminded me of the polar bear cub that I had once watched playing in and out of its pool at a zoo. This young creature plopped into the water, and clambered out again, time after time, varying this by sliding down a steep rock into the water, spread-eagled on its stomach or its back, or by rolling about in the water with untiring energy. Once or twice his mother followed him down into the water and they stayed out of sight for a minute or two. The keeper explained to us that she was trying to teach her cub to stay under water for longer periods. But he did not seem to enjoy his lessons much, for he escaped from her apparently as soon as he could and returned to his play.

The children would leap from the side of the pool or the diving boards again and again, sometimes entering the water feet first, more often head first, not doing any recognizable dive but turning and twisting their bodies in the air and entering the water at different angles and in different positions. Sometimes one of them would bounce and bounce and bounce on the springboard. On a certain day, one boy dived repeatedly from the side of the pool just in front of me, curving or twisting his body a little differently each time, and there was often an unconscious smile of pleasure on his face as he pulled himself out of the water. Most of the children were moving almost continuously but they did not appear to get tired, for they would stay as long as they were allowed to stay. It seemed to me that they were intent on discovering the possibilities for movement in a new element – water – and on making the most of the opportunities to learn the great variety of new movement through the air that having water below them made possible.

Even two-year-olds love to discover all about the nature of water, and what can be done in it as well as with it. The small learners' pool at the Peckham Health Centre was emptied every day and filled gradually during the afternoon to a final depth of about three feet. When the water was nine or ten inches deep, a selected group of two- and three-year-olds were allowed to play in it under supervision. (It was necessary for the adult in charge to be paddling in the pool with the children in order to be immediately at hand to put those who slipped over back on to their feet again: the heads of children of this age are so heavy in relation to their bodies that once they have inadvertently lost their balance it is difficult for them to get themselves upright again.) There was a small platform at one end of the little pool from which three very shallow steps led down into the water, except at the sides where the platform ended in a drop of about a foot (two or three inches above the water level). The 'old hands' would throw themselves into the air from this part of the platform, falling flat with a big splash, stomach first. But it took the children a long time to learn how to negotiate the steps and to keep themselves upright in the water. Later they would try sitting down in the water or crawling on hands and knees, until one day they found that the water would hold them up if they stretched out, keeping things under control and moving along by touching the bottom of the pool with their hands. Only two or three of the children learned eventually in the course of their play – no help or instruction was attempted – to trust to their knowledge that the water would support them sufficiently to succeed in floating on their backs.

In the process of acquiring general sensory-motor judgment, a child's muscles will also develop; but a well co-ordinated person is not necessarily a very muscular one. The converse is also true; one can build bulging muscles by doing prescribed exercises over a long period, and yet remain almost totally lacking in co-ordination and general sensory-motor judgment. One of my brothers grew very early and had reached his final height of 5 ft 11 in. by the age of fourteen. I remember congratulating him one day at that time on his muscular build. He must have been very conscious of being clumsy and a poor performer at gymnastics and athletics at school, for he replied that the size of his muscles must be due to the fact that they were always 'working against each other'.

There is a further reason for the large amount of time that children need to spend learning general sensory-motor judgment. It is that they grow, and therefore need to ensure that their knowledge keeps pace with the gradual alteration in their stature and proportions, and the increase in and distribution of their weight. It is not only that the child's muscles need to be stronger because of the increasing weight and length of his limbs, but also that the activity of all the parts of the body in the performance of any particular movement needs to be very slightly different week by week as the child grows. The manner in which gravity affects the body during any particular movement changes with the change in the proportions and weight of the body; and the child's directing sensory-motor intelligence has to be kept up to date with this changing data. Therefore the child that grows fast needs to spend more time doing this than the stocky or lightly-built, small-boned types.

One day in the playgroup, I made a note as follows:

On the first day of term after four weeks' Christmas holiday, when Sarah arrived, I involuntarily exclaimed to her father, 'Still taller!' She seemed to have grown several inches since I last saw her, and it is difficult to believe that she is only $3\frac{3}{4}$. During the week, she has been occupied in a great many different activities – never wasting a moment – but every now and then she returns to the slides, walking very carefully and a little uncertainly up and down them, or walking up and sliding down; and every morning she has asked, 'Can we do head-over-heels today?' [By this she means that she wants the slides and the mattress arranged as described on pages 37–8 above.] So each day after elevenses I have put the required apparatus up and it has been used with enthusiasm by most of the other children as well as by Sarah.

Most of my own family reach a height that is useful only for seeing over the heads of a crowd. At the age of twelve or thirteen, my elder son spent most of his fairly frequent spare-time visits to the swimming-pool in plunging head-first from the springboard in an energetic but what seemed to us a rather childish and dilettante manner. We were sorry at the time that he did not, as his elder sister had done, join a diving club and learn to dive properly, or else concentrate on swimming, for we were assured by the sports-master at his school that he had a future as a swimmer if only he would train. Now, however, having reached a final height of 6 ft $7\frac{1}{2}$ in. he holds himself well, moves gracefully, and finds new sports, such as ski-ing and surf-riding, and skills such as dancing, easy to learn, in spite of the undoubted handicap of his height. I believe that what seemed to us at the time to be time-wasting play was, in fact, one of the best means he could have used for maintaining and improving his general sensory-motor judgment and power of co-ordinated movement, during a period when he was growing faster than most other children ever do. Because of the speed at which his limbs were increasing in length, the boy's brain – to put it very crudely – did not know where his hands and feet were in relation to the rest of his body from one day to another, and was therefore unable to exercise its co-ordinating function effectively. He was giving it the necessary extra practice.

My son would have been unlikely to become a first-class high-board or springboard diver because of his unsuitable build; but, later on, when he had become a very good swimmer, his dive at the start of a race was a beautifully smooth and economical movement. It was also apparently effortless, though so powerful that it usually gave him a lead during the first length of the race. I am sure that the many hours he spent as a child *playing* in the swimming-pool, climbing trees, roller-skating, walking on stilts, and particularly his insistence in continuing this varied 'play' into adolescence and his refusal to spend the time at his disposal on training for any specialized forms of athletics, were the chief causes of his unusually good co-ordination and grace and precision of movement for one so tall.

Training in a particular sport cannot be successful beyond a certain point if the child or person being trained lacks general sensory-motor judgment. Therefore I do not believe that my son would have become a better swimmer than he eventually did if he had spent the whole of his time at the pool swimming 'lengths' – instead of only when under the eye of the school swimming coach. His muscles might have become stronger, but there would have been less co-ordination between his controlling sensory-motor intelligence, his proprioceptive and kinetic senses and his muscles, with the result that his swimming style would have been bound to suffer, and – because unnecessary or imprecise movements of the limbs and trunk slow up the progress of a swimmer through the water – his speed as well.

Easy, smooth, graceful and precise movement may be partly the reflection of temperament and attitude to life, but it is also the effect of the possession of general sensory-motor judgment; in fact, without the latter, feeling cannot be expressed adequately. Therefore ease and grace of movement is not by any means entirely a gift from heaven. It is learned. How successfully one does learn it depends partly upon innate factors and partly upon opportunity – but without opportunity, one cannot acquire it at all.

There are many different natural and manufactured environments that provide the opportunity. Of the latter, a swimming-pool is one of the best. The body is free in water – and momentarily free in the air when diving – to make a more varied selection of movements than those it can make when earth-bound; and the child is able, through making these movements, to increase and refine his power to move his body and its parts exactly and in every detail as he wishes from moment to moment.

Diving is an activity that shows up any lack of this power. I was watching the children in the swimming-pool one day, when a youth was being trained in 'springboard diving'. For at least half an hour the boy – aged about fifteen – was performing complicated and 'advanced' dives with intervals of earnest conversation with his instructor. He was muscular and sun-tanned, compactly built and yet slender, and he showed by his knowledge of diving that he was highly trained; yet almost every time he dived, he made some unnecessary movement or other that spoiled the line of his body in the air and its smooth entry into the water. For instance, he would slightly bend one knee when the other was straight, or hold one foot at a right angle to his leg when the other foot followed the curve of the rest of his body. That he was trying to make perfect dives was obvious. One could also tell that he knew exactly what he was intended – and wanted – to do on each occasion, but lack of the possession of fine general sensory-motor judgment marred the execution of his intention; and all the training that he had undergone did not make up for this. I believe that it would have been better if, in the past, he had spent more time playing and less on being taught.

Coaching and training have their uses. If a child is ambitious he may want to undergo a period of training under instruction at some time or other; but training can never be an effective *substitute* for the spontaneous, self-selected and self-initiated practice that occurs during play. Judgment in any field can only be acquired through the exercise of judgment. A child who performs prescribed exercises will learn how to perform those exercises more or less well, but that is all. The activity will not increase the speed at which he is able to learn different exercises, nor the grace and precision with which he moves. Training does not increase the power of the child's body of general sensory-motor knowledge to grow in response to new circumstances, as does play. It is as if the child being trained in a particular skill is suffering forced feeding with one type of food only, while the child playing in an appropriate environment is taking exactly what he needs, at the particular moment in time, for growth; or one could put it that he is growing a sturdy, bushy tree of knowledge which is capable of putting out a new shoot in any direction at any moment.

A child who has acquired a good basis of general sensory-motor judgment through playing on trees or rocks or in and over water, through sliding on ice or down sand-hills, or playing on apparatus such as swinging ropes or a trampoline will, when he has the opportunity to learn football, tennis or other games, or to be coached in athletics, swimming, diving, skating, dancing, judo or gymnastics, probably be glad to do so. He will also be able to make use of any particularly advantageous anatomical, physiological or psychological characteristics that he may possess such as a suitable build, stamina, the will to win, a 'good eye', or extra lung capacity. As for sports such as ski-ing and surf-riding, which do not entail the acquisition of a complicated technique and yet are infuriatingly hard to learn for those who, however muscular and fit, have 'bad' balance and poor co-ordination, he will find these easy, for he will be able to respond appropriately to the new situations in which he finds himself because they are related to those with which he is already familiar. Through his childhood play he will have developed a fine judgment of how to hold and move his body, and the ability to do so while moving fast and at a variety of angles, and to balance perfectly while making quick and subtle changes of direction; and he will have acquired a well-developed sensory judgment of distance, height, angles and speed. Therefore he will be able to respond instantly and appropriately in the new but related circumstances of ski-ing or surf-riding.

But one must always remember that a young person who specializes in a particular game or sport, and attains a high standard in it, will need to continue, while he is still growing, to spend some of his time playing – whether on skates, skis or a surfboard, in a gymnasium or a swimming-pool or on a dance floor or in the countryside – if he is to maintain his general sensory-motor judgment and therefore be able to improve the standard of his specialist skill. It should also be borne in mind that the first five or six years and the period just before and during the onset of puberty are times of rapid growth in all children.

People often confuse 'training' and spontaneous practice. Those who say that training a child in a particular skill before he has reached the necessary degree of anatomical maturity makes no difference in the long run to the standard of his performances are right, but they are wrong to conclude that the latter will be unaffected by the amount of time the child has spent spontaneously practising similar but more simple skills in the past. (If taken literally, they are in fact wrong in every respect because the training may have an adverse effect on the performance of the child.)

An often-quoted experiment was made by Gesell with a pair of identical twins aged ten and a half months. Twin A was given daily training in stair-climbing for six weeks, beginning at the age of forty-six weeks. Twin B was meanwhile given no training. After four weeks of training, twin A climbed the staircase 'with avidity and without assistance', and at fifty-two weeks she climbed it in twenty-six seconds. At the same time twin B was 'put to the test', and she at once climbed the staircase unaided in forty-five seconds. For the next two weeks both twins were given practice. At the end of the fortnight B was going up more quickly (in ten seconds) than A, and moreover, walking up, whereas A continued to crawl.

But, as one psychologist has pointed out, we are not told what twin B was doing while A was being trained. One wonders if there had been a doorstep in the twins' dwelling-place, or if twin B had managed to practise climbing on and off a footstool and perhaps from the footstool to an armchair when no one was looking. If something like this had been the case, and if twin B had thoroughly digested this bit of knowledge by the time she was offered the chance to attempt a whole flight of stairs, she would certainly have welcomed the new and timely opportunity with an enthusiasm that would guarantee quick learning. It is also possible that twin A was becoming more than a little bored by her daily routine of stair-climbing, was indeed suffering from a surfeit of stairs and needing greater variety in her diet.

There is another factor to be considered when assessing the results of this experiment. We are not told how the experimenters set about training the baby, but I suppose that she was encouraged or bribed by means of a reward of some kind, as well as being assisted in the beginning. And a baby will learn less effectively if his attention is mainly directed towards receiving a smile or a piece of chocolate than if he is climbing purely in order to satisfy his desire to learn how to climb, and therefore giving his attention wholeheartedly to the task in hand.

It is interesting that twin A continued to crawl up, whereas twin B soon began to walk up the stairs. This could be evidence of the fact that A had formed a habit of climbing in a particular manner because she had learned through being 'conditioned' rather than through digestion and so had acquired a mechanical, fixed-in-a-groove, dead-end piece of knowledge. B's skill, in contrast, had grown spontaneously and was therefore capable of further growth.

The moment at which it is easiest for a child to learn to climb stairs is the moment when he has reached the requisite degree of anatomical maturity, *and* has acquired sufficient general sensory-motor judgment through stepping on and off boxes or doorsteps and through scrambling about on banks or on other sloping surfaces. Only the child himself can know exactly when this moment has arrived.

CHAPTER EIGHT

Learning-activity 2 – Social

Learning to interact effectively with others is a complex process, inextricably bound up with the development of a distinct and integrated self, a sensitive awareness of the reality outside oneself and a spontaneous responsiveness to this reality. Moreover, the speed and efficiency with which one learns depends upon one's tendency to be selfish or generous, quick-witted or dreamy, and upon other character or physiological traits – as well as upon the opportunity that one has for practice in interacting with others.

However, there is one factor of which we can be quite certain: in this field of activity, as in the field of sensory-motor activity, children are born ignorant. To a baby under the age of six months, his surroundings are an extension of himself, or, more correctly, simply the temporary result of his activity, for he is not aware of himself as an object among other objects.

At five or six months a baby may begin to distinguish one face from another and may consequently become apprehensive of strangers, while up to this time any smiling face has been responded to with pleasure. He may show signs of terror or rage – at this stage apparently as yet undifferentiated emotions – if a face that has become familiar, suddenly appears unfamiliar to him because its owner is wearing a hat. From this age he may be shy of strange objects and people, but he will also begin to be interested in them. He will continue to use objects solely as functional nourishment on occasion, but he will become increasingly interested in the objects and the creatures themselves. For example, he will want to throw any object that appears to be throwable – a ball, a pebble, a teacup – in order to exercise his ability to throw, or simply in order to make a clatter, but he may also throw it because he wants to find out what effect throwing has on it.

He may hear, 'Don't! You'll break it!' But what does 'break' mean? He cannot know until he has heard and seen the cup explode in fragments on the floor.

In the same way a baby will want to discover, by using his senses upon them and by experimenting upon them, the nature and characteristic behaviour of other creatures. When he first encounters other children, he is totally ignorant of them. He does not liken them to himself, for he does not yet know much about himself. He finds out about himself and about them through interacting with them, in just the same way as he learns sensory-motor judgment by doing things that require sensory-motor judgment.

So a small child may treat another as he would a new and intriguing toy. He may want to watch the strange creature from the safety of the far side of mother; or he may want to touch him very gently, or to throw his arms around him and try to lift him, to pinch him, or stroke him, to kiss or bite him.

'Don't! You'll hurt him!' someone says; but what does 'hurt' mean in this instance? How can he know how it feels to be pinched or bitten if he has himself never been pinched or bitten?

A sensitive and intelligent child may remain ignorant for a surprisingly long time of the effect on others of actions such as these. Adults find it hard to believe that a three-and-a-half-year-old, who is so intelligent in many respects, does not already possess this seemingly self-evident knowledge; and, because many children choose to behave for much of the time as the adults around them want and expect them to behave, those that do not do so are often erroneously believed to be acting with malice. I do not mean to imply that perfectly healthy children are never guilty of malicious actions – only that the incidence and degree of malice may be less than is supposed.

Naturally, if a two- or three-year-old child has rarely played with other children, he may, on joining a playgroup, not yet know that children fall over when they are pushed, or that they may be as impatient for a ride on the rocking-horse as he is himself. One must remember, moreover, that he is likely to remain ignorant of these facts until he has had a few *battles* with other children over toys. Just as one becomes aware of others' opinions through discussing and arguing with them, so a child becomes aware of other children's feelings through wanting – and squabbling over – the same toy.

Recently a little boy of Ghanaian parentage has joined our group. He is two years and three months old, very strong and active, intelligent, curious, playful and determined. He is less well acquainted with toys than most of the other children were when they joined the group, and, apart from exploring the house and garden and pushing and pulling everything that it appears to him to be safe to push and pull and that responds interestingly to being pushed and pulled, he likes to open and shut doors and to use objects that are familiar to him, such as a dustpan and brush – which he wields effectively – and scissors, for his mother makes her own clothes. Apparently it gives him confidence, in this new and very strange environment, to exercise the skills in which he is already proficient.

During his first week or two in the group, he was hardly still for a moment. He would rattle small objects such as beads in their box and then suddenly turn the box upside down – but he would sometimes help to pick them up again. He would seize a paint-brush, dab at the paper, then at his hand, his shoes, the wall or the floor, or he would push the easel over. (Our easels invite a push because they consist simply of two pieces of hardboard joined together at the top and standing in a tray.) He would suddenly throw things – often over his shoulder without watching where they went; or he would throw himself to the floor and roll about. But he liked to sit in the Wendy House alone or with another child – sometimes for several minutes – 'pouring' from the teapot and 'drinking' from a cup.

He is cautious in his use of the slides and the climbing frame. For the first two weeks he used them rarely and did not trust himself to go more than about a foot from the ground. During the third and fourth weeks he climbed higher but very carefully and prudently. He strode away muttering to himself when he caught sight of the towering figure of my son with his long blond hair, but is not in the least deferential towards adults who have proved themselves to be friendly.

On arrival in the group, he was obviously completely ignorant of other children. As his mother said, 'He only knows Daddy and me.' His behaviour towards them, if they were the same size or smaller than himself, was similar to his behaviour towards inanimate objects; he investigated them and experimented on them in an impulsive and muscular way, including pinching, pulling and occasionally biting. We had to watch him constantly during the first few days, and sometimes to advise the victims to hit back. He was visibly surprised if they did so, and would pause a moment, apparently in thought, before turning to explore some other part of his surroundings. After four weeks in the group he is both more cautious and more confident in his approach to the children. He is, in fact, learning incredibly quickly how to enjoy the play-group, and the company of the other children. He has been asked not to throw or upset things, and in order to make our meaning clear to him we have sometimes taken things away from him. Now he will remain at one occupation for quite a few minutes and enjoys using the pegboard and pegs for their intended purpose instead of throwing them around the room. He realizes that the paper on the easel is meant for painting on, although he cannot always resist the temptation to daub other things.

One day after he had been in the playgroup for about a week, two or three of the children had made some 'swords' out of plastic meccano – very pliable and wobbly weapons – and they were playing at clashing their 'swords' together. Kuase somehow got hold of one for a moment and succeeded in joining in the game. This pleased him so much that, grinning broadly, he ran and literally leapt on to the rocking-horse – which up to then he had not had the courage to use – and then proceeded to rock himself carefully and attentively for a minute or two.

His mother appears to find him a great source of amusement, which is fortunate since his curiosity, determination and energy might otherwise have caused her nerves to snap in the constricted conditions of her home. Having watched his debut in the playgroup she asked the supervisor one day, 'Do you think he is a little bit daft?', a question which brought the strongest of sincere denials. Later she told us that, since he has been coming to the playgroup, he has been appreciably more gentle towards herself and more amenable than he was before.

I have described Kuase's behaviour for two reasons. It was easy to follow the processes that were going on in him because he acted so spontaneously and expressed his feelings so uninhibitedly in movement and facial expression. Secondly, he was, at the time he joined the group, physically strong and mature for his age and also *potentially* very capable; therefore his behaviour demonstrated very clearly the extent of his ignorance of the creatures, objects and situations that he found in the playgroup when he joined it, and also the speed at which he was learning judgment of every kind.

Young children can only learn about the world through their senses. It is necessary for them to experience events physically, and also voluntarily – that is, with interest and a desire to know – if they are to form realistic concepts. I was surprised when Dylan, at the age of twenty-five months, knew that Carolyn needed something to lean on if she was to be able to step into her wellington boot, and was moved to offer his shoulder for support (see p. 61). Later I realized that it was not because he was precociously intelligent or sensitive to the needs of others; rather it was because – firstly – he was at the time particularly intrigued by Carolyn and interested in her behaviour, and – secondly – being twenty-five months old, he had himself recently spent much of his time learning how to balance on two feet or on one, and therefore knew how difficult it is to stand on one foot without falling over.

It is likely that a child becomes aware of how things are for others through being occupied in digesting similar knowledge side by side and simultaneously with another child. For instance he realizes, as he climbs on the climbing frame, that he must hold on tightly or else balance perfectly, and it may be that he is at the same time becoming aware that the child climbing next to him must do the same. This may be partly the reason why no one gets pushed off the top of the climbing frame or out of the apple tree.

Adults may fear unnecessarily for the safety of a climbing child. A small child may be more capable of judgment in the situation than they would be, for he is attending wholeheartedly to the activity in which he is engaged and is consistently exercising a sensory-motor awareness that in them may have grown rusty.

Similarly, some adults think that spontaneity of movement exercised by a large group of children in a comparatively small and encumbered space must be dangerous. But small children are alive to the messages being sent out constantly by all their senses; and if they are in an atmosphere where there is nothing to be gained by 'showing off', and where they know they are responsible for themselves, there will be few bumps and bruises. It has been shown that, when children are digesting the knowledge of how to climb, jump, slide, swing and run, together with and among, and in and out and round about others, they manifest what – in the case of the children in the Peckham Health Centre gymnasium – was described by Scott Williamson as 'physical altruism'. The children in this gymnasium and Harry Harlow's rhesus monkeys (p. 59) were occupied in learning how to make exacting and exact movements and precise sensory-motor judgments in time and space, in the company of others doing the same thing. It was necessary for each, in order to achieve his purpose, to be able to anticipate the movements of all the other moving creatures and objects in his vicinity; and the child or animal became able to do this, because he himself was making similar kinds of movements.

The two-to-fives, playing in a free-choice and appropriately equipped playgroup, will also develop this faculty. It will take time because of the greater variety of activity that is going on in a playgroup and the greater variety of things they are engaged in learning simultaneously, but it is easier to develop this faculty – just as it is easier to learn to balance – when young. It is also safer for them to develop the faculty in a pre-school playgroup, where the penalties for not possessing it are likely to be less serious than they would be at a later date in unsupervised and unplanned surroundings.

It may be doubted if the faculty to be aware of, and to anticipate, the movements of a number of swiftly moving people is necessary to civilized man. In fact it is very useful when trying to board the correct suburban train at a large railway station during the evening rush hour. Perhaps, since men, women and children are increasingly forced to live, work and spend their leisure time crowded closely together, it will become more important than it is at present – even as important as it is to monkeys. It will be remembered that the young monkeys that were denied any opportunity to play together in the jungle-type playground during the vital age of one to six months turned out to be completely inept socially when adult. Apart from this it is evident that all healthily uninhibited children particularly enjoy developing this faculty in themselves, and this may signify that it is a faculty fundamentally important to human beings. Assuredly it adds to their ease and spontaneity in social situations and personal relationships.

It may be wondered why, since all children will sooner or later become aware that other children are flesh and blood like themselves and experience similar desires and sensations, I consider it necessary for them to do so as early as possible. The reason is that the earlier they can develop a basic knowledge of the nature and characteristics that children share, the earlier they will become aware of the differences between individuals. Furthermore, the early acquisition of social judgment will give them the confidence to take advantage of every opportunity that comes their way to play with other children, and therefore they are more likely to develop any potentiality they may possess for delicate and deep awareness of another's feelings and attitudes at any particular moment, and of the effect that their own behaviour is having on others. As we all know, the faculty to be aware of others' feelings and point of view is not by any means universal in adults – even in those who are kindly and well disposed towards other people – and the development of a person's innate potentiality for this may depend partly on the amount of opportunity that he has, as a small child, to interact freely with his contemporaries, while being actively engaged in similar learning-activities.

In my 'minute-to-minute records' (see p. 83), Tracy tries to lessen the hurt that she believes has been done to Jennifer by Dawn's expression of dislike. But the fact that a small girl of three may already manifest a well-developed consciousness of another child's feelings, combined with a strong desire for justice for others and the courage to act upon it, does not invalidate the above hypothesis. It can happen that a child possesses a strong natural tendency to develop certain qualities, and that this tendency is accelerated by the particular manner in which he is treated at home and by the example given him there, with the result that these qualities mature in him at an unusually early age.

In a free-choice playgroup the children gradually become more aware, through playing alongside each other, of the other children's sensations, desires and feelings; and when, sooner or later, they want to play co-operatively with them, they will take their desires and feelings into account. Some children are slow to do this, but since they do not usually want to play solo all the time, they begin, in time, to learn the art of co-operation and 'give and take'.

It is easier for a child to learn about human nature and about his own nature, and to behave spontaneously, responsively and appropriately, in a group of familiar children of his own age, than it is for him to learn these things in his family circle – however large that may be. In the latter situation his judgment is often clouded by emotions such as jealousy, or by the fear of being under-valued or disapproved of by those close to him; and he may also feel that he does not need to take account of reality because some-one will always be at hand to 'magic' things for him.

Because personal relationships are less intense in a playgroup, the child's emotions are less overwhelming and he can experience feelings of possessiveness, jealousy or fear in small *digestible* amounts.

I do not mean to suggest for one moment that children should be in a playgroup environment all day and every day. At this age children still need to be in their own homes and with their own families for much of the time. I feel sure that the children belonging to my group would make far less good use of it if they did not have, in the background, a home and family – however small – in which and to whom they feel themselves to be of particular importance. But a child also needs, from time to time, to be 'forgotten' by his family and out of their sight and hearing in a place where he can be an entirely freely-acting and independent member of a familiar group of his peers.

However, the acquisition of social judgment is only possible – even in a playgroup or nursery school – when supervisors and organizers are aware of the importance of freedom. If they are not, they may unwittingly make it very difficult for the children to develop this faculty.

This occurred to some extent in one playgroup that I visited. The children were given a period for free play with large toys.

Then, after a break, the tables were arranged in a big hollow square, and the twenty-five children were required to sit on chairs that were placed at the tables on the inside of the square only. 'Educational toys' were placed on two free tables and each child was allowed to come up and 'choose' a toy, and take it back to his place, where he was expected to stay for a certain time. The purpose of this arrangement was to assist concentration, and to avoid trouble – fights, tears and destruction or mixing up of the parts of the toys – but the *effect* was to minimize the contact of each child with the others, and thus to prevent them all from obtaining essential educational experience.

In a free-choice playgroup there will sometimes be tears, there will certainly be arguments over toys and occasionally fights. But these are all necessary experiences, through which a child learns a hundred things, and although some children may make a lot of noise and fuss, the emotions felt on these occasions are rarely deep and searing ones. As to the pieces of the jigsaws and other equipment getting mixed up, this is bound to happen to some extent, but supervisors should realize that a good proportion of their time *must* be spent in keeping the equipment in order, and should plan accordingly.

What it is quite unnecessary to fear, in the opinion of other free-choice playgroup supervisors besides myself, is that a general 'free-for-all' will develop, as long as – and this is important – there is available to the children at all times sufficient and suitable equipment for the learning-activity that they need.

It has been the experiences of the supervisors of well-equipped and genuinely free-choice playgroups that passions rarely run high; even momentarily uncontrollable anger seems rarely to be aroused, and temper tantrums are unheard of except in the case of very disturbed children. There may be a variety of reasons for this. Perhaps the children know that it will cut no ice with the adults and therefore will not get them anywhere; perhaps they do not expect so much of their friends and of the supervisor as of their parents, and thus do not feel so badly let down by them; perhaps they are so busy learning what they want to learn that to indulge in a temper tantrum would be a stupid waste of time. Perhaps the most important reason of all is that the supervisor, though from time to time she may have to restrain them from doing what they want to do, is in the fortunate position of only extremely rarely having to make them do what they do not want to do, and therefore, although they are often mildly frustrated, they never feel completely cornered or quite powerless to affect their lot.

The following is an extract from my notes:

I didn't see who had the small pull-along truck first, but when I looked, Richard, aged 3:1, was holding it, and then Iain, aged 2:3, began to cry. Since I suspected what had happened, but was not sure of the rights of the situation, I did nothing. After a moment, Richard put the truck down, placed a 'little man' in the driving seat, and handed the end of the string for pulling it to Iain.

In a free-choice playgroup, a child learns to act and to think, and also to *feel*. His sensory-motor and verbal and logical powers develop through use and the digestion of experience, and it seems to me likely that the growth of his sensibility and powers of feeling obey the same biological law. If this is so, it follows that the child needs to have the opportunity to feel, and to recognize in himself the feeling of, for instance, compassion or anger – or both at once – when he is in a position to act according to his feelings. It is undeniably good for him to be in a position to practise compassion when he feels it; it is probably also good for him to be in a position to direct his anger towards its real cause, so long as he does not expect to be shielded from the consequences of doing so. In the playgroup a child can discover the effects, both short- and long-term, that the expression of his feelings has upon others and upon himself.

Normally, as we have seen, he acts on his judgment of the situation as a whole and not in reaction to one part of it only. Consequently, as time goes on, he acts more and more often in a manner that is likely to produce the desired long-term results. He acts from the heart, but at the same time he learns to act with discretion and discrimination – that is, realistically and constructively.

The following example of behaviour in my playgroup shows two children exercising social judgment and practising the give and take of friendship. One day, Audrey Boyle called my attention to the fact that Michael was trying to teach James how to slide down the central pole of the climbing frame. Michael and James (see minute-to-minute records No. 1) were great friends and often played together. Michael was a year older than James but, at this time, half a head shorter. James, having grown so fast, found acrobatics difficult, but he was an extremely energetic and sanguine child, and had exceptional powers of concentration. He could, at this stage, climb very skilfully all over the frame, but had not yet had the courage to try to slide down the pole.

Michael apparently keenly desired that his friend should share the pleasure that he himself received from doing this, and spent time, energy and thought on trying to help him to learn until, after a few weeks, James was finally successful.

We frequently heard Michael urging James to 'do it like this'. Then one day he remembered that it is easier to transfer one's weight to the central pole if one is standing on a platform formed by placing a plank across the bars, half-way up the frame, than if one must stand on a perimeter bar and lean right over in order to reach the central pole, or – even more difficult – hang by one's hands from the top bars, wrap one's legs round the pole, and then transfer one's hands to it. We knew that this thought had come to him because on more than one occasion he asked the supervisor to bring a plank and place it on the frame and once he lugged one out of the shed by himself.

Michael did not seem to be motivated in the least by a desire to boss or to demonstrate his superiority; he merely did everything he could to make it easier for James. We noticed that when James began to play at something else, Michael would join him, apparently aware that James had had enough of learning to slide down the pole for the time being. He never stumped off impatient and disappointed, and so James was not made to feel a fool, and did not become dispirited or lose confidence in his ability to learn in the long run. On the next occasion when they were able to play in the garden – perhaps after an interval of a week or more, according to the weather – they both renewed their efforts. These were eventually rewarded, and James was able to swing himself onto the pole near the top, and slide to the ground with great enjoyment, if not yet with the grace and abandon of some of the other children.

Michael is a modest, very gentle and rather diffident child, shy and unforthcoming with grown-ups. He may, I fear, be the type who gets pushed to the wall in the classroom. If this happens and he loses confidence in his ability, it will be a pity, because he has considerable natural gifts; in particular, good powers of concentration and application, and a social and artistic sensitivity which have been nourished in a truly loving, though not well-educated or very articulate home. In the playgroup he was able to practise the *art* of friendship, and as a result his gift for affection began to develop into a talent for friendship that could in the future bring happiness to himself and others instead of being more often a source of pain to himself.

At the same time as he was acquiring this art, he was also acquiring many different sensory-motor skills, good hand–eye co-ordination and general sensory-motor judgment, balance and agility. This should, if he continues to find opportunity for the necessary practice as he grows, counterbalance any future deleterious effects on his self-confidence and any social disadvantages that his small stature might bring.

Michael was also becoming more at home with words. With adults he was slow to talk, but in the group he chatted with his friends very readily and talked to himself almost continuously. The children do not consider it odd to talk to oneself, so Michael was able to practise putting his experiences into words and describing objects and events without fear of ridicule, and sometimes his monologue developed into a conversation (see Chapter 4, Record No. 1).

In a free-choice playgroup the children's articulation of words tends to improve as well as their vocabulary, because they soon find that, in order to obtain the willing and effective co-operation of other children in an enterprise, they must speak clearly and pleasantly; they find that the kind of private language that mother understands is not good enough.

In a free-choice playgroup the children spend a very large proportion of the time in playing games of make-believe, either alone or with others. It is impossible to find out how much time they spend on this type of play as compared to play that teaches them about objects and materials and their uses, because so often they combine the two; for instance, they may be learning balance and skill in climbing on the frame or the 'slides' at the same time as they are playing at being firemen. When they are playing at family meal times they are practising hand–eye co-ordination.

A child finds make-believe play enjoyable because he relishes his *power* to imitate someone or something, or to recall – by reproducing it – a past incident, or to produce a comic or dramatic effect, or to tease. He also uses it as a means of learning about other people and events, and of experiencing emotions. One day, Piaget noticed that his daughter Jacqueline was fascinated by the sight of a dead duck that had been plucked and placed on the kitchen table. 'The next day,' he records, 'I found J. lying motionless on the sofa in my study, her arms pressed against her body and her legs bent. "What are you doing, Jacqueline? Have you a pain? Are you ill?" Silence, then, "No, I'm the dead duck."'

A small child tries to satisfy his curiosity about people and things by doing as they do. To this end he uses all his senses, including his sense of movement and his sensation of the relative position of the parts of his body.

A friend told me that at the age of five her daughter went through a period of about a week when she would often – at moments when she thought no one was looking – walk with a pronounced limp. Her mother found out eventually that she had seen a cripple in the street. The same child went through a period of pretending that she was blind; and I remember my own children wanting to be led by the hand while they kept their eyes shut. If a child can persuade someone to play this game with him, he will be able to feel in a small way how it must feel to be blind. The little boy who spends the morning 'being a coalman', and loading all his toys into a pillow case and carrying it about on his back, may be enjoying his power to do as 'the coalman' does, but he may also be enjoying the discovery of how it feels to carry a heavy load about on one's back, and to be forced to walk bent forwards and only able to look at the ground or sideways. A child may be trying to satisfy his curiosity about the coalman or the blind man or the cripple; and it is very likely that after 'being' these people, and having experienced the sensations that are produced in his own body by acting as they do, he does in fact possess a more objective concept of the life led by these people, instead of being only aware of the emotions, such as fear or admiration, that their presence or image may arouse in him.

I would suggest that this kind of play enables the child to see things in the round, from all points of view, instead of merely from his own. It helps him to grow beyond the egocentric position of infancy.

Incidentally, 'egocentric', as Piaget uses the term, does not mean self-absorbed; rather it means seeing things only from one's own point of view. The infant is not self-absorbed, he does look outwards; but naturally he knows things only as he himself sees them or in other ways experiences them. When the youngest of our children was four, her nearest sibling was an eleven-year-old brother of about 5 ft 6 in. in height, and the eldest two and her parents were all around 6 feet. When at this age she first began to draw people, she always began close to the top of the paper with a little round head; then she drew two long straight parallel lines to the bottom of the paper and finished with a large loop (foot) at the end of each line.

A healthily spontaneous child seeks nourishment for his concepts and his emotions as well as for his faculties. If he is successful they will become more realistic, subtle and comprehensive.

A child chews the cud of experience in order to make it more digestible; he re-enacts things that have happened to him or things that he has seen or heard about, in order to experience them more fully and to give them meaning – to digest them. In the case of very young children the happenings that they reproduce may be quite small snippets of their past experience rather than whole scenes.

They may reproduce the words and the tones of voice that they have heard used by people, apparently with the intention of experiencing the emotion that, it is evident to them, was felt by these people at the time and which had excited their curiosity and interest. When Dawn (see p. 81) said, 'Get *down*, Michael! *DOWN* ... AT ... ONCE!*' when they were both at the top of the climbing frame, she could not have been really concerned to make him do so, in spite of the strength of the emotion in her voice, for she took no notice at all of the fact that he did not obey her. Dawn has a highly effective intelligence and sometimes makes use of it to try to manipulate the other children, but on this occasion I think that she was not trying to exercise power over Michael. She simply wanted to experience the dramatic effect upon herself of saying these words in the tone of voice in which she had previously heard similar words used by an adult.

C. W. Valentine notes in *The Psychology of Early Childhood*:

Y. at 2¼
M. said at dusk, 'Pull the curtains to.' Y: 'Oo 'es – dark, very dark,' frowning and putting on a very serious expression, shaking her curls, puffing out her lips and cheeks. I fancied that there was an effort to experience the emotion by acting it. ... In playing with her dolls the little girl seems to enjoy not only the outward procedure of looking after them but the very emotion of tenderness.

Communal make-believe games have an added advantage: when two or three children are co-operating in a make-believe game they can learn how it feels to *be treated* as the character they have assumed. I remember a little girl called Wendy, three and a half years old, a particularly happy and serene, but also confident and energetic child, who had been a member of the playgroup for about a year when she acquired a baby brother. She showed no ill effects, such as a desire to attract attention to herself, for she was blessed with parents who made sure that her nose was not put out of joint. As it happened, there were some children in the group at the time who liked to play 'mothers and fathers,' and, for two or three weeks after the birth of her brother, Wendy joined this group and was always the 'baby' – a very young, helpless, passive baby (behaviour that was quite out of character for her). It seemed to me that her motive was mainly to satisfy her curiosity about babies by finding out how it felt to act like – and be treated as – a baby. I do not think that her behaviour was caused simply by a desire to exercise her power to lie prone and unresponsive like a new-born baby, because this desire would surely not have taken her long to satisfy, whereas she continued to play this game over a period of three weeks at least, whenever she had the opportunity.

I am aware that make-believe play can serve many purposes. It can be a means of compensating for the unpleasantness of real life or of restoring self-respect; there is no need to give instances of this because it has been well documented elsewhere. Children also use it in many individual little ways. One of my daughters, at about three years old, had a kind of familiar called 'Snakey'. I think he may have originated in a dream because I remember that at first he was a little frightening and unaccountable, but soon she turned him into a useful companion: 'I didn't do it. Snakey did it.' She was a sociable and talkative child, and when she could not think of any real-life topic, she used Snakey as a means of insinuating herself into the family conversation: 'Snakey said to me . . .' or 'Do you know what Snakey did?', sometimes deadpan – no doubt when she was thinking hard what it was that Snakey *had* done – sometimes with a twinkle in her eye.

Valentine's happy children played make-believe games at a very early age, as he said, 'from an enjoyment in the absurd and in the pretence itself'. As an example, he quotes the following extract from his diary:

> B. at 1:0, held out his hand to us saying, 'Ta', as if about to give us something. I held out my hand and he pretended to put something in it, then drew away and laughed. This was repeated many times, and I also did it to him, he holding out his hand for the imaginary gift. . . . At 1:9, when put into bed, he wanted to kiss a chair. When I held it up to him, he flung himself down in bed and pretended he was going to sleep. When I put the chair down, up he sprang again. Had me on like this a long time, laughing hugely.

But I think there was an element of learning here; part of the fun consisted in discovering how to 'have father on' more effectively.

So a child's motive for make-believe play may be partly or wholly a desire to experience what it feels like to be someone else or to behave in a certain way, or to be in a certain situation, such as in hospital, in a road accident, a policeman controlling the traffic, or the astronaut in his space-rocket. And even when other motives are involved, the children are likely to extend their knowledge of reality or their social judgment in some way or other, if their make-believe is co-operative. For instance, in a game of 'mothers and fathers', a child may choose the role of 'mother' in order to compensate for being in real life the smallest and least powerful member of the family, but in the course of the game she will obtain a better idea of what it is really like to be a mother, because her 'children' – unlike dolls – have wills of their own, and will not always be obedient. Again, the child that chooses to be 'baby' may do so because he likes to be made a fuss of, but will probably, after a while, better appreciate the utter helplessness and dependence of babies.

But I must underline the point that these games should be spontaneously initiated and carried through by the children themselves. Dramatization of stories after reading them may be a valuable activity in the junior school, but it is wrong to expect it of the pre-school child (probably also at the infant school stage). A child of this age may, after a lapse of time, spontaneously incorporate a character or an incident in a story that has particularly impressed him into his make-believe games, in the same way as he reproduces real events from his past experience, or plays at being a lion, a fish, a fisherman or a robot, but he does not naturally, as older children do, attempt to act well-known stories. I have tried, in the past, to encourage the children to act or mime the simplest of their favourite stories, but many would not co-operate and those who did became self-conscious and embarrassed. I am aware that a skilled teacher in a school-like environment might have quite a contrary experience, and I know that children aged three to seven can give an audience of parents great pleasure by their charming rendering of a Christmas play or mime. But I wonder if the *children* gain anything from the activity, or if at best it wastes their time, and at worst may help to kill their spontaneity.

If children are conscious of the presence of *critical* grown-ups, they may not engage in make-believe play. The supervisor of one group told me that the children only did it when they were inside the enclosed Home Corner and therefore felt themselves to be unobserved.

Children enjoy group make-believe games up to the age of eleven or twelve, though they may not admit this to older people. Long after the pre-school age, children love to 'be' brides and grooms, kings and queens, doctors or schoolteachers, in the company of their friends, and to try to discover, through 'being' these

176

people, a little about what adult life is like. Seven to eleven is the great secret-society age when children like to belong to a gang which has a secret code, meeting-place, passwords and, sometimes, rules of conduct. My children and their friends among the neighbours made use of the small underground concrete air-raid shelter at the end of our garden, an unpleasantly dark, dank and smelly place but, to their way of thinking, highly suitable for the meetings of the 'gang'.

In *A Group of Juniors*, Frances Tustin gives a fascinating account, including some verbatim reporting over a period of two or three months, of the activity of a group of eight- and nine-year-olds at a co-educational boarding school. The children often played in a disused quarry.

This is a friendly, sheltered place with all sorts of exciting possibilities for children to use in their play. It has a large circular patch of springy green turf. On one side is a high wall of sandstone rock which has natural caves and handy ledges for climbing. On the other side, opposite to the path, are several large trees growing on a bank with their roots exposed. These are thick and knotted and form a number of cubby holes. At the side of those trees is a natural sand-pit where the bank shelves away so sharply that the grass cannot get a roothold. On the fourth side is a grassy bank which is beautifully smooth for 'rolypolies'.

Here, they played solitary make-believe and 'group-fantasy' games, as well as, and often combined with, 'adventurous climbing and jumping, and sometimes intellectual play with words'.

Mrs Tustin found that, in their co-operative games, some of the more mature and balanced children acted with a very sensitive feeling for the needs of those who were less fortunate. For instance, 'Kevin, an unco-ordinated and unstable eight-and-a-half-year-old, is helped by Alan, also eight and a half but of unusual sensitivity and insight, to create a fantasy situation which is psychologically satisfying to him.' During a group-fantasy called the 'Monkey Game', which was often played in the quarry, Kevin said: '"I'm not in anyone's tribe. I'm just a stray one," and Alan says: "Pretend you're old and wise and live on your own," a situation which delights Kevin and helps him to bear his feelings of aloneness and of being different from the other children.'

Children of this pre-adolescent age need places in which they can play together away from adults. They need to be able from time to time to stop pretending to themselves and others that they are more grown-up than they really are, and to indulge freely in what they are aware may be considered babyish make-believe. They need places where they can build houses, dens, forts and wigwams, light fires, spontaneously mime and dance and sing, and exercise their powers of creative imagination uninterruptedly – places where mess and untidiness are allowed. They need places where they can simply talk undisturbed, as well as climb, swing and jump.

Mrs Tustin's charges were unusually fortunate in having a disused quarry as a playground. All similar places in the neighbourhood of inhabited areas should be preserved for children's use. But equally good play-spaces can be constructed within urban agglomerations if they are included in development or redevelopment plans, or if use is made of sites, such as steeply sloping ground, that are unsuitable for housing or commercial or industrial use, or if a part of a recreation ground or park is fenced off for the purpose.

But it is important to realize that children will be unable to make the most of such opportunities if they have not had the chance to acquire a healthy degree of social and sensory-motor judgment in their pre-school years and while they are still too young to make their own way to a playground.

If children are to develop their social judgment, their self-awareness and their responsiveness to the needs of others, they must, at all ages, have easy access to a place where their neighbours gather frequently for play. I do not mean to imply that children left to grow up in a community of children, as if on an otherwise uninhabited island, would develop truly human qualities. Children absorb the values of those around them, particularly the values of the people they admire and respect. It may well be that they need to have the opportunity to love and observe wise, mature and humane people if they are themselves to become wise, mature and humane.

Children need to be able to form relationships of varying closeness outside their families, both with their contemporaries and with adults. Often the regular play-leaders who look after and dispense the equipment and exert authority when necessary in 'adventure playgrounds' find themselves playing the part that an elder brother or uncle or aunt might play, of a disinterested, loyal, sympathetic and discreet confidant-adviser, or even a hero and therefore a model.

Dr Harry Harlow's rhesus monkeys were found to be unable to live peaceably and creatively together when grown, if they had been confined to the company of their mothers in a small cage during the vital period from one to six months of age. It seems equally likely that human beings will lead more tolerant, happy, effective and creative lives if, *as small children,* they are able to learn to interact confidently with their human and material environment. Ideally a child should be able to extend his environment for himself; he should be able to explore further from home and become familiar with a gradually widening circle of people and their activities and living space *as he feels able,* and to seek adventure and meet challenges and dangers on an exciting but manageable scale; in short, to learn through observation and practice how to live. He needs a home that is more than the space between four walls in which he and his parents sleep and eat; he needs a home neighbourhood – a territory that he can by degrees get to know intimately, and where the layout of the housing in relation to roads and streets makes sociability and neighbourliness possible.

CHAPTER NINE

Learning-activity 3 – Becoming Oneself

Being oneself is a faculty and, like any other, needs exercise if it is to develop. If a person had, from babyhood, always done what he was told to do – or been expected to do – and nothing else, and had never acted on his own initiative or according to his own desires – even in private – he would be nothing; he would have no self. Such a situation is inconceivable, and yet something like it does occasionally happen. It also quite frequently happens that a person is far less of an integrated individual than he might have been; he has no 'mind of his own', no power to digest experience, is adrift at the mercy of wind and currents and helpless in the face of misfortune.

Becoming oneself consists of:

1. Becoming a fully-functioning human being, capable of awareness and responsiveness on the sensory-motor and emotional planes.

2. Developing the natural aptitude and character and the 'vision' that is latent in every individual.

3. Developing spontaneity – by which I mean the ability to respond in a manner that is true to oneself as an integrated whole so that, instead of reacting compulsively to this or that force or mechanically to this or that irritation or being stuck in the railway lines of habit, one has free-will.

This is a tall order, or seems so at first sight. Does anyone ever develop all these qualities and powers? Yet, from a biological point of view, they are merely what one should expect in a wholly healthy member of the human species; they are the birthright, the potentiality of everyone. So one should rather ask, why do people *not* possess them?

There is no simple answer to this question; but it would certainly be less necessary to ask it at all, if every young child, from birth onwards, were to be free to choose for himself what he will pay attention to and what he will do, in surroundings that provide timely and appropriate nourishment for his developing faculties. Each time a baby selects something to respond to, or decides to do something because it is what he wants to do more than anything else, he is acting spontaneously, and nourishing his individuality and integrity.

The dictionary gives more than one meaning to the word 'spontaneous'. I am using it in the sense, not of acting 'on a sudden impulse', but of acting 'of one's own free will'. Indeed, it may happen that one reacts on the spur of the moment *un*spontaneously because one has allowed circumstances to dictate to one. Then, after a pause for reflection, or after a few seconds or hours during which one's 'digestive juices' have had time to work, one becomes aware of the total situation and of one's deeper feelings, and one becomes capable of acting truly voluntarily.

As we have seen, a baby's mouth at first sucks automatically, his limbs jerk and his eyes tend to follow any object that moves; but after a time it is apparent that he is selecting certain objects to watch, returning to them again and again. He is choosing what he will do with his hands and when he will 'kick' with his feet; he is deciding to suck or not to suck. No one can deny that a baby is acting of his own free will and is making a spontaneous decision when he unexpectedly interrupts his feeding in order to smile and gurgle at his mother, and then suddenly returns to his meal, or when he stops sucking his thumb in order to seize hold of his sister's curls or nose as she leans over him. In these cases he is responding as an integrated whole to his environment as a whole. He is making choices, thus nourishing his power to choose, and ultimately his power to be himself.

Just as the child can develop his sensory-motor judgment only by exercising it and his social judgment only by interacting freely with others, so he develops his spontaneity only by responding as an integrated whole to the whole situation as he is aware of it.

In an important sense, a person consists of the knowledge he has digested as a result of his experiences and activity. Expressed in another way, his *judgment is himself*: for judgment is acquired through the digestion of one's experience, and is therefore unique and specific to oneself. So a child is fully himself at any time only if he has developed the general sensory-motor and social judgment that he is capable at the time of developing. As we have seen, a child will do this if his environment consistently contains opportunity for the experience he is ready to digest, and if he is free to be aware of it. He will choose to do what he has newly become capable of learning to do.

Unfortunately it frequently happens that, from the second half of his first year onwards, a child's opportunities for doing what he is capable of learning to do are actually fewer than he had as a baby-in-arms. If his environment is not favourable for development, he has in fact no chance to exercise his ability for digestion of experience, and his judgment will remain embryonic. His promise will never be realized.

For instance, a baby will soon become bored with playing with his sister's nose and curls; they will no longer provide him with nourishment for his ability to catch hold of things. They no longer excite his curiosity because he knows exactly how they look and how they feel to his fingers and his mouth. He is no longer amused by the giggles and squeals of pain he has learned to produce by pulling them. He has learned everything about them that he is so far capable of learning, and so, if no alternative learning-activity is available to him, he might as well, from his point of view, go on sucking his thumb. At this stage, he is likely to be more interested in holding on to something that offers sufficient resistance to enable him to pull himself to a sitting position or even, having tensed all his muscles, to his feet.

In the industrially developed countries, small children are increasingly likely to spend their time in an environment which they cannot become familiar with through their senses, cannot understand, and in which they cannot, therefore, use their own judgment – nor even be allowed to try. Indeed a certain type of child, finding that his tentative efforts towards independence or adventure and experiment are frowned upon, may come to the conclusion that passivity is the best policy. Consequently he may do only what he is told to do, and not much of that. Then, when he is handed over to a school at the age of five, he continues to be mentally and physically passive, expecting someone else to take decisions and think for him – often to the despair of his teachers. But, in the modern world, a young adult needs to be capable of more difficult and far-reaching decisions than he would have needed in a more tradition-bound and less rapidly changing society, and it is necessary for our children to make particularly rapid progress in self-determination and judgment.

One can understand better what 'becoming oneself' means if one studies the manner in which young people who have failed disastrously to become themselves have been helped. At Finchden Manor, in Kent, England, Mr G. Lyward spent many years successfully helping maladjusted and delinquent youths onto the road towards a more mature way of life. He provided a temporary home, and respite from the pressures upon them, for boys between the ages of fourteen and twenty. They were sent to him – either privately on the recommendation of doctors and psychiatrists, or by local authorities – because schools could not manage them or they could not cope with school, or because parents or magistrates had despaired of them. They came labelled 'maladjusted', 'psycho-pathic', 'suicidal' and even, in one case, 'satanically sadistic'.

Mr Lyward talked little about his work, even to Michael Burn who spent several months as a member of his staff in order to write the fascinating book, *Mr Lyward's Answer*; but one day, as Mr Burn records, he exclaimed with pleasure when he saw half a dozen young men playing a childish ball game together outside the window of his sitting-room, and said, 'Why not let them have back their childhood?' He knew from experience that their only hope lay in shedding their sophisticated would-be adult masks and becoming wholeheartedly the children that they had never properly been allowed – or allowed themselves – to be in the past. He said: 'They have come [to Finchden] because they have failed to become seven-year-olds. However they may look and however big and cleverly they may talk, they may in truth be no more than seven-year-olds with an L-sign.'

As Michael Burn explained, these boys had come from a variety of backgrounds. Some had been smothered by parental solicitude, some had been expected to maintain too high a standard of beha-viour or to satisfy inordinate parental ambition; some had been deserted physically or emotionally. But all of them had suffered as children from not being able – out of fear of loss of affection or of more tangible ills – to act spontaneously according to their feel-ings and needs, or to follow their interests and their own purposes. As a result they had failed to develop any stable individuality, any power to direct their own lives, any emotional depth.

Many of them had tried to cover up – often successfully, for some were highly intelligent – by affecting a superficially sophis-ticated, hard-boiled or intellectual manner. But this skin-deep personality tended to develop more and larger cracks as they grew older. Some of them had tried to rebel against being deprived of their freedom to be themselves, but they were unable to rebel suc-cessfully because they had not – as Mr Lyward said on more than one occasion – been properly 'weaned'. However frustrated they felt about it, they were still dependent upon others to lead them; they did not have the power to find their own way. Therefore they succeeded only in dragging their feet, in adopting a negative atti-tude to life, and were constantly on the defensive and revengeful.

Almost all of them had a tendency to erect a barrier between themselves and their environment; it was as if they tried to protect themselves by wearing a suit of armour. The result of this was to cut them off from reality, but it did not usually succeed in achiev-ing its purpose of saving themselves pain and frustration, fear and confusion. They were inclined to walk about in their self-made prison, unaware of almost everything except what was going on in their own minds. They were in varying degrees incapable of responding to others; instead, they 'bounced off' people, automatically reacting to them defensively or else in a heartless or solely intellectual manner.

Most of them very soon recognized that Finchden Manor offered them a chance to rest from the struggle to behave as others wanted, or from the equally exhausting and ineffectual struggle not to do so. Here at last they were treated with respect as persons and as individuals with minds of their own. No one was trying to force them to be something they could not be, and they no longer felt that they were pawns in another's game or simply a nuisance. And at the same time they were not expected to be mature adults. They were, in fact, expected to play – in the sense in which the word is used in this book. So most of them stayed there voluntarily, until Mr Lyward considered they were strong enough to make their own way in the outside world. Some stayed a few weeks, many stayed several months or years. But, although they were treated as persons, it was often a long time before they could *be* persons at all consistently.

Mr Lyward's 'answer' was – very roughly speaking – to provide an atmosphere in which they could regain the spontaneity they had lost. This entailed encouraging them to be the small children that they really were beneath their tough or – sometimes – over-conscientious exteriors. He tried to make it possible for them to do what they really felt like doing, not in isolation but in relation to the community of Finchden Manor. Escape into an exclusive attachment to another boy or to someone in the local town was something he tried to prevent. If they must have a prop it was better that it should be one of the staff, who would, as soon as possible, remove his support and cause them to stand on their own feet.

But first, as he said, they had to become 'disarmed'. Only when the defensive armour, the pretences, the superficial cleverness or 'one-upmanship', with which they tried to compensate for the lack of a basic skeleton of character and individuality, had fallen away and they had begun to enjoy life and to look at it freshly and directly like a child, was it possible for them to begin to be aware of what was not themselves, and to relate to other persons.

This 'disarming' process took a long time. One of the reasons was that, after initially welcoming the free atmosphere, the boys found themselves unable to manage without their shackles. With no timetables or rules to keep (Mr Lyward did not even like to have public notices posted), those used to trying to conform felt lost; while those who had spent their energies in trying *not* to conform found themselves equally at a loss, for they had nothing to rebel against. They were free to choose for themselves and found themselves incapable of choice. One boy said: 'I wish there was something to do, but [hurriedly] I don't want to do it.' In reality the boys were free to play or work at almost anything they liked – for instance, to keep pets, make canoes or radios, organize entertainments and dances to which young people from the neighbouring small town were invited. The staff were willing to help them to do these things, but the initiative, application and continuity had to come from the boys themselves. The staff were qualified to instruct them in many skills and to coach them for examinations, but it was up to the boys to decide for themselves what they wanted to learn, to persist in a course of action or drop it as they pleased.

At Finchden they were thrown back upon themselves and teetered on the brink of a very painful realization, which was that behind the false front or armour there was nothing – or nothing but a very young, ineffective, indecisive little child. Some could not bring themselves to face this fact. Mr Lyward knew which ones needed to be let down lightly; he treated each boy differently, to the point of deliberate and obvious unfairness, but, although the boys grumbled about this, they did not at heart resent it, because it made them feel that they were being treated as individuals rather than as units of an undifferentiated crowd.

Mr Lyward or a member of his staff often had to sacrifice a great deal of time and energy to acting as an ever-available, womb-like retreat to one boy or another, but would try as soon as possible to manoeuvre him into becoming an effective, spontaneous member of the community comprising the other boys and the small staff of Finchden as a whole. When this had happened it was usually possible for the boy to leave Finchden shortly afterwards, make his own way in the world or perhaps to return to school.

Among the most difficult cases were those who, as Michael Burn says, had never successfully reached a stage of emotional development appropriate to a three- or four-year-old. They were 'camouflaged babies'. He describes a youth of twenty of whom one tended to think, 'this boy's intelligence is so high that he really ought to be at a university', and then, a little while later, the boy would lose his temper so completely that he was like a toddler in a tantrum, only more dangerous.

In this connection, a recent theory of one of the causes of schizophrenia is interesting: it is that the individual's real self has remained unformed, like molten lava which, from time to time, erupts through the outer crust of the false personality that he has allowed to be imposed upon him by those in charge of him during childhood. R. D. Laing noticed that the parents of patients often said something like this to him: 'He (or she) was so *good* as a baby and small child – so amenable – no trouble at all – always did as he was told.' From evidence such as this, Laing came to the conclusion that those who, as babies and young children, are temperamentally inclined not to assert themselves, may sometimes be liable to develop schizophrenia in adolescence – when they can no longer continue to be an appendage of the parent – unless their individuality is carefully nurtured. In *The Divided Self* Laing tells the story of one of his patients who proved unhappily to be incurable. As a small child, she had been everything her mother held to be good. (Her elder sister, in contrast, had – in her mother's words – 'always been self-willed', so much so that she had 'had to be allowed to go her own way'; she had become a normal adult.) During adolescence the favourite daughter became 'bad' and 'difficult', often accusing her mother of 'not having allowed her to live'. Later, she began to assert that her mother had 'killed a baby'. Then her family decided that she was not bad but mad, and sought professional advice.

Bruno Bettelheim has made the study and cure of autistic children his main life-work. He puts forward the hypothesis that some extremely sensitive children, if exposed to a certain environment, can find life so painfully humiliating that they try to experience it as little as possible. This prevents them from being further hurt, but also from developing, since interaction with the environment is necessary for development. Some, in fact, lose the powers they already have; for instance, they may have already begun to learn to talk, but stop and apparently forget the words they have already learned. Sometimes they succeed so well in closing themselves up against experience that they become insensitive to physical pain; Bettelheim reports one child who died from peritonitis without ever having given any evidence of feeling pain.

In the University of Chicago Orthogenic School, Bettelheim and his staff cured three-quarters of the autistic children who were admitted, to the point where they were able to go to an ordinary school, finish their education (some to degree level) and earn their living and function competently on their own in society.

Cure demanded, firstly, the constant offering of warm interest and respect from one or more particular adults for months or years on end. Secondly, the child had to be manoeuvred as soon as possible into feeling that he was to some extent master of his own fate, for he could not begin to feel that he was a person until he felt effective in some way or other. In *The Empty Fortress* Bettelheim says: 'Children suffering from autism and other less extreme forms of schizophrenia do not feel at all sure what is themselves and what is not themselves'; and it is through acting as an effective force upon things and people that they become aware of the distinction. They get a feeling of being an individual self and, at the same time, become more interested in what is not themselves.

These children appeared to feel that their environment was like an armoured car advancing upon them. It was only when, after some time in the school, they began to realize that the environment was something which could be influenced a little, that they came to have the courage to experience it and to make the first move back to health.

Hence it was axiomatic at the School never to force, or to appear to force, anything upon one of these autistic children. The danger was that they would immediately revert to their earlier state of thing-like insensibility, and all the patient attention previously devoted to them by their caretakers would have been wasted. Because they had always suffered from feeling overpowered and unable to affect their environment in any way, to feel yet again that they were being mastered and manipulated would have caused them to shrink into their shells once more.

It was also necessary to welcome with enthusiasm any activity whatever that was initiated by the child himself, however unpleasant to his caretakers it might be. This was easier to do than one might expect because *any* initiative on the part of a severely autistic child was a welcome relief, and made a little easier the almost impossible task of continuing to care positively for a thing hardly more alive than a mechanical doll.

As an example of the way in which self-determination and spontaneity were encouraged in the children, here are two extracts from the story of 'Marcia', who came to the school at the age of ten and a half. Before she came to the school she had, for many years, 'spent her days in mute, angry and frightened withdrawal. She sat on her bed for hours in a strange yoga position, her feet crossed under her, either motionless or excitedly rocking up and down.' For long periods of time she pressed shut her ears and sometimes her nostrils. 'When her forefingers were stopping up her ears, the little fingers would close up the nostrils. . . . Any bodily contact was angrily rejected, even a touching or holding of hands. Getting her dressed .required endless patience because her choices came only after endless rejection of what pieces of clothing we offered. Dressing was further complicated because she would let no one touch her. But since buttons and zippers were too difficult, she eventually commanded us to "fasten", though as always, in a whisper.'

When Marcia had been with us a little short of a year, she began to play a game, her only one – a game of being chased. For some time she played it only with Inge; then with Karen or Inge; and for the next two years with nobody else. 'Chase' was one of the first things she articulated clearly enough to be heard, though still in a whisper. There was nothing mutual about this game; she never ran after anyone of us, and we had to bend to her inflexible rules. But at least she needed us to play it. . . . The game, her contact with the chasing person, stopped immediately when she lost us out of sight. Nor could Marcia take the initiative of seeking us out. The game did not begin until chance brought us into her field of vision; only then could she invite us to chase her. Yet whoever chased her had to keep a careful distance because she could not bear any physical closeness. It would not only have killed her enjoyment, but the game itself. Likewise, for years, if we wanted her to have anything to do with us, we had to pursue her both emotionally and physically, always keeping our distance. . . . In Marcia's game, the distance she forced us to keep seemed designed to reverse her old experience: to prove that others can exist without being overpowering.

Later he writes: 'Marcia, who had been an autistic something, now became a somebody as she devised things to do on her own volition. Only then did other beings enter her world.' It was only after she had gained mastery of certain functions and objects and had begun to try and solve problems 'that some real interest in another being emerged and with it aggression, and also the ability for symbolic representation – that is, for true thought.'

It was also found that passively receiving the satisfaction of their needs did not help the children. Indeed, rejection of what was offered to them was sometimes a sign that a cure was beginning. 'They came to life only when we were able to create the conditions, or otherwise be the catalysts, that induced them to take action on their own behalf.'

188

These children had to be brought back to life by being gently, tactfully and very gradually manoeuvred into the position of asserting themselves. Normally a baby is active from the beginning, though in such a limited way that he may *appear* to be passive. As Bettelheim says, a baby is not suckled – he actively sucks; and soon, if he is hungry, actively seeks the breast or bottle with his mouth and head and hands.

If a baby's personality is to develop in a healthy way, at least some of his activity – not necessarily connected with feeding – must be effective and produce results. His view of the world and of himself will depend upon it. 'How his activity succeeds and the response it receives will significantly colour all his later attempts at self-motivated action.' He gets a feeling of being effective when he finds that his mother responds to his *expressed* needs; but, if she attends, however intuitively and efficiently, to all his needs without allowing him to be active in demanding anything, he does *not* get this feeling. Bettelheim says:

> What humanises the infant is not being fed, changed or picked up when he feels the need for it. . . . It is rather the experience that *his* crying for food brings about *his* satiation by others according to *his* timing that makes it a socialising and humanising experience. It is that *his* smile, when it is an invitation to play, results in being played with.'

Inevitably every mother will sometimes misunderstand her baby's signs, and there will also be occasions when she is forced to turn a blind eye to them. But a certain amount of frustration – 'manageable frustration', as Bettelheim calls it – helps the baby to become aware that an outside world exists. What is important is that his mother – and the rest of his family – want to please him and feel that it is good for him to be pleased. If he is to become a person it is necessary for him to be treated as a person – not as a thing. One must respect his feelings and desires and try to satisfy his needs as he sees them as well as how we see them. The baby will be incapable of treating his mother as a person in the same way, but will gradually respond to more aspects of her. Bettelheim describes the ideal mother-and-child relationship as one of 'mutuality'.

The lesson we can learn from this is that we are definitely not spoiling a baby by letting him feel that he has the power to get from us what he wants – our attention, cuddling or food – when he asks for it. On the contrary, we are making sure that we neither humiliate nor deaden him.

From the age of two onwards, however, every child needs to be increasingly frequently one of a group of other children where he will discover that he no longer wields a fairy's wand, and where he will find that, in order to achieve his purposes, he needs to take into account the fact that others also have purposes.

As we have seen, a well-equipped free-choice playgroup provides an environment in which a small child can become aware of a whole situation of which he is only a part. He can do this because both he and the other children are free to pursue their purposes, which are similar in that they are all engaged in acquiring the same kinds of skill and knowledge. Through active experience and observation, he can become more realistic about himself and others; and at the same time as he becomes increasingly effective and powerful, he learns that the world does not revolve around himself. He can grow out of his egocentricity.

In a well-run free-choice playgroup, individuality is promoted, but not eccentricity. This is because, in such an environment, a child can hardly fail to be aware of the *reality* of the situations in which he finds himself, and this means that he acts in a manner that *is to the point* as well as being specifically his own.

If a child is to grow into a self-directing and spontaneous adult, he must have the opportunity, all through childhood, of being self-directing and spontaneous. Therefore he must be free to act in fields in which he is capable, *at the time*, of exercising his judgment successfully. In a word, he must be 'weaned'. In common, but informed, use, the expression 'weaning' means making a baby capable of nourishing himself otherwise than solely upon his mother's milk, by introducing him to small quantities of one unfamiliar and less easily assimilated foodstuff after another, and by giving him time to learn to digest each new dish before trying another.

'Weaning', as used by Mr Lyward, and by Pearse and Crocker in *The Peckham Experiment*, means more than making the child accustomed to being away from mother. It means helping him gradually to become, in Groos's phrase, more and more of an 'individual of independent capabilities'. It means providing him with the opportunity to digest new kinds of functional nourishment as and when he is ready. One must know the kind of experience from which he is ready to profit, and see that he is exposed to it, and one must be prepared to wait patiently for him to decide for himself just what he will do and when he will do it. If one is to wean a child successfully, one must allow him to proceed from success to success – as he himself sees success – making it possible for him to *feel* that he is knowledgable, skilful and effective in those fields of activity that are attractive to children; and allowing him, within those fields, to form his own judgment, make his own decisions and choices, and be responsible for himself.

In the course of his presidential address to the 1970 national conference of the Pre-school Playgroups Association, Dr W. D. Wall said: 'Children grow well when their parents are growing well'. If a mother and child are confined almost exclusively to each other's company for too long, they may become parasitic upon each other and neither can grow. Sometimes the mother tries to live through her child, and may succeed in constituting an effective barrier between him and his environment. At the worst, this situation can lead to an effect on the child similar to the example of the incurably schizophrenic girl described by Laing. We all know of less tragic examples.

Occasionally it is the child who exerts a stranglehold on the mother. When a little girl spends most of her time alone with her mother, she may channel her desire to be effective into learning to predict her mother's reactions to events, and become extremely skilled at bending her 'round her little finger'. The child (girls appear to find the acquisition of this skill easier and more satisfying than boys) will test her skill by being as 'contrary' as she dares, knowing just how far it is politic to go. One four-year-old girl who joined the playgroup had become so addicted to the occupation of controlling her mother that she evidently preferred this activity to any of those offered by the playgroup – or thought she did. She was not at all a timid child and had not been entirely bereft of the company of her peer group. Sometimes she would walk into the room with assurance and play happily the whole morning; at other times, she would insist, without giving any reason, that her mother stay for a part of the session; and, occasionally, she had no sooner arrived than she would demand to return home; and her mother, with unconcealed annoyance, would comply with her wishes and take her home. It went on like this until, after about two months, her mother decided to give the playgroup up. A few months later, when the little girl arrived at school age, she showed no distress at all at having to leave her mother at the school gates. Evidently she understood that attendance at primary school was compulsory for all children and accepted the situation. In the case of attendance at the playgroup, it had been clear to her that the choice was hers, and she had decided against it. She had become dependent upon the presence of her mother for the satisfaction of her need to feel effective.

A mother-and-daughter relationship such as this is not uncommon, but it is more damaging to the self-confidence of the mother than to that of the child. In this case, the child had seen to it that her general sensory-motor judgment was reasonably well developed, she was not afraid of other children, and, above all, she had not lost confidence in her power to be an effective and independent individual. But many children suffer serious damage to their personalities and their mental health through being shackled to one person in an environment geared solely to adult life.

It is not, and never has been, possible for parents to wean their children without the assistance of a community of some kind, whether tribe, extended family, village or friendly and sociable neighbouring families.

The Pioneer Health Centre at Peckham provided ideal opportunities for weaning during infancy, childhood and adolescence. It provided the mother with the chance to renew or enlarge her interests and skills as well as enabling the child to find his feet, and gradually and smoothly to become himself.

For weaning during the particularly important years of early childhood a free-choice playgroup can be of invaluable assistance to parents. If the mother familiarizes it for the child by her presence for a while and continues to take an active interest in it, and especially if siblings and neighbours and friends attend or have attended the group, it can be an extension of home.

If, on joining a free-choice playgroup, a child has not been already irreversibly conditioned to depend upon others for direction and support or otherwise spoiled of his power to digest experience, he will act spontaneously and with awareness. At every moment he will be using all his senses and his co-ordinating intelligence on his surroundings as a whole. He soon realizes that he is free to behave as he likes; no one distracts him by calling his attention to this or that. He is as free as circumstances can make him from worry that he may do something unacceptable. He is not made to feel that, unless he is at all times busy and patently occupied, he will be forced to do something he would prefer not to do. A child may for weeks be physically inactive, but he is alert and alive all the time to what is going on, he is sensorily and mentally active: he is learning. Then, as his familiarity with the group of children and the equipment increases, he becomes more overtly active. He begins to trust his judgment. From then on, his judgment in every field of activity grows quickly, and the more it grows, the more acute and comprehensive his awareness of his surroundings and of what is happening around him becomes, with the result that he has a widening choice of activity and of functional nourishment. The centre-point of his attention may or may not change from moment to moment, but all the time he is aware of what is happening in a wide circle around that point. He is therefore continuously aware of a great many possible things to do or to think about, and at every moment he is choosing from among all these alternatives what he will do and how he will do it. He is inevitably exercising his power to judge, discriminate and choose on the mental, physical and emotional planes of existence, separately and in synthesis. Without strain or hurry or worry, he is continually making choices for himself. In this way he is becoming the unique person in action that his fingerprints would show him to be in physique. He is *selecting* bits of experience to digest and make a part of himself, and is therefore developing his own personal view of the world that is different from anyone else's and yet – because he is interacting with things and creatures that he is, at his age, capable of learning to know and understand – is as realistic and as objective as a small child's view of the world can be.

Mr Lyward, when asked what the word 'education' meant to him, said, 'It is a nourishing.' And I believe that this is exactly what happens in a free-choice playgroup. The children are, through their spontaneous activity in an environment planned for their needs, creating themselves, although, to all appearances, they are 'just playing'.

CHAPTER TEN

Self-confidence

Parents will not worry about whether or not they are exercising just the right admixture of indulgence and firmness if they are aware that the most important thing of all is to give their child every opportunity to *feel effective*.

From a very early age, the baby's great – perhaps greatest – joy is to exercise his powers. Knowing this, we must be sure that when he is awake he is not shut away all the time in a darkened room, but is lying somewhere where he can see and hear things going on. Even if he is so young that he cannot distinguish one object from another, he may want to follow with his eyes some interesting blob of light as it moves, and later he will want to discover which objects make which noises. We must also make sure that he has opportunities for feeling 'joy in being a cause' through success in getting his mother to talk to him or to feed him when he wants to be talked to or fed; or to have the satisfaction of achieving his intention to make his rattle sound more and more satisfyingly loudly. Successful activity is fuel to his desire to be mentally and physically active and effective; and it gives him the confidence to do what is necessary for the continuing development of all his potential faculties.

A young baby ignores a great part of his environment, for the simple reason that it is quite meaningless to him: he is selective of experience. Therefore we need not fear that he will be 'over-stimulated' if we pay attention to him, as long as it is responsive attention that we give: we should avoid distracting his attention from what he is already looking at or playing with. But he can be seriously harmed by being starved of food for his faculties and by the disregard of his wishes. Whatever anyone may say, we are certainly not spoiling him by allowing him to feel that he has the power to cause us to appear before him; on the contrary, we are building up his self-confidence. If he is to realize his human qualities and become a self-respecting person, we must respond to him as a person. If we simply do things to and for him, treating him as a thing – however precious – his self-confidence and his joy in being alive will wane.

A child's self-confidence is a precious thing, but far more vulnerable and precarious in some children than in others. Different children react to failure, rebuff or deprivation of functional nourishment in different ways. Some, as we have seen, wall themselves up. It is possible that certain people's obsession for revenging themselves on society may be due to a long-harboured resentment for the lack of appreciation and respect shown to them in infancy. Boastfulness and arrogance are known to be frequently signs of an underlying lack of self-confidence.

Some children, on the other hand, seem to be at the same time tougher, more sanguine and more modest than others. They make the best of things and remain hopefully on the lookout for whatever opportunities for successful activity may come their way. For example, a child who has been unable to form a mutually satisfying relationship with his mother may be able to compensate successfully for his earlier deprivation at a later date instead of remaining emotionally stunted for the rest of his life. Or a child who has spent his first years where there was no conversation and words were little used, and who therefore possesses a limited vocabulary, may, when he gets to school, take every opportunity to make up for lost time, whereas another may turn his back determinedly upon all intellectual nourishment. The child who has been deprived of the opportunity to acquire physical co-ordination, balance and agility may, whenever he gets the chance, try to remedy the situation regardless of bumps and bruises and even ridicule, whereas another will avoid all opportunities for learning in that field.

If children are able to realize their potentiality for general sensory-motor judgment while their centre of gravity is still low, they will continue to respond to opportunities to develop it as they grow taller and heavier. If they fail to acquire it early on, there may come a time when the gap in the sequence of development becomes unbridgeable. As a result, the quality of their behaviour in any activity entailing movement – even moving through a room containing a number of people and pieces of furniture – will be poor for the rest of their lives. They will suffer, at least during their childhood, from a sense of inadequacy and an inhibiting fear of being proved unable to respond effectively to the challenges of their environment.

I suspect that some children try to compensate for the damage done to their self-esteem in this way by trying to obtain power over others, and bossing or bullying more than they would naturally have done. Others, if their inherent ability and their environment permit, may devote themselves entirely to the acquisition of verbal dexterity and information. This behaviour may be socially acceptable but it does not promote health in the sense of wholeness. Happy with adults, such a child may shun the company of other children and, if forced to be with them, as in the school playground, may suffer agonies of fear. His parents may take his avidity for verbal information as a sign of superior intelligence and may not only painstakingly answer all his questions instead of putting him in a position to find things out for himself through active experience, but also, deceived by his knowledge of words, may expect intellectual performances from him beyond his power and thus weaken his self-confidence still more.

People may be unaware of the fact that vaguely understood words are an inadequate substitute for knowledge acquired through active sensory experience, and that a child whose mental activity is predominantly verbal is living at second-hand. A child who continues in this situation for long may – like the child who loses his self-confidence entirely – grow up with a personal 'world' that is based more on fantasy than on reality. He may always lack an awareness of things, people and situations as they really are; thus his thoughts and actions are likely to be inappropriate to the circumstances.

If we wish to preserve the self-confidence of children we must find out what kind of nourishment from his environment a young human being's basic powers need, and we must see to it that children have, at every stage, the opportunity to learn to do what they have become newly capable of learning to do. Being deprived of this opportunity is equally destructive to a child's self-confidence as his being continually urged to do what is not yet possible for him to learn to do successfully. Both starvation and forced feeding can ruin his digestion. These are the things that really *spoil* a child, for, if either continues too long, he will no longer know his needs. Therefore what he wants to do will no longer necessarily be what he needs to do for the healthy development of his faculties. He may tend to want to be taken in tow and have every decision made for him, or he may want constant entertainment or attention. His appetite for activity will no longer be a healthy one.

In order to make quite clear what I mean by 'healthy' in this context, I must add that a crippled or blind or mentally defective child can have a wholly healthy appetite for activity, *if* he is allowed to realize fully his prsent potential capacity in all fields of activity. If this happens, his confidence, self-respect, joy in being effective, and appetite for learning can be as unimpaired as in the case of a normally equipped child. I know a girl of seventeen with Down syndrome who is quite unlike the rather lifeless-looking children with this disorder one sometimes sees being led by the hand in the streets. She has been brought up in the country and as one of a family for most of her life, and she has been enabled to develop her potentiality fully. She is full of vitality, is independent and enterprising and, in a limited way, a responsible person. For instance, she travels by public transport to her school and back, although she does not speak intelligibly. She certainly has great 'joy in being a cause', which means that life is not easy for her mother, for this fully-grown girl tends to behave like a healthily noisy and mischievous child of two. But she is outward-looking and seems to be alive to everything within her capacity. Naturally, she does not go uncorrected by her parents, and at times must be physically restrained, perhaps indeed more often than would be necessary if she were less fundamentally spontaneous. But one feels that she is incomparably happier and more fulfilled than if she had lost confidence in her ability to interact effectively with her environment and had, as a result, become dulled and passive.

It has been said that the creatively original person is one who, among other things, has an unusual sensitivity to the applicability of known facts to new situations. It seems to me that this is another way of describing a person who possesses a living body of knowledge that has grown through the *digestion* of experience. Facts that have been selected because of their interest and relatedness to what one already knows, and have therefore been digested, are likely to be always available. Their possessor does not need to keep his eyes fixed on them in case they are lost; he can afford to look outwards towards the changing scene, and so will be aware of any situations to which his knowledge may be applied – and of any further 'food for thought' that may be available.

Now a young baby's attention *is* directed outwards towards his environment – although at first he will be aware only of a small part of it. He is outward-looking for two reasons. Firstly, his biological urge to exercise his faculties and to become familiar with his environment has not yet been weakened by the fear of failing in his own eyes or in those of others. So far, he is innocent of the experience of rebuff or of failure to achieve his desires and intentions. Secondly, his environment has, so far, been worth looking at; for the first few months of his life the most ordinary of experience is grist to his mill; his body-of-knowledge is so small and undifferentiated that he does not need a great variety of mental food from which to choose.

But since one's faculties do not thrive on repeated doses of the same food, the baby's environment must expand and grow in step with the growth of his powers. If his environment remains always quite unchanged, there will come a point when it holds no interest for him and he may therefore stop attending to it. Equally, if it changes so fast and so drastically that he is unable to interact successfully with it or affect it in the smallest degree, he may find it less humiliating to stop trying. In either case he will at best be only intermittently outward-looking, so that there is little interaction between himself and his environment and 'the healthy spiral of development' will slow down.

A baby's powers must be allowed to grow smoothly, which is another way of saying that he must be allowed to learn to do what he has newly become capable of learning to do. As soon as he has formed a mutually satisfying relationship with his mother, he needs opportunity to form different kinds of relationship with different kinds of people. As soon as he has become aware of the existence of objects, he needs the opportunity to handle and investigate a *variety* of objects. As soon as he has become able to wriggle, or crawl, or hitch himself along on his bottom a little way, he needs to be allowed to practise the art of moving his body from one place to another and he should not be confined for long to his pram or his chair. As soon as he can walk he needs to be allowed to climb; as soon as he has become interested in making distinguishable sounds, he needs to find that he can obtain a response and should be *answered* – in his own language at first – not continually talked *at*. In short, he needs to know that he can be effective in many fields of activity.

If we do not allow him to become daily more effective in these ways and also to feel that we share his joy in his growing power, we deprive him of self-confidence and self-respect.

Towards the close of his book *Lives in Progress*, Robert W. White writes, 'A person's conception of himself is nourished partly by the way others treat him and the things they say about him, but the heart of his self-feeling is in what he feels able to do.' This is as true of small children as it is of anyone.

The tragedy for children nowadays, among both the comfortably off and the impecunious alike, is, as Beatrix Tudor-Hart points out in her wise and instructive book *Learning to Live*, that very often they find that a happy and successful relationship with their parents is incompatible with a successful relationship to their physical environment – one excludes the other. A small child finds that his parents do not approve of his walking along the very edge of the kerb, jumping down into the road or climbing up and down other people's doorsteps on the way to the shops, or of his efforts to satisfy his curiosity about objects and to exercise his manipulatory skill inside the shops. Most of the time he is confined within the four walls of his home where his efforts to become competent in skills requiring violent movement, or causing noise, may upset the neighbours or the rest of the family, and have to be stopped.

To a child, approval of his spontaneous activity means love. Love that is expressed in care for his safety or for his future happiness, or even in constant attention or in *unsolicited* demonstrations of affection, means little or nothing to him. He needs the manifestations of love that increase his self-respect, and he may find that, in order to obtain this 'love' from his parents, he must suppress his instinct to do the things that will lead to the growth of other powers that are necessary to his self-esteem.

Béla Mittelmann writes that, during 'the second and third years the motor urge dominates all other urges', and that the 'evolution of self-esteem is intimately connected with motor development'. He says that 'restriction of mobility occurs because parents are anxious or because the child's self-assertion troubles them', and lists the horrifying results that this can have in different types of children: 'lasting injury to the parent-child relationship' in some, and 'severe anxiety reactions' or 'dependence' and 'self-hatred' in others. From experience I know that this language is not too strong.

But it is not only that a child needs to move, he needs to move well. As we have seen, he needs and wants to acquire a more and more precise control over his movements and co-ordination of his sensory, muscular and nervous systems, and he can only do this by moving – in a progressively more adventurous manner – for several hours a day. He needs to encounter all sorts of hazards, obstacles and challenges to his skill, and to be able to decide for himself which to overcome and which to circumvent, and to be entirely responsible for where and how he moves. It is very important to him to feel 'able for the next' as an Irish friend of mine put it, in this sphere of activity; his self-respect requires it.

Surely it is also true that a young man's self-respect and self-confidence are enhanced if he knows that he is capable of shinning up a drainpipe or a lamp-post, or of hauling himself over a high wall or leaping a lower one.

A small child can become fettered by a consciousness of his lack of general sensory-motor judgment. No matter how permissive the environment in which he finds himself, if he has lacked opportunity to learn to move with precision, speed, balance and agility, he might as well be dragging a ball and chain. We may say to him: 'Here you are; go ahead and play!' But if he has no confidence in his ability to enjoy active play, he is not free to play.

In my playgroup at one time there was a tall, well-built and potentially intelligent boy of four and a half who would only play with jigsaw puzzles and – most skilfully and imaginatively – with small building blocks. Day after day, this was all he did. He was tense and self-conscious – often shooting a sidelong glance at the supervisor. He was no trouble, always quiet and busy. Out of doors his activity was, in contrast, aimlessly and clumsily energetic – mostly he just ran about – and gave one the impression of a child younger than he actually was, whereas indoors his behaviour was superficially 'grown-up'. He was with us for only three or four months, and although towards the end he became a little more relaxed, and occasionally tried – very gingerly – to use the slides, he never learned to use any of the climbing apparatus with enjoyment; nor did he paint or join in make-believe or rough-and-tumble games with the other children. He preferred to play safe and stick to the one or two occupations in which he was confident of success and which, it appeared, he knew from experience were acceptable to adults.

Another four-year-old, with whom I had a fleeting acquaintance, neither walked nor ran but always proceeded at a shambling kind of jog-trot – perhaps acquired through having to keep up with his mother as she pushed his baby brother's pram on hurried expeditions to the shops. He would not attempt to climb the easiest part of the climbing frame, designed for – and normally used by – two-year-olds, 'because I might hurt myself'.

The only way to help such children is to enable them, without any self-consciousness or guilt, through many hours of 'babyish' play, to make up for lost time so far as their general sensory-motor judgment is concerned. This can be done in a free-choice playgroup, because the children are not critical of the behaviour of their fellows, unless it is anti-social. They have no idea of age, and even differences in size do not mean much to them, so that they do not remark upon the fact that a five-year-old is doing what one would normally expect a two-year-old to do.

More forceful, happy-go-lucky and perhaps less sensitive children succeed against all odds in becoming competent in the field of general sensory-motor activity; but it is sometimes at the expense of a happy and easy relationship with their parents and other adults, and this can inhibit the development of their power for sensitive and responsible social relationships.

I believe that the serenity, poise and easy friendliness that were observed to be characteristic of the children at the Peckham Health Centre were due to the healthy self-esteem in which they rejoiced, and that this was, in part, the result of the many hours they had chosen to spend playing in the 'gym', the swimming-pool, on roller-skates and so on, and in part due to the fact that the Centre was just as much *their* Centre as it was the adults', and that they mixed socially with the members of all ages of other families. The children's self-confidence allowed them to be forgetful of self and correspondingly aware of, and responsive to, people. One element in the mixture of cause and effect may have been that many of the adult members were also happily engaged in developing their faculty for general sensory-motor and social judgment: learning to swim and dance, for instance, and making friends and dozens of acquaintances. They had gone back to being children themselves in their leisure time, in that they were learning the basic skills of human beings, and were therefore better able to understand and respect the children and their activities.

A small child needs to acquire a familiarity with other small children that will enable him to feel confident of acting appropriately towards them. Every toddler is curious about other toddlers, but when all the contact he has with them is to see them pass by in their push-chairs, or firmly held by the hand in a shop or other crowded public place, he cannot become sufficiently familiar with them to be able, later on when he goes to infant school at five, or to a nursery class at four, to approach other children and respond to them with spontaneity. This may delay indefinitely the moment when he is able to begin to develop social judgment and spontaneous and easy personal relationships.

In the two fields of sensory-motor and social activity, a young child is capable of becoming autonomous. Quite obviously, there are areas of activity in which he cannot be allowed to judge for himself. To expect him to decide when to cross the road, or at what time he should regularly be in bed, or what his mother should buy and cook for the family dinner, would be foolish, because he cannot at his age possess a knowledge of the factors involved. He cannot judge the speed of an approaching car or lorry, nor does he know abstract facts such as the number of hours' sleep he needs, and the time at which the family needs to be up and doing in the morning, nor the amount of housekeeping money in hand. He does not know how hungry he will be in three hours' time, nor his own and the rest of the family's dietary needs. In these cases, he would not be judging in the light of experience; he would be acting entirely on guesswork, fancy or caprice. To have to try to take decisions of this kind would not nourish his power to judge, nor would it make him more knowledgable and effective. Indeed, it might be as bad for his self-confidence as it is if we insist that he decide which shape is an 'A' and which is a 'B' before he has developed the necessary visual judgment.

Only in situations that are beyond his comprehension does it do a child any good to know that someone else is in control of him. For instance, he does not need the 'security' of knowing that someone else is always there to protect him from himself – from his 'uncontrollable emotions' and so on. He needs rather the feeling of power that the successful exercise of self-government and self-direction gives him. When he is playing freely with other children, the successful achievement of his purposes will require the exercise of self-control. He will also learn to know himself and – without realizing it – to direct his powers of emotion in the same way as he directs his physical activity. Within an at least partially familiar animate and inanimate environment, it is good for him to feel that he is responsible for himself.

There is one situation in which the youngest toddler can be completely autonomous, because he can be at the same time independent and successful, and that is when he is climbing upon some suitable object or surface. ('Climbing', for a very small child, includes scrambling and sliding on sloping surfaces, swinging from his hands, jumping or stepping down from boxes, crawling upstairs and easing himself down from one step to another.) As we have seen, he can be relied upon to use his judgment successfully when he is in a situation in which he can depend entirely upon the information concerning that situation that his sensory-motor system is giving him from moment to moment. This is the case when he is 'climbing'. He is deciding for himself where to place his hands and feet and how to hold his body in order to balance, and he is deciding how far and exactly where to climb; moreover, he is deciding what he will do with his whole body and not only with his hands and his eyes. He feels self-respectingly responsible for himself. It is probable that, at the toddler stage, 'climbing' enhances a child's self-respect and self-confidence and joy in life more than any other sensory-motor activity.

Many children are inevitably bound to lose confidence in their ability, at one stage or other, to learn higher mathematics, for example, or to make a speech that keeps their audiences convulsed with laughter, because they do not possess these particular gifts. But it is difficult to see any reason at all – except lack of opportunity for play – why children should, at any stage, lose confidence in their ability to control the movements of their limbs, or to respond to, and communicate with, their fellow human beings, although the words they use may be few and simple, their grammar almost non-existent, and they may make abundant use of gestures.

In trying to nourish a child's self-confidence, we must guard against telling him indiscriminately and absentmindedly that he is 'doing fine'. Since he knows very well when he has or has not done what he intended to do, such behaviour on our part must in the long run cause him to doubt our sincerity. Rather, we must show him that we approve of the fact that he is doing what he wants to do, and share his joy when he is successful. We must also be sure to give him time to become familiar with his material and human environment and with his own powers. (The more he feels at home in his skin and in his surroundings, the more confident and enterprising he will be.) And finally, we must ensure that he is free to choose for himself – in circumstances in which he is capable of making a choice that is based on knowledge – what he will do and how he will do it. In these circumstances what he does will be what he needs to do for his development as a whole and, moreover, he will have the satisfying and necessary feeling of being capable of choice and will, therefore, enjoy and welcome the freedom to choose.

The Jesuits are reputed to have said: 'Give us a child till he is seven.' I would say rather, let a child be a child till he is seven. In one Far Eastern country, this is what happens – or did at one time. Children were indulged and made much of, and were quite free of the traditions of behaviour, rules and conventions that were binding on adults, until they were seven. At that age they were expected to grow up rather suddenly and take on responsibility, such as minding the younger children. I have noticed that children whose self-confidence and spontaneity have not been eroded seem to make a sudden jump forward in maturity at about that age.*

Although, in the West, we no longer dress tiny children like miniature adults, we still often expect them to behave like 'little Christian gentlemen' even though we may not use that particular

---

* I believe that children should not have to move on from one school to another just when they are about to make this jump forward in development which often includes the mastery of reading and writing. A change of school at 8+ or even 9+ would be better.

expression. One must appreciate the child as an individual and as a self-respecting personality, and, at the same time, appreciate the fact that he is a child. Children need the love that shows itself in overt approval of at least some of the things that they do on their own initiative.

A small child, whose parents expect behaviour from him that is beyond his powers and who express distress and horror at his acts, may try to restore his self-respect by attempting to (as he thinks) *force* them to respect him. One small boy of two and three-quarters, an extremely intelligent, sensitive, strongly-built, energetic and capable child, distressed his mother by his behaviour in the playgroup, where he was still a beginner in the art of playing happily and co-operatively with the other children. For instance, she showed her horror when he clouted a smaller child on the head; and the tone of her voice as she finally said, 'You are *too* bad. You'll not come here any more,' must have been a shattering blow to her son's self-respect. She told me that she did not know what to do about his growing 'disobedience' at home; latterly he would often hit her and kick her, and when she came into the room he would begin to throw things about, particularly books and objects that belonged to her, rather than to him. She also told me that, although he was afraid of dogs and cats, he would gesticulate aggressively and shout at them as long as they kept their distance. This gave me the clue to the mystery of his behaviour. Evidently this child's reaction to fear was a positive but not, owing to his tender age, a very sensible one. He feared that he was losing his mother's respect, or perhaps it was simply that she made him feel vaguely afraid and he did not like to feel afraid. Whatever it was that he felt, his reaction to the feeling was rather similar to his reaction to dogs and cats: he was trying to show her that he was a force to be reckoned with. If the mother had been a person of less civilized habits, a vicious circle might have arisen, till the child became 'out of control' and delinquent.

This is an example of one of the many difficulties for mother and child that may arise if the mother is helping to supervise the children in the playgroup. The advantages to society of having mother helpers or father helpers actually present in playgroups greatly outweigh the disadvantages, but it certainly adds to the responsibility and work of the supervisor.

It is not difficult for parents who understand their baby's needs to provide him with an environment that nourishes his power to digest experience up to the age of about twelve months. During his second year it is possible but needs care. But, under present-day living conditions, when their child reaches the age of two – in some cases one and a half – it is usually impossible for them to give him opportunity for learning-activity that is as satisfying to him as playing with a rattle or a wooden spoon, waving a handkerchief about, or learning to make a new sound was to him at the age of six months, *unless* there is public – or co-operatively organized – local provision of the appropriate space and equipment for communal play. Somehow it must be made easier for toddlers to enjoy the company of other small children in an environment that offers opportunity for attractively adventurous play within reach of their mothers. (By the last phrase, I mean that the mother should be within the child's reach and not only the other way round.)

Also, it must be made possible for those two-year-olds who are ready, and for all three-year-olds, to play regularly for two or three hours, at least three times a week, in a group of others of preschool age, under the knowledgeable but self-effacing supervision – *not* the direction and control – of *some person other than their parents.*

Playgroups are not luxuries, nor are they needed only by children living in unsuitable housing conditions or with parents of inadequate material, emotional or mental resources. Free-choice playgroups provide developmental opportunities that are needed by *all* children – opportunities that they can, in industrialized countries, only rarely obtain elsewhere.*

In a well-planned playgroup a child does not feel bound to be occupied. He may simply sit and watch the other children; they will not bother him because they are intent upon their own activity and because they do not think of him as being unhappy simply because he is inactive. And so he does only what he feels confident of doing competently; therefore he achieves his intentions and gains confidence in his judgment. The children walk into situations confidently, but not blindly. They are not blinded to reality through being preoccupied with the effect they are making on others – they are not intermittently watching an adult out of the corners of their eyes to see if he approves of what they do – and so they are free to be aware of the *total* situation. They soon learn the limits of their powers, but they are confident of extending them. The children feel encouraged to continue to act sponta-

---

*One hundred years ago, 'doorstep play' with the neighbors' children was available to the two-to-fives or they could go out to play in the charge of slightly older children, just as they still can in the more 'undeveloped' corners of the planet.

neously while they are in the playground and, judging from the reports I have had of how some of them behave after leaving the group, they continue to act in the same manner in new situations whenever possible.

In the planning of a pre-school playgroup the needs of the children are paramount. So it can be situated where there is no need to consider the comfort of elderly people; all mechanical artefacts and electrical gadgets that are beyond the understanding of children of this age can be excluded or placed well out of reach. A playgroup can be planned to be a place where children may – for two or three solid hours – use and learn to trust their own judgment and thus grow in self-confidence.

PART III

Necessary Provision for Play

Introduction

Perhaps mothers (or indeed fathers) would not feel that their time and talents were being underemployed by staying at home to look after a child for two or three years, if they were to realize how important, for his future happiness and worth, is a baby's present physical, mental and social *activity*.

Society must change its attitude; it must treat the rearing of a baby as the valuable and important form of employment that it is. The job requires knowledge and a relaxed, leisurely, unpreoccupied frame of mind. It does not require 'higher' education or a trained mind, but it does require some form of instruction and practical experience, and the availability of advice from people who know traditional baby lore and have sifted from it that which is based on fact and reason and is apposite to the needs of babies in all societies and civilizations. People no longer grow up with lots of babies around them; and furthermore, we cannot any longer afford to practise and learn by experience on our elder children, when families consist of one or two children only. Therefore a course of instruction in the developmental needs of babies and small children should be a part of the school curriculum for all students aged fourteen or fifteen, who should also have the opportunity to work for a few hours a week as assistants in adventure playgrounds, playgroups or day nurseries, or to assist the mothers of large families or registered child-minders. Since knowledge promotes interest and interest appreciation, this might engender in people an enjoyment of the activity of children and an appreciation of their needs.

A free baby-sitting service might be given by these students to young parents living in the neighbourhood of their homes. It is surely no hardship to do one's homework or watch the television in someone else's house, and one should not accept any payment for it. This is important because people with young children often have a lower income than at any other time of their lives except old age.

We cannot expect anyone to undertake the work of child-rearing with enthusiasm if it means almost completely renouncing the company of one's fellow adults and all opportunities for nourishing one's own mental and emotional faculties. So we must see to it that besides a baby-sitting service there are neighbourhood centres that provide a meeting place for people of all ages and opportunities for communal leisure occupations. For the sake of the health of their relationships, young couples must be able to enjoy their leisure time together and to make friends in common.

It is also our duty to see to it that parents are able to wean their children, for unless we do this, it will be impossible for any parent to be a good parent. At a certain stage, animals push their young away to find their food for themselves. A century ago most mothers could say, 'run away and play and come home at sun-down', aware that some of the people living and working in the neighbourhood would know the children by sight and name and would feel a certain responsibility towards them.

Playgroup supervisors, play leaders, nursery-school teachers and youth leaders should realize that their primary function is to help parents to wean their children.

CHAPTER ELEVEN

Then and now

People may even now assert that planned, supervised and publicly subsidized provision for play is unnecessary on the grounds that 'we did well enough without it in the past'. But if they look back to their own childhoods – and certainly if they remember the stories told by their parents and grandparents of *their* own childhoods – they will realize that children were much freer to find nourishment for their basic faculties when they lived in more natural surroundings and, above all, before the age of ubiquitous high-speed motor traffic. When questioned, middle-aged people will frequently recall that they spent their leisure time as children 'on the moors beyond the town', 'in a wood outside the village' or 'in the meadows of the farmer over the way'. And even those who grew up in cities could wander the streets in search of adventure, company, and all sorts of interesting happenings and information without being in danger from traffic to anything like the same degree as would be the case today.

In the village of my childhood, I can remember hoops, tops (simple metal-tipped wooden ones which were spun and whipped with a piece of string or leather thong attached to a stick) and marbles being played with, each in turn according to the season of the year, in the widest part of the wide village street, although it was a part of the main road between the county town and another large town. When a vehicle approached, either it went round them or the children moved a little closer to the verge.

We lived in a 'village', my husband in a 'town', but I doubt if there was much difference in size and importance between the two – indeed *we* still had a cattle market on Thursdays. During the First World War, his mother was busy running their jobmaster's business in the absence of her husband at the front. They possessed a small garden, and a yard with a coach-house and stables for half a dozen horses; he remembers watching the horses being groomed, helping his elder brother to work the chaff-cutting machine, and the superlative place for play afforded by the hayloft. But this was not all: from the age of three or four until a few weeks after his seventh birthday – when the family moved from the district and he was sent to a boarding school – his playground included the streets of the little town, the mound crowned by huge old trees which covered the site of the old castle, and the heathy 'common' that skirted the town. He spent his time exploring as the fancy took him and playing 'touch last', hide-and-seek, and 'Indians' with his elder brother and neighbouring urchins; he is not sure whether it was at this stage, or later, that they made themselves bows and arrows, but he remembers clearly that they had 'spears' and cap pistols. They climbed trees after birds' eggs, always hoping to come across a bird's nest. Probably they rarely succeeded, because the time they found a duck's nest in a bit of swampy ground close by the road to the station remains a vivid memory. It was down Station Road that they rolled in 'soap-box' carts which were always coming to bits and requiring to be mended with hammers and nails.

He and his brother enjoyed rolling downhill in a barrel. The yard sloped towards the road, and they would crawl into the barrel on the level space at the top of the slope, rock to start themselves, and roll down the yard, through the gate, across the road, and finish up against the opposite verge. This road leads to the next small town, and is now a busy main road, but in those days apparently you could hear before you started to roll if anything was coming.

My husband was nearly four years younger than his brother and, after the latter had departed for boarding school at the age of eight, he played on his own or with the neighbours' children. His mother remembers that, when she wanted to call him in from play, she usually took her bicycle with her, for then the warning cry, 'Billy Stallibrass! yer mother's looking for you!' would probably cause him to appear, as he loved to ride home on the saddle while she pushed and guided the bicycle. If she did not bring the bicycle and he was not very hungry, he would be off, and she would have difficulty in catching him.

At one time he had a nursemaid but, besides being a very 'good sport' and not much more than a child herself, she was lame, and also 'she could not climb trees'.

At four he went to a small private school for a few hours every day and he learned to read before he was five; but there was all the rest of the day for play, and it is the play that he remembers. He remembers also the people for and to whom he ran errands and the shops where he bought sweets and the caps for his pistol and cap-bomb, and particularly the saddler who made and mended straps and bits of harness in the intervals of serving his customers, and who could talk with his mouth full of needles and pieces of twine.

Naturally the forge was a fascinating place and the blacksmith, who shod the enormous cart horses, a hero. The metal hoops, with which the children played, frequently came apart at the join, and this provided an excuse for visiting the forge and watching, while waiting for the blacksmith to find a spare moment in which to mend them. I had had only wooden hoops and they had seemed to me to be rather unexciting toys, but my husband informs me that the metal ones were a different thing altogether, for they could be steered quite precisely with a metal hook on a wooden handle, and he remembers the satisfyingly loud scraping sound that the metal hook made on the metal hoop.

In Victorian and Edwardian times, if the stories that one hears can be believed, even extremely 'well brought up' little girls in their frilly petticoats were only 'seen and not heard' for a certain proportion of the day; for the rest of the time, they were able to be where they were neither heard nor seen by censorious adults – though there may have been sympathetic ones around who would stop them from running into any serious danger but who could be trusted not to report their escapades to those in authority. It seems evident that in those days parents, however insistent on lady-like behaviour, were less worried about the dangers into which their small girls might run if allowed out of their sight.* My mother relates how she and a girl cousin would compete to see how long they could cling to the back of the loaded hay-wagon as it swayed and jolted along the rough lanes, and how she and her elder brother used to play on the roof of the big Victorian mansion, repelling a besieging army of 'Boers' from behind the parapet. She remembers also a most attractive hayloft to which one could retire, and – even on wet days – be happily out of sight and earshot of the grown-ups.

In those days young children in every class of society were less continuously under the strain of being in tow to their parents – or adult child-minders – and, as a result, felt less bewilderingly at one moment the focus of the adults' attention and, at the next, a nuisance and a tie. Perhaps children had less free time but they had more opportunity for really free play. Before they were old enough for school, or after school work and their other tasks were finished, they were able to co-operate with other children – siblings or neighbours – in adventurous enterprises; consequently, without anyone noticing, they developed agility, resourcefulness, enterprise,

* See, for instance, Gwen Raverat's *Period Piece: a Cambridge childhood.*

self-reliance and judgment. To the toddler, the 'world' was waiting beyond the kitchen door and he was free to satisfy his curiosity about it and to test his courage as and when he felt able.

As little as twenty years ago there were numerous 'bomb sites' in London which made attractive playgrounds. Our two eldest children were able to explore the vast overgrown gardens of several bombed houses that were left in their ruined state, for some unexplained reason, for many years after the war. It was possible to allow them to cross the main road between our house and these gardens by themselves from the age of seven or eight. Nowadays one must sometimes wait for what feels like five minutes before one can venture to cross this road, and few children under the age of eleven or twelve would have the necessary patience – let alone the judgment – to do so on their own. When our elder children were eight or nine it was possible to allow them to walk by themselves into the centre of the town after school, to visit the library or the swimming-bath or to see their friends. They not only played hop-scotch on the pavement but used roller-skates, bicycles and stilts, and bats and balls on the road itself outside our house at all times, and not only on Sundays. The cul-de-sac adjoining, which is on a hill, was fun to roll down on a home-made go-cart or trolley. Now both streets are lined all day long during the week with parked cars; and motorists seeking short cuts shoot along them.

An elderly couple who live in a quiet cul-de-sac, lined by small terraced houses, told me how, from their windows, they had watched children inventing games which were passed on from the older to the younger ones over a period of thirty years or more, but now that the street had become an unofficial car park, the children played there no more. Yet there has been no increase in the number of alternative places for play. In a town which has a population of nearly a quarter of a million people, no 'adventure' or 'junk' playgrounds have been provided, as in some Greater London boroughs, although in our part of the town there are several parks – mostly elegant and formal ones, or conventional recreation grounds. Further towards the perimeter of the town there are two public parks consisting of heath and birch and pine-covered gravel hills. The hills are broken up, forming miniature valleys, ridges, and steep-sided hollows and hillocks ideal for all sorts of stalking and hide-and-seek types of games, and many of the trees are climbable. But surprisingly few children play there. At weekends, when we often walk there, we rarely see children who are not decorously accompanying their parents on a little stroll.

213

During the week it is often quite deserted. Perhaps these natural playgrounds are too far from the more densely populated parts of the town, perhaps parents fear 'the roads' or 'sex maniacs', or perhaps children have lost the taste for adventurous play, and prefer to go 'window shopping'. My eldest two children played there for hours with their friends, the next two less frequently; they were discouraged by being told by the park-keeper that tree-climbing was forbidden, that there was a bye-law to that effect, and that a visit to the public library would verify the fact. The children carried out his instructions, asked to see the bye-laws at the library and found that it was in fact as he had said, and we did not choose actively to encourage disrespect for the law. Incidentally the park-keeper's or 'ranger's' uniform was very similar to that of a policeman.

I am told that at weekends the casualty department of the hospital is crowded with children with broken limbs. But I do not believe that this necessarily means that they have been climbing trees or scaling walls; the last two broken limbs of which I have heard among the children of my acquaintance were caused, in one case, by being tripped up in the school playground and, in the other, by the child simply running along a path. The fact that so many children break their limbs at weekends does not necessarily mean that they have been 'getting up to mischief' or being particularly adventurous; instead, it could signify a low level of general sensory-motor judgment in the child population.

As Anthea Holme and Peter Massie say in their study, sponsored by the Council for Children's Welfare, of children's play needs and opportunities, 'play provision should be thought of as an essential service and as such be planned along with the rest of the neighbourhood. ... Continuous propaganda must be used to convince adults in the community that children must have space of their own and freedom to play there and that this cannot always be on someone else's doorstep.'

In their book they make detailed suggestions as to the part that both officials and the public might play in order to make successful child-rearing possible in an urban society, and mention imaginative schemes that have already been initiated and maintained both by groups of private individuals and by local government departments. Lady Allen of Hurtwood in *Planning for Play* describes some of these in more detail, as well as play facilities that have been provided in other countries.

The following proposals for the creation of an environment in which future generations can grow up healthily is based on the

214

results of their research as well as on the experience of myself and my friends.

At this point a few definitions of the types of play facility referred to may be necessary.

1. *Adventure Playgrounds* (or 'junk playgrounds') originated in 1943 in Denmark, where there are now a large number. In Great Britain and the U.S.A. there are several, mainly run by voluntary committees; sometimes they are short-lived because they make use of land awaiting redevelopment, or because of lack of money or difficulty in finding suitable playleaders. The best of the latter have often had a varied experience of life and employment. The Dane who so successfully developed the use of the original 'junk playground' at the instigation of Professor C.Th.Sørensen had been both a nursery-school teacher and a seaman. The playleader's job is to provide help when requested and plenty of material for building, to know roughly what is going on, and to take care of the tools and materials and the natural features of the ground, but not to lead or in any way to organize the children. He must be, in Lady Allen's words, aware of the children's 'deep urge to experiment with earth, fire, water and timber, to work with real tools without fear of criticism or censure' and of 'their love of freedom to take calculated risks'. Naturally these playgrounds all have different features, but in every case the people organizing them aim to provide something different from the conventional playground with its stereotyped equipment that provides no scope for creativity and invention, and satisfies few learning-needs. In most of them a large hut or some other building provides opportunity to play in bad weather, and some sort of provision for arts and crafts, dressing up, acting or dancing is made. Usually they are fenced off from the public view in some way because they are inevitably something of an eyesore.

2. *The Greater London Council (GLC) 'playparks'*. These were started in 1960 and are similar to adventure playgrounds. There are now about thirty of them and they are organized over-all by a former adventure playleader from within the parks department. The playleaders are usually recruited from the teaching profession with student assistants. The two 'playparks' I have seen are fenced-off portions of two of the larger London parks. They are spacious, and good use has been made of natural features, sloping ground, trees and banks and bushes. They contain exciting but simple apparatus for free gymnastics and acrobatics, sometimes erected by the fourteen- or fifteen-year-old boys and girls with the help of the playleader, or ropes have been suspended from the

largest trees. Equipment such as stilts, trolleys, trucks and large building blocks that have been proved to stand up to long and continuous use in all weathers have been imported from Scandinavia, and some are now being manufactured in England. Some of the playparks have notices at the gate asking parents to keep out. They usually contain a hut for indoor occupations and for storage, and an area especially planned to suit the needs of the younger children with a sandpit and a paved or asphalted space.

3. *The GLC 'One O'clock Clubs'* are for the under-fives and their mothers. Mothers can bring the baby along as well and can sit and talk, or play with the children. They are always expected to stay within the area of the park and to be responsible for their own children, but the children play with the equipment and materials provided by a trained playleader.

4. *'Playgroups'* provide indoor – and when possible also outdoor – supervised play for under-fives only (although sometimes five-year-olds for whom there is no room in the infant school are to be found in them). Usually they are open in the morning three, four or five days a week. A number of the best-equipped are organized in 'deprived areas' by the Save the Children Fund and are open to all children at a nominal fee. Other organizers are forced to charge a fee that covers the rent and heating of a hall, equipment and replenishment of materials, and a small but regular payment to the regular staff. Hundreds of playgroups started and run by parents have been helped with advice and encouragement by the Pre-school Playgroups Association.

Maintained nursery schools provide all or half-day supervised play, but are few and far between.

By law, all 'child-minders' must be registered with and inspected by the local health department. In our borough, this body distinguishes between child-minders and playgroups; but playgroups and the most old-fashioned and narrowly educational establishments for under-fives are lumped together under the heading 'Playgroups'. Therefore it is necessary for parents to insist on seeing what goes on in their nearest 'playgroup' before enrolling their child.

Even those children who are fortunate in belonging to a playgroup need also to be able to play at home within the family ambience. 'Doorstep play,' as Holme and Massie call it, is important; and, as in some 'new towns', houses should be surrounded by pedestrian precincts which include small spaces where the younger children can play at odd moments when mother is busy indoors. Overlooking these play spaces there should be seats for grandparents or other friendly elderly people (some old people like to watch small children playing). Seats would also enable mothers or fathers to enjoy the equivalent of the neighbourly 'over the fence' conversation during leisure moments.

School-age children can be expected to play further away from the houses and where they will be less likely to disturb sleeping night-shift workers or sick people, but they should be able to reach a playground that offers opportunity for a variety of types of play without crossing any dangerous roads.

It is necessary that every child over the age of five or six be able to reach a supervised playground of the 'adventure playground' or 'playpark' type from his home unaccompanied. It is also very important that there should be an even larger number of unsupervised playgrounds.

Sweden specializes in the provision of imaginatively designed unsupervised playgrounds. Unlike 'adventure playgrounds', which are preferably hidden from sight because of their concentration on the use of junk and on the opportunity for creation and destruction, these playgrounds should be open to the public view, but sheltered – or partly so – from cold winds.

Those responsible for designing housing developments or re-developments and for planning the utilization of open spaces should be on the watch for any small corners or larger unused spaces that could be transformed into unsupervised play areas. The smaller, more sheltered and sunny and more irregularly shaped sites might well be equipped in such a way as to attract *small* children and their mothers. Older children will also appreciate having a small 'kick around' area, and a stand, from which hang a climbing rope, trapeze and gymnast's rings, really handy to their homes. Where there is a larger level area but not enough space for a full-sized playing field, playgrounds for older children should have a hard-surfaced rectangular space for playing impromptu games of five-a-side football or other ball games, and which could also be used for roller-skating, playing 'ice hockey' on roller-skates or 'polo' on bicycles. Bollards, strategically placed, can double as goal posts, and as hazards around which to skate or cycle, or they can be used for leap frog. On at least one side there should be a long, high wall against which to play ball and do handstands and which will provide shelter from the wind. On the other side there should be horizontal rails at various heights and a pair of parallel bars, and in a corner a really high stand – such as are seen in private and public gardens and on beaches all round France – from which are suspended a trapeze, gymnast's rings, a climbing rope or pole, and a rope ladder. It is important to keep the surface of such playgrounds in good repair.

If there were enough of this type of playground, older children would be less likely to invade the playgrounds designed to attract the younger children, spoiling their fun and breaking the equipment.

The playgrounds intended for younger children should be surrounded by a low fence or by thickly planted prickly bushes and entered through a gate, so that mothers can relax, knowing that their toddlers cannot easily wander on to a road. As a minimum they should contain (a) a hard-surfaced area upon which the children can use their own wheeled toys such as scooters, tricycles and doll's prams, (b) a sand-pit, (c) some *simple* and *low* apparatus upon which to climb, scramble, slide and swing, and (d) seats placed in sheltered and both sunny and shaded positions, and a solid table or two, with space for prams nearby. A small shelter in case of rain, toilets and a water tap and basin must be included unless the playground is a very small one, intended only for the families living in the immediate vicinity. Grass, shrubs, trees, flowers and a paddling-pool would be luxurious but very welcome additions.

The best type of slide for such a playground is one that is supported by a mound covered with grass, or cobbles set in concrete. The children can climb up the cobbles or a plank laid against the mound but just free of it, and, on the other side, slide down a wooden or metal slope, preferably wide enough to take two or three children at once. In the playpark in Battersea Park, London, a few years ago, there were two slides of different sizes made by laying a three- or four-foot-wide sheet of some rustless metal against a bank. These were, I observed, very popular. For small children the mound need be no higher than three feet if the slide is continued for several feet along the ground at the bottom.

Swings may be tyres slung horizontally or vertically on ropes, or a single thick rope knotted at the bottom. They should not be the kind into which a child must be lifted as into a cage, and pushed. The swinging area could be surrounded by a low wall (useful for walking along or climbing over) or a railing (useful for the smallest to swing from by their hands and for the slightly less small to turn somersaults over) which would lessen the danger of a toddler running full tilt into a moving swing.

Small children like curving paths to follow and changes of level to negotiate, bushes to play among and, if possible, a very simple 'house' for the 'mothers and fathers' type games and a 'fort' (*not* necessarily on a high platform). They will also enjoy a climbing frame like mine, or a metal 'bridge', and 'stepping stones' (but not those made of sawn chunks of tree trunks because they tend to become slippery).

These playgrounds would need to be regularly inspected and cleaned and kept in good repair, but the local authority should not be legally liable in case of accident. Holme and Massie report that, in Stockholm, notices are posted at the entrance to all public playgrounds to the effect that 'the play material is for the children who use it at their own risk'. They also say that 'most Swedish school children and many of pre-school age are insured by their parents against accidents for the small sum of eight shillings a year'. But the provision of more varied and interesting places in which to play is not likely to cause an increase in the number of accidents as long as the children are not, as a result, subjected to increased danger from traffic. On page 89 of their book there is an interesting footnote:

> An unpublished Accident Survey of London playparks and conventional playgrounds found that in 1964 there had been an average of one broken limb per playground per week; in that year there were none in the playparks.

Wherever they exist within or in the neighbourhood of towns, bits of broken, unlevel ground, rocky outcrops, wooded gulleys or hillocks, disused quarries or opencast mines – the latter drained and made sufficiently safe for reasonable seven-pluses – should be made use of for playgrounds.

All sites that are unsuitable for buildings can be used: in North Kensington, London, a play-space has been created under the arcades of a motorway. Sites awaiting development can be and have been used temporarily. Prefabricated buildings for playgroups have been designed and used. Moreover there are such things as 'toilet vans'. In Copenhagen recently, it was observed that children loved to play on building sites, and arrangements were made to use a corner of some of the larger ones as temporary, supervised playgrounds.

Another essential provision in every built-up area is an indoor swimming-pool, to which children can go in order to play in and out of the water as well as in order to learn to swim and for training in swimming. These pools must be equipped with springboards (not necessarily boards for high diving) and the surrounding surface should be of a non-slip material so that running dives can be allowed. There should always be two pools, one reserved for learners. The latter should be fingertip to shoulder depth (that is graduated from about 1 ft to 2 ft 6 in.).

However, it will be useless to instal good play facilities for the older children if most children have lost their capacity for really educative play by the time they are old enough (five, six, seven, eight, nine, ten, eleven?) to go out of the house on their own. Therefore it is vitally important to provide places where toddlers and their mothers can meet together within a short distance of their homes, opportunity for doorstep play, and neighbourhood free-choice pre-school playgroups.

We know also that children grow well when their parents are growing well, and that children acquire social graces when their parents exercise the same. Therefore centres where neighbouring families can spend their leisure time sociably and creatively are also a necessary educational provision. Children can no longer watch the cobbler, the blacksmith, the baker, the carpenter, the ploughman, the milkmaid or the tinker at work, but it should be possible for them to observe a similar pride and satisfaction in achievement emanating from the amateur musician (pop or otherwise), dancer, potter, painter, actor, dressmaker or raconteur; they should have the opportunity to watch the leisure occupations of the adults and adolescents in their neighbourhood. This means that there must be a building as well as an open space where the people of the neighbourhood can meet and which is large enough to house the equipment and provide the space for the leisure activity of all age-groups. The warden of such a centre must be a person of wide interests and knowledge. Perhaps a nominal family membership fee should be charged.

The Peckham Health Centre might well serve as a prototype for such a community centre. But in one or two places different schemes are being tried: in some areas where a new comprehensive school is needed, 'Community Schools' are being designed and built that are intended to serve the dual purpose of a school and a community centre for leisure activity. Holme and Massie state that in the London borough of Camden an attempt has been made to 'integrate the child into the community' by creating 'Community Play Centres' which are designed to 'attract the whole family'; this, they say, 'emphatically includes the youngest members'.

The GLC's 'One O'Clock Clubs' have been a great success and have increased in a few years from the original experimental one in Brockwell Park to twenty-eight in 1970. Mothers and babies need a place where they can meet of an afternoon, come rain or shine. Ideally it should be a place where husbands and older children can join them when on holiday or off duty, and at weekends.

However, while working and waiting for the realization of the larger schemes, we can immediately, in every region, put into effect smaller ones, such as the One O'Clock Clubs, both adventure playgrounds and the unsupervised kind, and playgroups. Many parents are becoming very much aware of the need for these for their children, and are willing to devote time and energy and as much money as they can afford to establishing and running them. These public amenities need only a little help from public funds – especially after they are established – but that little sometimes makes all the difference between good provision and no provision at all. Understanding by people as a whole of what is needed is as important as money.

Children spend only a small proportion of their total waking hours throughout the year in the expensive care of trained teachers – and so they should. More and earlier school is no substitute for proper facilities for play (apart from being a bigger drain on the public purse). The amount of interaction with other children of various ages available to the children during the school day – even in the modern English primary school – is not enough to nourish their social judgment and their spontaneity; nor is the time spent in the school playground and in PE lessons enough to nourish their agility and general sensory-motor judgment.

Teachers who are trying to teach in a way that encourages healthy function, trying to foster individuality, initiative, the appetite for mental activity and the desire to discover and create are often fighting a battle that is lost before they begin because the children have no opportunity to exercise these qualities during the years before they start school: infant school teachers say that many of their new recruits have little or no spontaneity, curiosity, or delight in being effective, and even, that it is necessary to *teach* them to play. This points to the fact – among others – that it will be impossible to evaluate any new primary school teaching methods until there is proper provision for play for all the two-to-fives.

CHAPTER TWELVE

The Role of the Adult in the Playgroup

'Supervisor' is an unattractive word, but I can think of no better title for the adult in charge of a playgroup. 'Teacher' is obviously wrong. 'Playleader' also gives the wrong impression, because a playgroup is, above all, a place where children can make a beginning in finding their own way in life. In secondary schools and in the upper halves of primary schools, the teacher must lead, in the sense of transmitting his enthusiasms for culture and the particular techniques required in present-day civilizations, and by opening up to the children, by word of mouth, the avenues they must follow if they are to obtain these things. This is, as we have seen, neither necessary nor advisable in a pre-school playgroup. Perhaps 'caterer' would be a good title for the adult in charge of the children, because her job is to obtain the 'food' and place it on the table, so to speak. She makes it possible for the children to digest the mental and emotional nourishment that they need if their basic and essential faculties are to grow. She must so arrange the environment that each child can easily help himself to the particular pieces of nourishment that he may need at any moment. Occasional suggestions by word or action – which the children *know* are genuinely meant only as suggestions – as to the v ie to which a piece of equipment might be put is all the direct help with the process of cultivation of their dormant faculties that the adult in the playgroup should give to the children.

The adult in the playgroup has the pleasure and the privilege of watching the children grow, of watching their faculties, their knowledge, judgment and individuality develop. It is exciting because all these things can grow very rapidly between the ages of two and a half and five. But it is the adult's responsibility to see that the playgroup is a place where growth can happen.

So what does the adult in the playgroup *do*? We try to keep *all* the children free to digest the nourishment needed by their faculties at this age. We make it possible for there to be a free flow of interaction between each child and the environment that is created by the spontaneous activity of all the children. We try to ensure that each child is uninterruptedly free to be aware – and to grow ever more deeply and precisely aware – of his environment as a whole, and, at the same time, of his internal environment, or total body of digested knowledge to date. For, if this is the case, he will be able to create – through a process of synthesis of elements from his inner and outer environments – both himself and, in part, the environment of the whole group. He will grow in individuality and thus add richness and newness to the little 'world' that is shared by the other children while they are in the playgroup. He will add appropriate new items of food to the common menu, as no adult can do.

But if this is to happen, we must take the plunge and, right from the beginning, allow complete spontaneity of movement and behaviour – with the minimum of adults getting in the way – and thereafter exert eternal vigilance in order to preserve it. Also, right from the beginning, we must be sure that the children have the materials from which they can produce growth in themselves and in the environment. Therefore the SELECTION, MAINTENANCE AND 'DEPLOYMENT' OF THE EQUIPMENT AND THE PLANNING OF THE SPACE IN WHICH THE CHILDREN MUST MOVE ARE THE CONSTANT PREOCCUPATIONS OF THE PLAYGROUP SUPERVISOR.

Selection of Equipment

When choosing equipment the chief criterion must be simplicity and adaptability: e.g. the length of vinyl flooring that we place on the bank in our garden (see p. 52). When describing equipment, the word 'adaptable' is used in different senses. For a playgroup the equipment should be adaptable in the sense that, although it is itself arranged in a similar manner every day, it can be used in a number of different ways by the children, and, ideally, both by the youngest children and by those who wish to invent, and become skilled in the performance of, difficult 'tricks'. If it is adaptable only in the sense that it can be arranged or put together by the adults differently from day to day, it is of little use in a playgroup, since both the experienced small athlete and the most prudent or self-distrustful novice will wish to repeat exactly the activity that he had begun to try out the day before.

Our climbing frame (described in Chapter 3) is an ideal piece of equipment, being both simple and supremely adaptable. Unfortunately, as things are, this particular type of frame can be used by few playgroups because it cannot be folded up and put away in a cupboard. One hopes that the day will come when all playgroup premises will include an indoor or outdoor space where large climbing apparatus can be left permanently in place, or failing that can be left in a corner covered with a tarpaulin, roped and padlocked.

Our originally makeshift indoor 'slides' – described in Chapter 3, pp. 31–2 – have proved to be superlatively adaptable. The slides found in most public playgrounds are just the opposite; they are large and pretentious, but are so shaped that they can only be used in a sitting position and at a speed that is dictated by the shape of the slide – fast at the top where they are steep and tailing off at the bottom where the slide is curved so as to end horizontally. One cannot climb up them nor run down them, nor leap down them, nor go down them very slowly, controlling one's speed by holding on with one's hands, nor become acquainted with them gradually by climbing up a very little way to begin with. One cannot descend them on one's stomach or upside down or sideways, nor 'ski' down them in one's socks, nor, when descending in a sitting position, steer oneself by controlling the relative angles of one's trunk and legs. They provide a thrill, but this soon wears off. (Slides that end a few inches above the ground also limit the child to a sitting position.) In the long term, children much prefer playthings which increase their skill and sense of competence, and which provide them with opportunities to use their powers of invention, to those that simply provide a thrill.

It is important to find out exactly what kind of equipment it is that children can easily learn to use on their own without help. The first essential is that the child must be able to become familiar with its possibilities SIMPLY THROUGH THE USE OF HIS SENSES AND HIS INTELLIGENCE UPON IT AS HE USES IT. Our climbing frame would be a less safe piece of climbing apparatus for very young children if they were able to reach the top of it by means of a walled-in easy staircase, for in that case it would be possible for a child to arrive at the top without realizing how far from the ground he had come.

Similarly, a climbing frame with a platform on or near the top may be more dangerous than one without, because the children, while standing on it, will be less vividly and uninterruptedly aware with all their senses of the distance between themselves and the ground, than they are when they must support themselves without intermission by balancing on one bar and holding on to another. They may, as a result, tend to jostle each other if several are together on the platform. As it is, if a child is to climb even as high as the second rung of our frame, he must in the process have learned a little about climbing and about height. The same thing applies to our other pieces of climbing apparatus, such as the tent frame and the indoor slides. In the case of the latter a child must have climbed *up* one of the planks if he is to reach the top of the carpenter's bench and be able to slide down again – there being usually no other way of getting there.

An experiment (described by R. D. Walk and E. J. Gibson in *Psychological Monographs* in 1961) was performed by psychologists in order to discover how early an infant can 'discriminate a visual drop'. Several babies at the crawling stage were placed in turn on a table over which a strong sheet of clear glass had been placed, so as to cover the table and to project two or three feet beyond the edge of it. The baby's mother stood beyond the projecting sheet of glass and called him, but it was found that the babies did not crawl over the glass towards their mothers beyond the limit of the table edge. It was, however, incidentally observed that, as the babies crawled about over the glass, they would sometimes allow the back halves of their bodies to pass beyond the edge of the table. As long as they were not looking at the drop, they were unaware of it. They were unaware of it because they were in these circumstances unable to obtain information about it through any other sense but sight. If the glass had not been there, it seems to me likely that, even if they were moving backwards – provided it were slowly enough – towards the edge of the table, they would not have fallen, because the sensation of a sudden absence of support to their feet and shins would have warned them in time that their feet were projecting beyond the edge. Babies at the crawling stage should, of course, not be allowed to crawl about on tables. Climbing apparatus for small children should be designed so that they do not get themselves into a position where a knowledge of the class of objects 'table' is necessary. Indeed, no generalized knowledge should be necessary, nor the power to represent past events in imagination. All the child needs to possess, if the apparatus is suitable, is the power to exercise all his senses, as well as his understanding of movement, position and balance. Very young children should climb barefoot and as free of other clothing as possible, so that they can more easily make use of their senses.

From one point of view, good playgroup equipment can be divided into two classes. Both serve the child's purpose of cultivating his sensory-motor judgment. But one kind also encourages invention and creation, while the other is valued by the children mainly because it requires the learning of a precise discipline; examples of the latter are bicycles, scooters, roller-skates, jigsaws, inset shapes, 'hammer pegs', beads and laces for threading, and certain constructional toys (such as 'Escor').

Other constructional sets and building blocks belong to the first type, and also sand, water, dough, clay and dressing-up materials.

Some things come into both categories: scissors, pencils and paint-brushes and paints require the mastery of a specialized technique but, when this has been acquired, can be used creatively. This applies also to climbing frames and tricycles.

Because he has formed a habit of asking for help, a child on first joining the playgroup may ask the supervisor for help in mastering a skill such as riding a bicycle or using scissors or doing a jigsaw puzzle. But one must remember that if one accedes to his request and is successful in helping him, one will rob him of the satisfaction eventually to be obtained from mastering the thing for himself; and if one tries to help and fails – as is often the case – one may simply prolong the frustration he feels *and*, what is more, pre-vent him from turning to a learning-activity with which he could spend his time more satisfyingly. Occasionally, if he is very im-portunate, one may have to try helping him in order to prove to him that one cannot help him. Even more exceptionally, cases occur in which a little help – probably less than he is demanding – may give a child the confidence to make a start with something that he very much wants to attempt but does not dare. (See the example on p. 228 below.)

Maintenance and Deployment of the Equipment
The supervisor must be aware of the need to keep the equipment, not only in perfect working order from day to day, but also handy from moment to moment and ready for use. Therefore, she will reassemble – or see that her assistants reassemble – the pieces of a constructional toy that have become dispersed, or re-position the parts of a piece of equipment that have become displaced by one child, so that it is ready and attractive to another. This is not at all the same thing as indiscriminate 'tidying up'.

In order to make it easier for a newcomer, a very young child or one particularly lacking in self-confidence to do things success-fully by himself without help, she may frequently need to re-arrange the equipment after it has been used by more practised children; for instance, she may have to put the trapeze on to lower hooks or the slide at a less acute angle. She will make sure that there is always clean paper on the easels and clean paint in the pots; she will be ready to return the dough to the 'pastry' table or the sand tools to the sand-pit, or the household goods to the Wendy House. Incidentally, she must see that those who wish to use the latter as a house have a chance to do so, and may therefore sometimes – not necessarily always – find it necessary to eject the big boys who are using it for a fort, or   – preferably – provide separate accommodation for the 'mothers and fathers' on the one hand and for soldiers, robbers, etc., on the other. A friend told me of an occasion when she saw several girls sitting in a row watching some boys who were removing everything from the Home Corner. The latter having lately often been occupied by characters for whom it was not intended, she asked the girls: 'Do you mind this?' and they replied: 'It's all right, we're moving house.' This particular piece of growth of the children's resilience, resourcefulness and ability for social co-operation would not have occurred if there had been a rigidly enforced rule in that playgroup that the Home Corner must never be used for anything but a house, and the furniture never be used for anything else, nor removed from the house on any account.

The avoidance of cramping and restricting rules makes more work for the adults: we must realize this and accept it. In the above instance my friend would most likely have been obliged, after the children had moved on to another game, herself to return all the things to the Home Corner in order to maintain its attractiveness to other children in the group.

The children should not be required to put things away when they have finished with them as a general rule, because the *enforcement* of such a rule would spoil their ability to decide absolutely spontaneously what they will do from moment to moment, and would prevent the creation, by the children as a group, of a dynamic and organic – and therefore nourishing – environment such as I have described. However, children will more often return a thing to its place of their own accord when they have finished with it if each thing has its own place into which it fits easily and neatly. Cupboards or shelves designed for 'self-service' and divided into niches or cubby-holes can be made especially for this, as at the Peckham Health Centre. If necessary for storage purposes, they could stand on castors and have doors which locked. As these 'display' cupboards or shelves would probably not hold the whole stock of smaller pieces of equipment belonging to a group, the things displayed could be changed once a week; or it might be preferable to change them every three or four weeks, the reason being that children like to repeat the same activity on several consecutive days in order to make quite certain that they have got a skill 'in the bag'. I leave some of the most popular things permanently displayed.

That the equipment should be arranged in the same manner for some days running is sometimes of very great importance. Pat Thurston, who runs a free-choice playgroup, told me about a little girl who appeared to be incurably timid, following Pat or one of her assistants about like a shadow whenever possible, doing very little and showing no sign of enjoying herself. She seemed to be unable to overcome her fear of being among the other children, unsheltered by an adult. From watching her, Pat guessed that this little girl wanted very much to use the 'assault course' (a combination of such pieces of apparatus as a simple climbing frame, slide, plank walk etc., that was quite often built for the children to use at this playgroup) but that she did not dare to venture far enough away from an adult to do so. So one day Pat helped her to climb over it. After she had been helped two or three times, she felt able to do it on her own with Pat standing nearby; and having succeeded, she was full of joy, dancing up and down in her glee.

But the little girl's mother, though concerned at her daughter's lack of confidence, did not understand and could not be convinced that what she needed above all else was to feel able to rely on her ability to move safely and surely among all the other rapidly moving children, and to climb and jump with skill. The mother simply reiterated: 'She has plenty of toys at home.'

During the following weeks, the little girl gradually gained more confidence, but had entirely lost it again on her return from a spell in hospital. After a time she left the group without having recovered her ability to enjoy being part of it. Pat told me that on looking back, she realized that this child would have progressed much more quickly, both in skill and in self-confidence, if the 'assault course' had been put out and arranged in a similar manner for several days running, so that she would have been able to start the day by repeating the skill that she had successfully acquired on the previous day and then progress to doing something very slightly more enterprising or complicated. As it was, the opportunities for activity were varied from day to day; for instance, the assault course might be arranged differently or not erected at all for a few days, by which time the little girl's confidence in her ability to climb over it would be likely to have completely evaporated.

So, when deciding how to arrange the equipment and what opportunities for activity to provide each day, one must carefully balance the children's need for variety against their need to consolidate a skill. The latter need is not confined to the unusually timid child: a very adventurous and inventive child may need opportunity to repeat his efforts to perform a particular gymnastic 'trick' or other self-appointed task, many times in a morning over a period of several days, before he is satisfied, and feels that he has achieved success. This does not mean that a child will necessarily want to spend sixty – or even three – minutes consecutively on the same activity; it means that he needs to be able to *return* frequently to the same learning-situation over a period of minutes, hours, days or weeks. I think that in a free-choice playgroup it is even more important that the material surroundings and the children should be the same from day to day than that the adults in charge should be the same, as long as the latter's attitude to play is similar. This is because the children are learning primarily to relate to the whole situation comprised by the material environment, the children as a whole and as individuals and their activity, and only incidentally to the adults as individuals.

It is important that EVERY CHILD HAS ENOUGH TIME IN WHICH TO DIGEST THE NOURISHMENT FOR WHICH HE HAS, AT THE MOMENT, AN APPETITE.

One mother removed her small daughter from my group after a few months and sent her to another playgroup where the tendency was to direct the children and make sure that they were continuously busy and occupied with this or that – or entertained. The mother explained to me that she thought her daughter was 'unfortunately the type that was happier with less freedom'. Perhaps this was true of the little girl at the time, but I believe that if her mother had waited a bit longer, she would have grown to enjoy the freedom to use her own initiative as much as all the other children did. The fault, I now realize, was mine because, owing to the size of my waiting list at the time, I was taking this child and some others for only one afternoon a week. I realize now that children who attend a group for only one day a week usually benefit very little, and occasionally fail to settle at all; seven days is a long period for a small child, so that every time he comes to the group it is for him almost as if he were starting afresh. It is important that all the children, especially the younger ones, should attend three times a week and preferably on three consecutive days.

It is particularly important that SOME KIND OF SIMPLE CLIMBING APPARATUS SHOULD BE AVAILABLE TO THE CHILDREN FOR AT LEAST HALF OF EVERY SESSION SIMULTANEOUSLY WITH A VARIETY OF EQUIPMENT OF OTHER KINDS. This ensures that there will be moments when it is unoccupied, and therefore attractive to a 'newer', younger or less confident and skilled child (see Chapter 3, p. 37). If, on the contrary, the climbing apparatus is put out only for a short time, it is likely to be continuously used by rapidly moving and – to the inexperienced child – super-efficient children.

When I was visiting various playgroups, I happened to arrive at one during their 'free-play period'. There were about twenty-five children in a good-sized hall. Three or four small tables holding some books, jigsaw puzzles and table games had been put out at one end of the hall, and at the other end there was a small folding climbing frame with slide attached – and that was all. A large majority of the children were crowded on and around the climbing frame and slide, a helper stood close by – a seemingly necessary precaution because of the dangerous overcrowding of the apparatus, although it is doubtful if, close as she was, she could have intervened in time to prevent an accident. Six or seven children sat playing at the tables. Another helper said to me: 'There are always some who prefer quiet occupations.' I could well believe her under the circumstances obtaining at the time, because only the more skilled or happy-go-lucky children would have dared to use the frame and slide among such a crowd. This faulty planning was, as it happened, quite unnecessary in the case of this group, because they possessed a large shed full of equipment of all kinds and a beautifully spacious hall.

A free-choice playgroup need not necessarily be a small one. It is possible – but not easy – to provide the right kind of play environment and atmosphere for as many as fifty children at once, in a sufficiently large hall. I visited one run by Mrs Mary Extence, and very impressive it was. I made notes at the time on the method of organization used. Four low tables, each formed from three or four small tables pushed close together and therefore large enough for a dozen children to sit at, were placed at widely-spaced intervals in the centre of the hall, one for dough, one for constructional toys, one for jigsaws and one for cutting out and sticking. In one corner of the hall there was a large sand-tray, in another a water-trough, in another a 'book corner'. A folding climbing frame and slide occupied a large space; a trunk full of dressing-up clothes stood open by the wall, as well as a large box of building bricks and another box containing other toys. Along one wall there was a row of painting easels and next to them a small, very low and strong seesaw. On the roomy stage of the hall there were dolls, cots and beds to fit them, and small household tools and furniture.

At any one moment, most of these things were being used by the children and, at the same time, other children were pushing and pulling trolleys and prams, and riding scooters and tricycles, threading their way with incredible skill between the groups of children around the tables and those engaged in playing with sand, water, paint and so on – and also between other pushers and riders.

There was a continuous hum of noise, but perhaps because of the height of the ceiling, it was not at all overpowering. Four adults were unobtrusively doing the necessary chores, such as wiping up the water that was spilled from the water-trough, sweeping up the sand, helping when necessary to put on or remove the painters' and water-players' protective clothing, removing the finished paintings and pinning up fresh paper. Each assistant had been allotted a part of the hall in which to serve the needs of the children. Mary Extence was always available to anyone – child or adult – but kept herself sufficiently free of duties to be aware of what was happening everywhere.

Neither she nor her assistants seemed to be expecting to need to intervene between one child and another or to interfere in any way.

The secret of the success of this group seemed to me to be the amount, variety and appropriateness of the things that were available throughout the morning for the children to do, and the fact that the equipment was positioned well and similarly from day to day; plus the respectful attitude to play of the adults in charge, and their willingness to trust each child to know what was good and proper for himself to do at any moment.

The general picture on that particular morning was of spontaneous and happy, but purposeful and serious, activity. One received the impression that each child respected the purposes of the others and therefore 'did as he would be done by'. For this reason the disruptive and apparently quite purpose*less* behaviour of one little boy attracted my attention: he would snatch things from the other children, knock their buildings down or even suddenly sweep everything off a table. I asked one of the helpers if his physical appearance belied his age and if he was much younger than he looked, and I was told that his behaviour was not at all typical of him; in fact, that he was not himself because that very morning his mother had suddenly been taken away to hospital. His reaction was not to weep or complain, but to vent his rage from time to time in senselessly destructive action.

Good selection and organization of the space and equipment can make it unnecessary to ask the children to do what they do not want to do, and almost unnecessary to ask them to stop doing what they want to do. Experienced playgroup supervisors will know many small practical ways of minimizing the imposition of rules and reminders. For example, painting easels can be placed at some distance from a too attractive wall; protective covering can be spread on the floor under and around the easels and the water and sand-trays; overalls with sleeves can be put on the children when they are playing with these things and, unless they have a strong objection to it or the temperature precludes it, shoes and socks and other unnecessary clothing can be removed.

Unintentional anti-social behaviour between one child and another can be minimized by such actions as arranging the room or hall in a similar manner every day so that the children are at home in their surroundings and know where they can expect to find things. Failing a high-ceilinged hall, or walls which absorb noise, one can perhaps provide a quiet room to which children who are distressed by noise can retire when necessary. All objects can be excluded which are at the same time not really necessary *and* easily broken or can be used as dangerous weapons. Objects that are both necessary and potentially dangerous, such as hammers and saws, can be placed in one particular corner and a watch set over them.

The Supervisor's second most important duty: the provision of freedom

In a playgroup *all* can be free for two main reasons: (*a*) opportunities to do what all children of this age want to do are abundantly provided, and (*b*) the children are supervised. After the organization of the environment, the important part of the adult's job is to hold herself ready *at every moment* to ensure the safety, peace of mind or freedom of a child. That is why she tries to be continuously aware of what is going on in the whole of the play-space, and avoids becoming entirely involved with any one child or group. She cultivates the ability to attend to one child while at the same time keeping over-all track of what is going on all around. The omniscience she thus possesses enables her to act wisely on the occasions when the children's inexperience makes action on her part necessary. She must watch and listen continuously – or listen when she cannot watch and vice versa. It is not easy to be untiringly observant of the whole situation, nor to be, as Sybil Marshall put it, 'poised on a pinpoint', ready to act in response to a child's need, yet never intervening or helping unnecessarily. It is difficult to remain inactive for long periods without letting one's mind wander; or one may easily become involved in absorbing conversations with the other helpers. The temptation to relax one's vigilance may even increase with experience, because one learns that, for most of the time, the children do not need one at all.

The following is an example of the kind of thing that may occur when the adults neglect to watch the children even for a few minutes. In one playgroup the climbing frame is out of doors and not visible from the indoor play-space. One day, the children had their elevenses indoors, but one little newcomer, who had not yet grown to enjoy sitting in close proximity to a crowd of his fellows, was allowed to take his biscuit and eat it outside, and he climbed to the top of the climbing frame and sat there quite happily. When the children indoors had finished, a few of them rushed out to play while the supervisor and her assistants cleared away or lingered over their coffee for a moment. When an adult went outside, she found the shy newcomer cowering terrified in some bushes. He had been so thoroughly frightened that he would have nothing more to do with the playgroup – that is to say, he had not, after a month, yet returned to the playgroup. But all that had happened was that two or three of the children had seen this boy perched at the top of the climbing frame and had 'shot' at him with some 'pretend' guns that they had made from a constructional toy earlier that morning. No doubt the fact that he showed fear and ran away made them feel pleasantly effective; but, being themselves quite unafraid of being 'shot at' by their companions, it would have been impossible for them to be aware of the extent of the panic they had caused him to feel. If an adult had been present, she would have stopped this innocent game as soon as it began to have such unfortunate and unexpected consequences.

What is freedom?

In a well-organized free-choice playgroup a child is free to please himself, and, as he knows, so are all the other children. He knows that he cannot count on being shielded from the consequences of his actions, and so he quickly becomes a realist as far as life in the playgroup is concerned. He acts with discretion and discrimination, and becomes resourceful and capable in many fields of activity. In the playgroup he no longer has an attendant mother who foresees his every need, and tries to make his world just as he wants it – or else can be bullied into doing so. Nor are there plenty of under-occupied helpers ready to put things right for him immediately they show signs of going wrong, and so he has got to accept reality and make the best of it. For instance, Susan (see Chapter 4) is self-reliant and resourceful in the playgroup: she does not complain or make a fuss when her 'baby' does not behave as she thinks a baby should or eventually walks out of the game. On one such occasion (p. 98) she quickly finds a replacement, and on another (p. 93) finds another occupation. When Mark (p. 98) is obviously very disappointing as a 'baby', she perseveres with the game, doing her best with the material at hand. Yet, in the company of her mother – a near-perfect mother – she is inclined to be complaining and dependent, expecting that everything will be exactly to her liking.

It occurs to me that the sudden regression into babyish whining and dependence that we have observed in some children when mother comes to fetch them home at the end of the morning may be the temporary effect of tiredness, as a result of two and a half hours of uninterrupted exercise of so many faculties and powers, including self-control and respons-ability.

The children waste no time in crying for the moon. And, since they quickly become knowledgeable about their surroundings and their own powers, they tend to attempt the possible and, therefore, to be successful; as a result they obtain a satisfying feeling of effectiveness.

Their realism includes a knowledge, obtained through observation and experience, of the kind of behaviour to which the other children or the adults are likely to object. They take this knowledge into consideration when deciding what they will do from one moment to another. On one occasion, a very young child was slowly, and with concentration, pushing a scooter along the path. Then I saw one of the bigger boys stride up to him very purpose-fully and in a manner that made me conclude he intended to ap-propriate the scooter. However, when close enough to touch the younger child, he hesitated, while turning his head sideways a little way in my direction *but* not far enough to be able to see whether or not I was watching him. Then he turned in the opposite direc-tion and went off – equally purposefully – towards the climbing frame. It seemed to me that something like the following had flashed through his mind: 'This small child will probably make a fuss, in which case Mrs Stallibrass will very likely make me return the scooter to him, and I shall have wasted my time. Better to go and climb on the climbing frame, where there is plenty of space free, and where I shall enjoy myself almost as much as on the scooter.'

In order to ensure that *every* child is free to digest nourishment according to his present need, the supervisor encourages certain traditions of behaviour connected with the use of the equipment. Probably the most important of these is allowing a child to finish what he has begun, so that if one wants a toy or piece of equipment that is at present being used by someone else, one waits until he has finished with it – queueing up if necessary – or makes do with a second-best. Also she makes it plain, if it is necessary, that one should not push a child who is climbing or jumping, or push a child – at any time – backwards, that there should be no throwing of sharp, knobbly or heavy objects in the direction of other children, no splashing them with paint or dousing them with water, and that one should not destroy another child's handiwork without his permission. These conventions are encouraged, but not presented as rules, nor are children who disregard them automatically reprimanded or made to feel ashamed.

As conventions, they are in fact extraordinarily easy to establish. I believe the reason for this is only minimally that the children wish to please the supervisor. Rather, in the case of the younger children, it is because they soon become aware that they are weaker and slower than the other children, and that it is in their own interests to observe them. Many of the older children seem to see the sense of the particular conventions noted above, and to understand that the observance of them is in their own *long-term* interests. Or, as in the example given above of the boy who restrained his impulse to take the scooter from a younger one, a child may realize that since the supervisor is present the observance of one of them is in his own *immediate* interests. This child was exercising a control over himself of a similar kind to that which he might exercise when restraining an impulse to climb higher, or to jump further than he knows is sensible; he was simply acting in his own best interests.

The children, while they are in the playgroup, are not inhibited by the fear of failing to live up to the expectations of others, nor by the vague and indefinable fear of doing something unacceptable. They are in an environment that they know and are capable of understanding, and they are inhibited solely by the facts of the situation. For instance, they may be inhibited by the fact that the slide is slippery so you cannot walk up it without holding on to its sides and pulling; by the fact that you are not yet capable of getting yourself to the top of the climbing frame and down again with safety and enjoyment and that therefore you must be content for the time being to go only halfway up; by the fact that, if you take the knife away from the pastry-table and use it on something else, it is likely to be taken away from you by the adult in charge; or by the fact that Jill will not continue to be your 'baby' for long, if you take no notice of her expressed desires, nor John continue to 'wrestle' with you, if you are rough and hurt him.

When there is complete freedom of interaction in a knowledgeably planned environment, the children become able to anticipate the consequences of their own and others' actions more and more reliably. They learn the best means of achieving their ends; and they become aware of the exact nature of their own needs in both

the short and long term. They do things that are specifically apposite both to their own needs as a whole and to the present circumstances as a whole. They become discriminating and selective.
They become capable of choice.

Therefore, organizers of free-choice playgroups need not fear
that hysterical and indiscriminate running, shouting and bashing
will continue for long after the opening of a group. It is important,
however, to remember that this will depend on how well the children's real needs are catered for. For instance, one must make it
possible for those who want above all to acquire the power to throw
to be *able* to throw in a specified place and with and at specified
objects; those who particularly want to pour water over things or
to practise punching or wrestling should have legitimate opportunities for so doing.

We must be quite clear what we mean by freedom. It has been
said that, in a good playgroup, the children are free to play spontaneously, but are not free to fight and bully, scream, or break up
the equipment and toys; or that free-play does not mean licence
for all to do as they like. These statements are a little ambiguous,
and I wonder if they may cause people to suspect that the children
in a well-run playgroup are not in actual fact entirely free.

The truth of the matter is that the children *choose* at every moment exactly what they will do and how they will do it. I believe
that they feel perfectly free to do as they choose; but, *in* choosing
what to do, they take all the facts of the situation into account –
including the likely reactions of the supervisor.

Inevitably they will sometimes choose to do things that are
anti-social, and that is why they must be supervised and why we
hold ourselves ready to judge quickly whether or not to intervene.
If a child is behaving, or seems about to behave, in a manner that
causes or appears likely to cause another child real distress, or is
seriously against the interests of the group as a whole, we stop
him – or the other children may stop him. In fact the presence of
the supervisor adds to the children's freedom far more than it
subtracts from it.

Why is it that in a well-equipped and arranged free-choice playgroup it is only rarely necessary to correct or direct a child, or to
exert moral guidance in any more or less subtle form, or hedge the
children in with rules? The answer is that we provide the children
with plentiful opportunities to satisfy their need to become self-
governing, powerful and effective. And, because of the spontaneous, multifarious and continuously interweaving activity in which
the children are together immersed, they are able to become aware

of their needs and of the means of satisfying them that are available. And so on the whole they behave at any one moment in a manner that is *specifically* appropriate to their needs at that moment as growing, developing organisms – in other words, healthily. Thus, unless a child wants to box or wrestle or engage in some other trial of strength or skill with another child more than he wants to do anything else, any kind of clash with another child will be likely to appear to him to be a waste of time. Also screaming, purposeless movement, or indiscriminate destruction will seem unsatisfying and pointless to him – at least after a short time. Incidentally 'fights' are often perfectly good-tempered affairs, consisting of make-believe boxing or wrestling, and are probably undertaken for the sake of the physical contact or for an excuse to roll about on the ground, as well as for the sake of the skill involved; therefore, so long as tempers are under control, there is no need to stop this kind of play.

So we see that if the supervisor has attended sufficiently to the most important part of her job, which is the planning and organization of the environment according to a knowledge of the needs of children of this age in general, and to good guesses of the needs of each individual child in the group from day to day and moment to moment she can to a large extent avoid the necessity of obstructing the all-important flow of interaction – of awareness and response – between each child and the total environment of the playgroup.

When in charge of children of this age, one should ALLOW NOTHING TO INTERFERE UNNECESSARILY WITH THE CHILDREN'S OPPORTUNITY TO BE IN DIRECT RELATIONSHIP WITH THEIR ENVIRONMENT AND THUS TO EXTEND THE RANGE AND DEPTH OF THEIR AWARENESS AND TO BECOME CAPABLE OF ACTING WITH REALISM AND SPONTANEITY OR FREE WILL.

How to foster free will

Just as the supervisor tries to be uninterruptedly aware of the total situation herself, so she tries to make this possible for the children. That is why she avoids attracting a child's attention to herself or in any other way distracting him.

She also avoids doing anything that might make a child self-conscious. For instance, to ask a child – even a newcomer shyly watching the others – 'what would you like to do?' may have an effect on him similar to that which my exhortation to '*think*' once had on one of my daughters when I was trying to teach her to read. It was obvious to me that she immediately began to think ever so hard about herself thinking, so that my remark had the opposite effect to that which I intended; it caused her attention to be directed to herself instead of outwards onto the words on the page.

It goes without saying that the supervisor is careful never to draw the attention of the rest of the group to the behaviour of any one child. She does not loudly or emphatically dispense either praise or blame, nor make overt comparisons between the skill of one child and another; and she never tries to encourage a child to make greater efforts by saying: 'Look at Peter, *he* can do it.'

If a shy, timid or self-conscious child realizes that no one – neither child nor adult – is in the least critical of him or even concerned in any way about what he does or how he does it, he is likely to choose to attempt some extremely simple task and, having achieved it successfully, proceed to something a little less elementary, and thus to make progress.

When a newcomer is excessively timid and one has waited in vain for some time for him to leave his mother's side, it may sometimes help if one places him at a table with some dough or a simple table-toy in front of him with which he can ostensibly be playing while he watches. This may make him feel less conspicuously doing nothing, and, therefore, more free to watch and listen. Apart from this it is best to leave him strictly alone in the hope that before long some interest will catch him unawares and absorb his attention to such an extent that he forgets himself and his fears. Moreover, if we leave him alone he is more likely to find something to do that he can, in his opinion, do successfully, than if we choose for him; for we cannot know exactly what his capabilities are, nor what he would consider as success. When he feels he has been successful in doing whatever it was that he intended to do, his self-confidence will begin to grow; he will feel a little less inadequate, a little more competent and, therefore, a little more confident of success in the future. To feel a strong desire to attempt to do a particular thing and to have the courage to fulfil his desire will be satisfying in itself, and will enhance his self-respect. One must ensure, however, that opportunities for successful achievement are easily available to him, so, however old or precocious he may be, it is advisable to place a very 'first' jigsaw puzzle or a wooden pull-along train in his vicinity; and it will be wise to put the slide on to the lowest support at a moment when the 'old hands' are otherwise occupied. Because a healthy child is motivated mainly by a desire to be effective, the way to encourage health in a child is to make it possible for him to get a taste of the feeling of effectiveness.

However, his desire at that moment may be to touch or speak to one of the other children, or to be successful in obtaining a smile from another child; we do not know. We can be quite sure only of one thing; he needs to become aware of his learning-needs, and we do not help him to do this by choosing an occupation for him or by repeatedly suggesting this or that.

The children, on entering the group – except for those among the older ones who have become petrified, as it were, or a slave to habit – quickly become aware that they are free. They are also aware that everyone else is free; and this may be a little frightening to some, and they may, as I have shown, spend a long time watching before making up their mind to act. Usually they find the opportunities for activity so enticing that their fear is overcome, and it is rare for a child to cling to the supervisor for protection.

In fact, in a properly equipped free-choice playgroup, the great majority of the children very soon regard the adult simply as a useful provider of opportunities for learning-activity and a guardian of fair play. They do not often court her praise. There is little competition for her attention. The occasional call, 'look at me!' is often addressed to no one in particular or simply to himself and means, 'I can do this.' As soon as mother appears the same phrase is spoken in a tone that expresses an urgent need for a response and may be reiterated with growing passion. Because no one present gives a hint of having a preconceived idea of what they should be learning or of the standard they should have attained in any activity, or even of expecting them to be visibly occupied, they are quite free to be aware of the surroundings as a whole and of their own learning-needs.

In a free-choice playgroup, instead of being preoccupied for any reason whatever by self-consciousness, the child's whole attention can be directed instead towards the things and activities and the creatures that are of interest to him at the present moment. He can be completely alive to what is going on around him and to all the possibilities for action, interpersonal as well as on and with objects, and is free to respond according to his desires. He does what he needs to do, including just thinking and feeling; interest and appreciation shine out of the faces of some of the children as they watch the others.

He is self-conscious in the sense that he is very much aware of what he is doing and of his feelings, and of what he is experiencing through his senses; but he is not self-conscious in the sense of looking at himself through the eyes of other people and seeing himself as he thinks they see him. Being free of self-consciousness and quite spontaneously active, mentally and physically, also enables him to acquire a far more realistic idea of his own capabilities and of the real nature of the objects, forces and creatures around him than he would have if he were trying to behave according to the expectations of others.

This applies to almost all the children almost all the time. But occasionally there is a child who tends to 'show off' or is at least partly motivated by a desire to impress the supervisor. Some have manifested a certain amount of self-consciousness even after belonging to the group for two years. I believe that, just as some children are inherently more enterprising, more persistent or more obstinate than others, some have a predisposition to be self-conscious – in the sense of looking at themselves from what they imagine is the viewpoint of others. This is a handicap, for it may spoil a child's power of digesting experience; it may prevent him from being continuously aware of his environment as a whole and from being in direct and spontaneous relationship with it. Probably nothing can be done to remove this defect, but it can be aggravated by overtly critical adults. It can also be minimized by allowing the child to become as knowledgeable and as skilful as possible, but never being impatient or forcing the pace, and never criticizing him or extolling his virtues before others.

I do not mean to imply that a child should not be conscious of self in the sense of being aware of the body of knowledge within him which has grown through his digestion of the environment in the past; but a healthy child is not inward-looking only, for, in that case, he would soon have nothing at which to look; he is aware of both his environment and his internal environment.

Many people attach great importance to the necessity for the adults who staff playgroups to be *warm* characters; but I think that one can easily overdo the warmth and motherliness. Naturally one always welcomes each child with a smile and a word of greeting, and one does not spurn a child who asks for a cuddle at any moment or who holds fast to one's hand. But children require air as well as warmth.

The adult in the playgroup must beware of being a 'Pied Piper' and stealing the children away from themselves and their potentiality for growth. Those children who are apparently quite happy to be directed or entertained, or who are over-dependent upon the approval or attention of adults, are precisely those whom one should be particularly careful to steer clear of.

I have heard it argued that, since the children take suggestions from each other, it cannot be wrong for us to suggest to them what to do. This is a fallacious argument, because the relationship between children of about the same age is on a totally different footing from that which exists between a child and an adult, whether one has the charm of a Pied Piper or not.

The discovery that, on the whole, the playgroup children would obey me much more readily than my own children did at a similar age made me realize how careful one must be. Small children may feel bound to react positively to one's most diffidently expressed wish, or else, occasionally, negatively and do the opposite. In either case they are not freely selecting the functional nourishment they need. This does not mean that the supervisor must never suggest a new activity or a new use for the equipment, but if she does, she must be as sure as it is possible to be that the children feel as free to disregard her suggestions as if she were one of the children herself.

What, above all, the small child does *not* require is entertainment, jollying along and the smoothing out of his path. He may have learned to expect this of his mother: the playgroup offers him the chance to learn to do without it.

So the kind of bright and breezy behaviour described by Brenda Crowe in her report of her three years of visiting playgroups up and down the country, is – or could be in its effect on a child – almost criminal. She writes,

At first glance, a playgroup may be most impressive; in a calm and peaceful atmosphere, the children are all busy, and the adult in charge may be delightful. Only slowly does one begin to register what is happening as one listens to the pleasant voice saying, 'Now, who hasn't made an ashtray for Daddy yet? Peter! Come on, there's a chair free now. Are you going to make a round one, or a square one? John! You've had a long turn on that see-saw now, what about Jane having a turn? Sarah! What are you going to do? Would you like to play with the sand? No? Well what about the water? No? Well, we must do something mustn't we? Come on, you come with me and we'll look at a book.' In the nicest possible way she is 'ordering' everyone, until in the end they just sit, or stand, passively waiting to be told what to do.

The children will at times find the supervisor useful as a listener or as a provider of information, but one should be highly suspicious if they pay one *much* attention. It might mean that their environment is providing nothing more interesting upon which to nourish their faculties, and so they are forced, *faute de mieux*, to exercise their wits on you. The other day I happened to be watching – from a little distance – some small children playing in an enclosed playground in London. I discovered afterwards from an assistant – to whom I talked over the hedge – that the playground belonged to a day nursery. A motherly-looking woman was walking slowly up and down the length of the playground, holding a very small child by the hand. Quite a number of slightly bigger children were keeping pace with her and I idly wondered why. I watched more carefully. After a bit my companion remarked, 'That woman is a bit free with her smacks.' I explained what had that moment become clear to me: it was a game. The children were ostentatiously sucking their thumbs as they walked along near her, and as she made to knock their hands away from their mouths they dodged the blow or skipped out of the way. There were a few pieces of play equipment around, including a very small climbing frame and slide – by which a bored-looking young girl was stationed – but was hardly used at all while we were there. Presumably the older children had exhausted all the possibilities of this equipment and found teasing Mrs X more rewarding.

On the further side of the hedge, there was another playground. This one belonged to a nursery school and in it stood – sadly alone and empty because it was during the school holidays – a good selection of large pieces of apparatus, including a climbing frame similar to my own – BUT with the central pole carefully sawn through at the top and bottom and removed!

Any activity that requires leading, such as singing, reciting nursery rhymes, cooking or even listening to stories should – apart from being quite voluntary – occupy only a small amount of the precious two and a half hours of the playgroup session. Some children may welcome these activities as a restful interlude from the hard work of being actively themselves among a large number of other children also being themselves, and of digesting a variety of different kinds of knowledge simultaneously. We should be aware that this may be their sole motive for participating in activities in which an adult takes the lead.

We may not realize the extent of our power for good or ill. Simply by taking the centre of the stage, an adult can all too easily nip in the bud the children's power to acquire free will.

One day I visited a small private school – listed as a playgroup – for children of two to five. There were fourteen children in a small room. The teacher's skill was fascinating to observe, but it was the skill of an entertainer; her 'patter' never flagged. Some of the children looked amused, but a few of the smaller ones looked utterly blank most of the time, and all of them gave the impression of being marionettes animated by the teacher's will and skill, some responding verbally and physically in the manner required, others hanging limp and lifeless. The adult's manner was jolly and light-hearted and gentle, and she stopped to listen to those who volunteered bits of information – however irrelevant to the subject of her discourse. But the children's contribution to the talking consisted mostly of the replies that her leading questions obviously required and of obliging laughter at her jokes, and even this amount of animation was limited to a few of the older ones. Half the children were only partly there – 'partly living'. I do not doubt that the teacher succeeded, as she told me, in teaching many of them to recognize and name their letters and numbers, to recite nursery rhymes and sing songs and Christmas carols, and, in one or two cases, to read a little. But all this was superficial – and purely verbal – knowledge. It was like painting green oranges with orange paint instead of waiting for them to ripen. From watching the class I gained the impression that they – or the more 'cute' ones among them – were mainly learning to say and do what grown-ups in general expect them to say and do; and some were simply learning to remain for long periods quiet and completely passive.

At one point, the teacher said, 'Now, we'll do some exercises to get rid of some of that exuberance over there' (I had not noticed any), and proceeded to spend ten minutes trying to get them to do an exercise with their arms. The youngest two or three failed to imitate her at all and the rest waved their arms vaguely and half-heartedly. Then she led them in jumping up and down on their toes until a mother arrived, and a child cried, 'Here's my Mummy.'

These children were not gasping for air or struggling; they were neither rebellious, nor apparently positively unhappy. Yet they had been caught in a trap. How had it happened?

Most three- and four-year-olds, although still capable of knowing what they want and need to do in order to nourish their faculties and their individuality, feel the need for the approval of adults. The small child, handed over by his mother to the care of another adult, wants this adult to approve of him, and so he quickly adapts his behaviour to that which he guesses the adult would find acceptable. Apart from this, he may have been told that he is a big boy now and he is going to 'school'. Newly arrived at pre-school playgroup or kindergarten or nursery school, he accepts whatever comes, because he thinks of 'school' as a step towards 'being grown-up'; therefore as a 'new boy' he is particularly amenable and malleable. If it appears to be the done thing to do, he will quite happily wait to be told what to do and when and how to do it. Then he is caught, for at his age the approval of his peers is not enough, and it takes a very self-assured four-year-old indeed to be a successful rebel when the adults in charge are skilled and persuasive teachers.

However, he does not usually complain; he makes the best of it in one way or another, either by being very 'good' or 'clever', or by abstracting his attention and reserving his energy for the time when 'school' will be over.

Most playgroups provide considerably more freedom to play than this. But we are not giving children the opportunity to choose for themselves when we say, 'now choose what toy you would like to play with and go over there and play with it,' with the hope – that is obvious to the child – that that particular toy will keep him happy for at least five minutes. Nor do we do so when we present him with particular decisions – decisions of our choosing – saying, 'which would you rather do, this or that?' For one thing, he may not want to do either of the two things, and being incapable of choosing between them, feels inadequate and worried; and for another thing, we are insisting that he narrowly focuses his attention on one point, to the temporary exclusion of the rest of his surroundings from his awareness.

If, on the other hand, the child can just *be* with other children in an environment that is rich, varied and appropriate, and in which he is at home, he will not be self-consciously weighing the pros and cons of this or that alternative, he will act spontaneously and according to his specific need. He will be continuously making choices, but easily, without any feeling of pressure or any *conscious* effort.

The authors of *Children and their Primary Schools* (the Plowden Report) write: 'The baby depends on environmental stimuli for his development, and these need to be varied and complex if the full range of normal behaviour is to be developed. It is the function of the educational process to provide these stimuli from the moment of birth onwards.' This statement is absolutely true as it stands. But one must look at it carefully and notice that they use the word 'stimuli' and *not* 'stimulation'. A baby needs a stimulating environment, in the sense of plenty of interesting things, people and opportunities for activity to which he may respond *at will*, but we should be grossly misled if we were to take the authors of the Plowden Report to mean that we must continually attract the baby's attention to ourselves or to the stimulus of our choice, re-gardless of his interests and desires of the moment, and thus dis-tract him from doing what he needs to do, and, in the long run, prevent him from *knowing* what he needs to do in order to develop healthily.

Probably most people agree by now that we should not give the children in a playgroup 'formal' teaching, but many still believe that the children must be *busy* the whole time. Perhaps in many cases playgroup organizers act on this assumption because they fear that 'the devil may find work for idle hands to do'; and they may be quite justified in their fear in the poor conditions with which many must make do – lack of money for equipment, un-suitable premises with totally inadequate storage space and no pos-sibility of leaving anything permanently in place. But I have heard it advanced, as a matter of principle, that a nursery teacher should aim to keep each child attached to herself, as it were, by a piece of remote-control apparatus. One expert in primary education pub-licly adjured helpers in playgroups to watch the children for signs of flagging interest in order to be ready to proffer an alternative occupation. She wrote, 'the young child may be completely ab-sorbed in his play for short periods, but at intervals he will look to the nearby adult for encouragement and he needs her to stimu-late his interest whenever he tires of what he is doing at the moment.'

This attitude seems to me to be based on a misunderstanding of the process of learning. How can a child be himself in spontaneous relationship with his environment, how can he be comprehensively aware of his environment and of the nourishment that it may con-tain for his faculties, and be able to digest – that is, select and absorb – it, if he is continually distracted in this way? To behave in this way towards the children would be to treat them as if they were sick and, what is more, as if they were incapable of becoming healthy. The majority of the children in a playgroup are still potentially healthy and will be capable of digestion and of free will if we give them the opportunity; and this is just what we would *not* be doing if we were to make all their choices for them and continually loom up and place ourselves *between* them and the nourishing environment that we have carefully provided.

Dealing with ill-health
Very occasionally there is a child in the group who is unable to make good use of freedom and who feels compelled to take it out of the other children and spoil their enjoyment. One is forced to

follow him around trying to divert his attention to more harmless play, but one should recognize that one is attempting to deal with something pathological and treating the symptoms of the disease, not curing the disorder itself. We know that we are unlikely, through our intervention, to be helping the child towards health; we are only trying to prevent him from spoiling things for the other children.

Sometimes this unfortunate state of affairs is reasonably short-lived, but occasionally a supervisor finds herself with a problem that may be insoluble. The following is the kind of thing that can occur. A mother with a strong and vivid personality and very definite ideas about how children should behave is in fact ignorant of the needs of small children. Her son is very dependent on her love and approval, and is also capable – perhaps unusually for so young a child – of strong affection. As a result, although (or rather because) he has, like his mother, a strong will, he behaves in her presence as she would have him behave. He is rarely anything but docile and polite, is always gentle with his baby brother, suppressing any jealousy he may feel; he is never aggressive and tends to restrain his urge to run and climb and jump and shout and give rein to his curiosity and his desire for mastery and power. Because of his preoccupation with doing only what will be acceptable to his mother, he keeps a close watch on himself, with the result that he has not only repressed his emotions but has become inward-turned, and unaware of and unresponsive to his surroundings. He has rarely responded to his environment according to his own feelings and desires, and so has achieved no autonomy, spontaneity or integrity. His mother thinks he is a wonderfully self-controlled child, but in reality he is controlled only by his fear of losing the approval that to him signifies love as long as he is with his mother, and he *is* with her all day and every day.

So when he joins a free-choice playgroup at the age of three and a half or four, this child is aware neither of his own developmental needs nor of the opportunities present in the environment for nourishing his faculties; he is therefore not interested in the learning-activity with which the other children are occupied. Because his mother is not there and will not return for two or three hours, the weight of his fear is lifted, and his urge to become powerful is released in a blind rush. Instead of having the normal and healthy, gentle but persistent urge to develop all his latent powers, he is driven by a desire for indiscriminate and immediate power over the other children and the adults in the playgroup. So he rushes hysterically about, interfering with the other children's activities, creating havoc and distress and defying the adults. As soon as his mother appears his behaviour changes and she finds it impossible to believe the accounts of the playgroup supervisor.

A child like this might be a very serious problem in a free-choice playgroup. He is not so much 'maladjusted' as over-adjusted to a particular environment, so that he is incapable of acting appropriately in a different one. He is no more 'weaned' than the child who, equally hysterically, clings to the nearest mother-substitute. Perhaps, if he had been able to join a free-choice playgroup a year or so earlier, his condition would not have become so serious. As it is, the only possible course of action – short of excluding him from the playgroup – would be to employ a helper to devote herself entirely to preventing him from disrupting the activities of the other children by keeping him constantly occupied, and by being always ready to forestall his aggressive and destructive intentions.

A child whose growth has become stunted and warped will, in the free atmosphere of a free-choice playgroup, behave in strange ways, but, as long as he confines himself to such inoffensive activities as, in one case, carrying a small box of treasures around while muttering to himself, or, in another, intermittently shrieking like a baboon and growling his only intelligible phrase – 'bloody hell' – his behaviour is apparently taken for granted by the other children. It is only when unusual behaviour includes interference with their activities – as when the first of the two children referred to above would give a sly push or a punch to another child when my back was turned, or when the second would collect all three scooters together and try to prevent any other children from using them – that they make any comment. The children seem to follow the example of the supervisor in being uncritical of their fellows. At this age, as we have seen, they have adopted few of their elders' conventions or, rather, they do not adhere to them when they are in the playgroup.

An unfounded fear
One should not be influenced by the fear of undesirable behaviour spreading from one child to another. If the children are occupied in doing something that they really want to do, they will not be tempted to stop doing it in order to imitate another child's activity unless the latter seems to them to be particularly interesting and rewarding, or unless a great deal of attention is paid to it by the adults. The use of 'naughty words' is certainly an activity to which it pays to be deaf. Sometimes in my group there has been

a mild epidemic of the repetition of one or other 'bad word'; but if no notice at all is taken of it by the adults, it is usually of very short duration, and sometimes does not spread beyond one child. Occasionally the children find it fun to try to get a rise out of the supervisor, as long as they do not have to put themselves out much in order to do it. For instance, at the period when my group consisted of two girls and nine or ten boys, several of whom were particularly energetic and noisy, I remember being momentarily confounded – very obviously, no doubt – on two or three occasions, because the whole group would take up the shouting that had been started by some of them, until the din was appalling and making myself heard became an impossibility, but they grew tired of this activity after a minute or two.

Ensuring the peace of mind and safety of all

As others besides myself have discovered, things can be safe for children in a free-choice playgroup that would not be so in a group where the children are organized and 'directed'. The reasons for this are that, in the former case, the children are at every moment deciding for themselves exactly what they will do, and where, when and how they will move, and are never relinquishing responsibility for themselves; therefore, they are much more likely to be wholly alive to their surroundings and uninterrupedly using all their senses to keep themselves informed about their physical circumstances.

I was reminded of these facts one day when a health visitor visited our group. In our playroom a metal vice is attached to the end of the carpenter's bench and projects beyond it, the metal handle hanging down below it at about head-height for the children. This end of the bench is close to the door so that the children must pass within two or three feet of the vice when going through the doorway. The health visitor thought that this was dangerous. I found myself surprised by her judgment because to my knowledge no child had banged himself against it in twelve years. Later, it occurred to me that in different circumstances she would have been right. If, after having been playing under the direction of a teacher for an hour or more, the children had been conducted as a party to the lavatory and had gone through the door in carefully organized single file, it would have been quite likely that one or other of them would have hurt his head against the handle of the vice. Being under orders, so to speak, they would have abdicated the responsibility for themselves and for others in favour of the teacher. They might feel that there was little point in paying careful attention to their surroundings when they had so little choice as to when, where and how they moved. They would know that the teacher did not want them to be diverted by any attractive alternative from the occupation that she had chosen for them at that moment, which was to 'go upstairs to the toilet', and, therefore, it would be less frustrating to put on blinkers, as it were, and let the teacher take the reins.

It is the same when the children are climbing: if someone – particularly a parent or someone in authority – is standing by encouraging them, offering advice or otherwise trying to help, an accident is much more likely to happen than if they are absolutely free to choose for themselves what they will do and how they will do it.

At the Peckham Health Centre, selected three- and four-year-olds, who had become accomplished in the use of the simple climbing apparatus provided for them in the 'nursery', were allowed to use the gymnasium, under the supervision of myself or another student, in the early afternoon before the arrival of the school-children. Here, they would make amazingly good use of apparatus designed for adults; the more experienced would climb to the top of the ribstalls and also to the top of the 15-ft-high 'window frames' and stay there, from time to time hanging from the top bar by their hands, or shouting down to the others. Yet, to quote from *The Peckham Experiment* (p. 185), 'no accident of any kind happened to any child under five years of age during the period the Centre was open,' (May 1935 to September 1939).

An environment that is safe for adults is not always safe for small children; on the other hand, one that is safe for playing children may be less safe for preoccupied and absent-minded adults. Beatrix Tudor-Hart, in a description of her nursery school, noted the fact that there were some stone steps leading from the playroom into the garden below, which had iron railings at either hand, but that the children would frequently ascend and descend them on the *outside* of the railings.

The supervisor must know WHAT IS AND WHAT IS NOT SAFE FOR CHILDREN OF THIS AGE. A conventional swing is enjoyed by the older children, but can be dangerous when there are very young children in the group, because they are not yet aware of the pendulum action of a swing and, when it is being used very effectively by an older child, may run past it just at the wrong moment. The danger can be lessened by substituting, for the heavy and sharp swing seat, a tyre slung either vertically or horizontally on a rope or ropes, or else a rope ladder. The latter can be used as a swing as well as for climbing: the child puts his head through the 'window' between the two lowest rungs and sits on the lowest – or, if his legs are longer, on the second rung. He will thus be able to reach the ground with his feet and swing himself, which he may be unable to do from a swing seat. In a large playground, a low rail can be placed around the area in which the swings are situated. It will be useful for turning somersaults but will stop a child from running full-tilt into the swing.

'Carpentry' needs to be watched particularly carefully; it seems to be necessary to remind children very frequently that, when one is sawing and the wood is held in a vice, it is not necessary to hold one's free hand close to the part of the wood that is being sawn.

If something is persistently used for undesirable purposes it may have to be removed altogether for a period. I have had to do this once or twice, very regretfully, with the building toy 'Connector'. At that time the group was almost exclusively male, and the children used it only for building realistic 'guns' of all kinds. It is impossible to stop children from playing with improvised guns of one kind or another altogether, but it seems to me that 'guns' can become a habit which it does no harm to try to break from time to time. I do not encourage toy guns being brought into the group. For that matter, I try to exclude personal toys of any kind because they can cause distress if they are broken. My particular objection to 'guns' is partly the inevitable concomitant nerve-shattering noise, but mainly my fear that eyes may be harmed when children are running about with them in their hands and jabbing them in each other's direction, as they will persistently do, although without the least intention of hurting anyone. Used in this way, the 'connector' rods were potentially dangerous.

Aggression

There will be occasions when the supervisor has to exert her authority in order to preserve the safety or the peace of mind of a child, but they will be surprisingly few in relation to the total amount of activity, providing that (*a*) there is enough of the more popular apparatus to prevent overcrowding, (*b*) the apparatus has been selected and arranged with knowledge of a small child's power of judgment, and (*c*) the children are free to be aware of and responsive to their surroundings.

The supervisor must have a realistic attitude to aggression. She must *expect* all children to be aggressive in one way or another at some time or other, and so not be offended by it.

There are a great many causes of aggressive behaviour; a complete list and description of them would fill a book. Therefore it is surprising that in a free-choice playgroup such as I have described, the children are on the whole friendly, forebearing and gentle.

One of the causes of aggressive behaviour in children is their desire to be effective and powerful. One might think that in a well-equipped free-choice playgroup the children have the opportunity to feel effective and powerful in so many ways that they will not need to exercise power over other children. But this is not so: even the most gentle child will occasionally want to test his ability to control others.

There are some children who may need watching particularly carefully. Sometimes there is a child who, in some way or other, is made to feel frustratingly impotent at home, and he may take every opportunity to assert himself and make his presence felt in the playgroup. There is also the inherently 'bossy' child who likes to organize the other children. But if these 'aggressive' children also obtain a healthy enjoyment from acquiring mastery over their material environment and over their own limbs and muscles and there is plenty of scope for this, they will only occasionally spoil the pleasure of the other children.

Sometimes there is an older girl whose favourite occupation is 'mothering' in a rather forceful manner, and occasionally one of the smaller children may have to be rescued from her continuous attentions. Here again, there is no rule about it, for the would-be 'mother' may find a 'child' who likes nothing better at the time than to be mothered. I remember one such pair; the little boy Benny seemed to miss the older girl when she left the group, and to be for a time at a loss. Nine months later, however, he had completely changed in character, enjoying rough-and-tumble games with the other, bigger boys, and was quite a resourceful initiator of activities. His earlier period of dependence on the older girl had apparently done him no harm, and for her it had been a godsend. She was an only and fatherless child who was 'mothered' every minute of the day at home, either by her grandmother or by her mother, who had a full-time job, or by both together. They rarely took her desires into consideration, 'for her own good' but also to make life easier for themselves. When she began to unfreeze and loosen up in the playgroup atmosphere, she also began to throw her weight (which was physically considerable) about in a maladroit manner, and to plague one or two of the younger children who did not want forceful mothering – until she found Benny.

A child who occasionally commits acts of physical aggression upon others may be exercising his curiosity, or may simply be trying out his physical powers. The fact that one's instincts may lead one astray on encountering a situation of this kind was graphically brought home to me on one occasion. 'X', an extremely sensitive and gentle three-and-a-half-year-old, very tall for his age and still covered by a good deal of baby-fat, pushed a rather top-heavy three-year-old, 'O', down on the lawn and sat on her. The little girl 'O' attracted this kind of treatment for some reason and had already, two or three times that morning, been treated in a similar manner by others. I was occupied at a little distance when I heard 'O' shouting for help and, without taking into consideration 'X''s personality and character and the fact that he had never done this kind of thing before, I shouted angrily to him to stop. The next day his mother rang up to say that 'X' was inexplicably determined not to come to the playgroup, and so he remained. I did not see him for two or three weeks until one day I met him and his mother in a shop. I said 'Hallo' to 'X' and he said without preamble: 'I won't push "O" again.' But he did not return to the playgroup.

In retrospect, I realize that I should not have expressed any disapproval of 'X''s actions, nor even been in such a hurry to rescue 'O', for 'X' was merely trying to see if he could do what the other boys had done and would probably not have continued to sit on her for more than a few seconds after she had begun to protest. Also, I believe that 'O' felt more anger than fear when she was treated in this way; moreover, it was quite obvious that occurrences such as this did not seriously interfere with her enjoyment of the playgroup. Through my undiscriminating action I had quite unnecessarily robbed 'X' of self-confidence, and of a few months of the playgroup.

I have noticed that small children can take from each other with equanimity – or be only momentarily upset by – a considerable amount of what an adult might consider to be physical ill-treatment; whereas they can be really worried by verbal threats which an adult – and most children – would not consider to be seriously meant. For instance, at one time, two or three of the children liked to build what they called 'prisons' when, towards the end of the morning, they played with the large 'Adventure Playthings' building blocks – at other times used as display shelves. These children would persuade some of the younger ones to be 'prisoners' for a few minutes. Some children happily joined in the game, but one child protested fearfully. The oldest child in the group at the time, who happened to be rather timid in some ways himself, found it satisfying to tease this child, and made a great point of threatening to put 'S' in 'prison'. 'S' was really frightened and one day came up to me as soon as he arrived in the morning and, on the verge of tears, said 'I don't want to be put in prison'. Perhaps a play-group consisting of twenty-five children or more has an advantage over a smaller one such as mine, in that in the former it is easier for a child to escape from the attentions of a particular child if he so wishes.

Combining age-groups

The presence of the supervisor as ultimate authority ensures the freedom of the weaker individuals to do what they want to do. This does not mean that she automatically flies to the defence of the youngest. It does no good to either party if the older child is forced by the adult to give way to a little one just because he is little. Moreover, the younger children will be happier when they have learned to accept the fact – already accepted by most younger members of large families – that they are weaker and slower and less expert than most of the other children, in the same way as they accept the fact that they are too small to reach up to the lowest branch of the apple tree. In fact, the younger ones do quite often uncomplainingly put up with a certain amount of queue-jumping on the part of the bigger ones and, if they are pipped to the post in obtaining a desired piece of equipment, may quite unconcernedly and cheerfully find an alternative occupation. Every child's freedom is inevitably limited by the freedom of all the others, but in the process of developing his faculties and individuality, each child – as we have seen – may enrich the environment of the others and thus increase their choice of activity. This means that the freedom of each increases as much as it curtails the freedom of every other, and the smaller and less experienced child benefits from the example of the skill, ingenuity and creativeness of the older and more practised children. In a well-equipped free-choice playgroup there are advantages as well as disadvantages in being one of the 'little ones'.

Because many children do not complain when their wishes are frustrated by the other children, the supervisor may intervene without being asked to do so on occasion, whereas she may very frequently simply advise patience on one who loudly complains. A request for help is never automatically granted.

In the case of the biggest, oldest or most ruthless children in the group, the advantages they can gain by refraining from spoil-ing another's enjoyment may not be brought home to them by

253

circumstances so forcefully as they are to the smaller and younger ones, and it may therefore sometimes be necessary for the supervisor herself to do so. It is her task to do this without making the offending child feel guilty or self-conscious, and without making him or the rest of the group feel any less free to do what they want to do. In a free-choice playgroup it is possible to restrain, correct or advise a particular child without distracting the other children in the least, because the children do not wait upon the supervisor for direction, nor are they more aware of what she is doing or saying than they are of the activities of any of the children.

During a discussion on the age at which children should enter a playgroup, I heard the following piece of 'evidence' put forward in favour of the age of three. It was said that the children who had joined the group in question before their third birthday had, after reaching the age of four and a half, acquired 'behaviour difficulties' and become a problem. The deduction was made that they had suffered from being separated from their mothers too soon. I think that there was a quite different reason for the fact that at this age they began to behave in a manner that was undesirable to the supervising adults. It seems to me very probable that, after two years in the group, the children had exhausted all the legitimate means that were provided for developing their effectiveness, knowledge and skill.

The supervisor must make sure that THOSE WHO HAVE BEEN SOME TIME IN THE GROUP HAVE THE OPPORTUNITY TO CARRY THEIR SKILLS A STAGE FURTHER. They may need more effective carpentry tools, or more interesting 'junk' with which to construct original artefacts, or real clay instead of dough and plasticine. They may need materials with which they can play 'shops' as in the infant school, such as a set of old-fashioned kitchen scales, toy money, a 'cash register' and paper bags in which to wrap the goods. They may need equipment of the simplest kind – such as a 'first' (one-to-five) abacus – to encourage counting, and the opportunity to begin to connect figures with numbers. They can do this most effectively on their own, if they can already count up to twelve, by playing with wooden clock faces with detachable numbers and movable hands together with a clock (possibly made of cardboard) with fixed numbers as a model. Some may enjoy moving to music of a simple kind, or beating time to it on percussion instruments, a little singing or – in a few cases – simply listening to records.

But above all these older children will most certainly welcome the opportunity to perform more difficult feats of balance and agility and muscular strength, and to exercise their creative imagination and ingenuity in these fields. The rough-and-tumble games of make-believe that boys of this age enjoy – and occasionally inflict on unwilling participants – are mainly a vehicle for this type of learning. I find that we have no trouble from physically overweening and exuberant four-year-olds in the summer when the children can play in the garden most or all of the morning, using the climbing frame, apple tree, rope-ladder, trapeze, gymnast's rings, swing, seesaw, rocking boat, steerable trolley, 'tent frame', the vinyl slide on the bank, and the bicycles and scooters.

During a recent cold and wet spring, when we had two four-year-old boys who were very fond of boxing and quite effective at it but who did not always confine themselves to boxing each other, I hung a small sack stuffed with newspaper from a knob that happens to protrude from the ceiling in the hall near the bottom of the staircase. This proved to be much appreciated – and not only by the two for whom it was installed – and the indiscriminate biffing on the part of the latter stopped almost entirely.

It is said of children such as these, 'they are ready for school.' If by this is meant they are ready to learn to read and write, they may or may not be ready for school, but they are most certainly ready to experience greater challenges to their wits, their ingenuity and their resourcefulness, and to exercise general sensory-motor and social judgment in more demanding circumstances: in short, to 'be themselves' in a group that contains older children. Children of four who have been in a well-equipped free-choice playgroup from the age of two-plus have often acquired sufficient knowledge and judgment to be able to look after themselves in an adventure playground or a playground that is less closely supervised than a playgroup. Highly competent 'rising-fives' need the opportunities for developing their faculties offered by a shallow swimming-pool, space for roller-skating, or for using bicycles, scooters and 'soapboxes' on wheels on slopes and bumpy ground and where there are trees, bushes, bollards or other obstacles to be circumvented. At this age they may already want to build dens, keep pets and light fires. One of my sons had a passion for lighting fires at the age of five and six, which he would certainly have indulged in secret — and therefore dangerously – if he had been forbidden to do so. But my hope that, by encouraging him to make fires, with the proviso that I should know when and where he was doing it, I would shorten the life of this craze, was vain; it seemed to last for ever.

The girls in my playgroup enjoy becoming skilled acrobatically quite as much as, if not more than, the boys (and are incidentally less interested in becoming skilled at boxing, wrestling and throwing); but it seems to me that, because of their apparently keener interest in people, girls are better at finding alternative means of satisfying their desire for competence and power. And, when opportunities to acquire general sensory-motor ability are lacking, they may make less obvious nuisances of themselves. However, they may engage in a more subtle form of interference with others, using their tongues instead of their fists as weapons, and quietly managing and manipulating some of the others. In my own group I have heard a four-year-old girl slyly inciting one boy to hit another, and already at this age some begin to say, 'you're not my friend any more', or 'if you do this' or 'don't do that, I won't be your friend.'

So, if there are insufficient opportunities for the four-year-olds to learn the skills that they hold dear, both boys and girls may exert too much power in one way or another over the younger ones, and it will be difficult for the supervisor to keep all the children free.

Children need the kind of nourishment that a playgroup provides from about the age of two and a half. And in my experience – limited to a small playgroup – if there are no children in the group at the time suffering seriously from emotional ill-health, a two-year-old can look after himself in a free-choice playgroup quite adequately.

It is, of course, important at this age (but may be necessary at any age) for the child's mother to familiarize the new surroundings for him by her presence in the playgroup for the whole session on one or several occasions. It may also be necessary for her to absent herself for very short periods at first, telling the child that she is going away but will return soon; and, in fact, returning a few minutes later, increasing the period gradually. Occasionally a child may need the presence of mother in the playgroup for several weeks.

In my playgroup we have had, over the years, at least four children joining the group just before or just after their second birthdays, who had an older brother or sister already in the group. None of these has needed his mother to remain with him for more than a few minutes on a couple of mornings. In these cases, the playgroup is already a part of the child's home in the sense of being a part of the experience of the family, and he may already have sometimes returned home most reluctantly with his mother, after leaving the older brother or sister in the group.

Whatever the age of the child, a mother must be prepared to stay sitting quietly in the room or hall for as long a time as is necessary for the child to begin to appreciate the attractiveness of the playgroup, and to become familiar with it, but she must also be prepared, when she has done this, to wave goodbye one day to a furiously weeping child, struggling in the supervisor's arms. This is hard for the mother; but most children, having made a protest in this way, will be perfectly happy a few moments after she has gone. Some persist in sulking for longer, and occasionally a four-year-old will 'have a pain' or 'feel sick'. In my experience, those who let their mothers go quite happily after a reasonable settling-in period are almost as likely to be two-and-a-half-year-olds as four-year-olds. Being suddenly left with complete strangers can be terrifying to a child of almost any age, if he has never learned to trust any adults other than his parents, or if he has, on a previous occasion, experienced what has appeared to him to be final desertion by them, as in the case of sudden hospitalization.

The boundaries of the supervisor's job
The adult in the playgroup is a weaning agent. She helps parents to make it possible for the children to learn to digest experience. In a playgroup, a diet that is at once varied and rich, and suitable to this age-group, can be provided as nowhere else.

As long as one is knowledgeable concerning the developmental needs of children it is, in my view, much easier to be a good playgroup supervisor than to be a good parent. Parents and the ambience they create, and their example and expressed feelings and opinions, are inevitably an essential part of the child's 'food'; and a parent may not be able to do much about it if he does not have – metaphorically speaking – much flesh on his bones.

It is also easier to be a good playgroup supervisor than to be a good schoolteacher because much less technique is required. A teacher in a primary school nowadays does not have to teach, so much as to make it easy for a child to discover things for himself, but nevertheless, it is a teacher's duty to do his or her best to see that the child discovers how to read and write before the age of nine or ten or eleven, and that he obtains a basis of the knowledge that will enable him to behave competently and usefully in our technologically advanced society.

The playgroup supervisor, on the other hand, is there to make it easy for the child to acquire only the kind of competence that all healthy children will desire passionately to acquire, whatever their background, tastes, temperament and inherent ability may be. It is not incumbent upon her to make the children into anything that they may have no desire to become.

I believe that one should not try to impart 'culture' to children of this age even when one knows that their home environment is devoid of it, unless one is absolutely sure that it is not at the expense of things that are more important to children of this age. Our primary – and absolutely essential – *raison d'être* is to enable them to feel confident in their sensory-motor and social judgment and in their power to be themselves, within a group of others who are also being themselves. If we can do this they will enter school at five with confidence in their power to interact effectively with their fellows and with adults, and to learn what they want to learn. Because they have, so far, acquired skills and knowledge through digestion, their appetite for learning will be unspoiled and keen, and if the school offers them the opportunity to continue to learn through digestion their appetite for knowledge will grow to include a taste for some at least of the skills and the culture obtainable at the school.

It is hard on schoolteachers if the child's home gives him little cultural background; but their task will be easier if, when he starts school, he is alert, and alive to his surroundings and on the lookout for the nourishment he needs for his faculties, and if he enjoys a healthy self-respect and is capable of 'spontaneity', in our sense of the word. The cultivation of these qualities is exactly what we in playgroups can do for the child, but we may fail to do it if we try to anticipate the work of the school. Nothing should divert us from providing the children with the essential opportunities for growth that they can obtain only through playing absolutely freely in a suitable environment and in a familiar group of their peers.

There is one other essential need – normally provided for in the home – which a playgroup supervisor might be sorely tempted to satisfy at the expense of the needs described above. It is largely agreed that reading is better learned after the age of five, but no one doubts for a moment that children should be able to talk before they reach school age – not necessarily grammatically, but in phrases and sentences that are comprehensible. There are unfortunately some children whose parents fail to do their duty by them in this respect and who reach the age of five knowing only a small number of words in their own mother tongue, as well as a number of children whose mother tongue is not the one used in the schools. In these cases, if playing in a free-choice playgroup for two or more years would not give one of these children sufficient opportunity to acquire a reasonable vocabulary before starting school (and I have not enough experience to know whether it would or not), then these children should be taken, in small groups, out of the playgroup itself, into a separate room for short periods and conversed with, sung with and played with by adults or older children especially detailed to do the job. It would be quite wrong for the supervisor or her assistants to spoil the atmosphere and the organic structure of a free-choice playgroup by talking to these children to the extent that would probably be necessary; it would break the direct relationship of each child with the whole environment provided by the group, and therefore prevent the children from finding exactly the nourishment for their faculties and for their individual personalities as a whole that they are capable of digesting at any moment. It would interfere with the process of digestion and, therefore, with the nourishment both of the individual and of his environment – the group as a whole – and might change the playgroup from one in which the children become themselves as effective two-, three- and four-year-olds to one in which they were simply being entertained and instructed.

It seems to me that if children have the opportunity to become competent and spontaneous and self-governing four-year-olds they are more likely to become competent, spontaneous and self-governing seven-year-olds, even if, at the latter age, their environment chances to be inappropriate and stultifying. For this reason I believe very strongly that the well-intentioned person who uses the precious hours of playgroup or nursery school to prepare the children for 'big school' – in the sense of getting them accustomed to being organized, to acting identically with a crowd of others, or to sitting still and acting or speaking only when and how they guess the teacher wishes them to behave or speak, because they may be required to behave in this way when they go to school – is wholly misguided. Even if the school to which the child proceeds at the age of five or eight turns out to be a barrack-square type, he will be no more unhappy there if he has developed an inner core of individuality through making choices and decisions for himself, than if he has become a piece of soft and shapeless clay, pliant to the hands of anyone wanting to try to cast him in a common or prematurely adult mould. He may suffer frustration at times, but he will at least know how to enjoy any moments of freedom he is allowed. He will also have learned how to learn – in the sense of thoroughly digesting – the things that interest him. In short, if he has at any stage become accustomed to knowing what he needs for the nourishment of his faculties, he will be more likely to continue to do so even under difficulties. In any case, State infant schools are rapidly becoming places where such qualities as self-reliance,

initiative and spontaneity are welcomed, and a sheeplike con-
formity discouraged.

Now and again one comes across a child who insists on learning
to read at four or five, or one who is fascinated by the idea of numbers, or an infant musician or poet, or one who has learned from a
parent the names of dozens of flowers or some other form of culture, or some who already exercise genuine Christian virtues and
have a keen sympathy for others; but we should never *expect* any
of these things in a four-year-old, and we should beware of the
temptation to spot interests, abilities or qualities that usually only
develop very much later. In fact, when a child is precocious in one
way or another, we should take particular care to see that he has
plenty of opportunity to develop the more common-or-garden
faculties that we know all children need to develop at this early
stage. We must apply Montessori's theory of the 'sensitive periods'
for learning skills through which children pass, over a much wider
field than she herself did. In short, our aim in a pre-school playgroup should be to nourish and care for the roots of the sapling so
that they will be able to grow thick and spreading, and thus be
capable of holding the tree firmly upright however tall it may grow.

I cannot bring this chapter to an end without including the
following quotation from Sybil Marshall's *Experiment in Education*.
She was speaking of her experiences as sole teacher of a village
school consisting of about twenty-five children aged five to eleven,
but the passage describes exactly how an adult in a free-choice
playgroup may feel. 'All kinds of things were happening over
which, it seemed, I had little control; or, to put it another way, it
appeared to me that if I were to exert any control, as I had until
then understood the meaning of the word, I should not only nip
the buds, but parch the very roots of a wonderful flower I had
discovered growing under my feet.'

Conclusion

In the course of an interview reported in the press some while ago, J. B. Priestley said,

> I am very pessimistic about the way the world is going. I think it's been going this way for a long time; from the time of the industrial revolution. I think the reason it's gone wrong is really very simple: it offers secondary satisfactions instead of primary ones.

I agree, but cannot help thinking that people have made the world go that way because that is how they want it. They seek secondary satisfactions because they are incapable of enjoying primary ones.

Perhaps if we stop stifling our children's urge to develop their primary human powers, they will be able to enjoy primary satisfactions, and they and their children will want to and succeed in changing the direction in which the world is going.

I will try to summarize the contribution that this book makes to the science and technique of child-rearing.

A child is born with an urge to realize his potentiality for being a competent and effective human being (White). At two years old, he knows no better than the polar bear cub (described on p. 155) what he will need to be able to do when adult, but he has practised stepping on and off the front doorstep until he is satisfied with his skill, and now he knows that he wants to learn how to jump with both feet together from the doorstep to the ground with ease and precision – and so on. Nature – or the effects of natural selection – has ensured that from birth a child will act – environment permitting – in a way that will develop the basic faculties needed by a member of the human species in order to survive and flourish in a state of nature. These include the faculty to recognize objects and to judge their distance and size, to distinguish sounds and make them himself, to move every part of his body, and his body as a whole, precisely as he intends to move them, and to co-operate successfully with other human beings. A child born into our civilization will not need to develop these faculties fully in order to survive to maturity and rear the next generation. But a child is only *happy* if he has daily evidence of the fact that he is growing in ability in fields of activity such as these; without it, he feels worthless because powerless and ineffective; with it, his self-confidence blossoms, and so his urge to develop his human powers to the limits of his potentiality will be continually reinforced.

The food and drink of faculties is exercise, but not just any exercise. Unlike bodies, faculties and powers cannot digest exactly similar items of nourishment over and over again. A baby will recognize the specific nourishment needed by his faculties at any moment if it is present in his environment (Piaget, and Scott Williamson and Pearse). But if the latter is boringly limited and unchanging or if he is not allowed to choose for himself what he will pay attention to and what he will do, his faculties will be starved and will consequently remain embryonic. If his opportunities for necessary activity are insufficient, a child may become afraid – with reason – of failing to achieve his aims; for fear of further hurt to his self-esteem, he may avoid activity in this or that area of experience and thus may ensure his own inadequacy. Through organizing the environment NOT the child, we can see to it that the circle is not a vicious one, but is – as it should and can be – amiable.

A still healthy baby is interested in things that are intriguingly new but that have a certain similarity to things with which he is already familiar (Hebb). He is attracted to opportunities for physical and mental activity in which with effort – more or less effort according to temperament – he is capable of success. A small child needs an environment that he can extend at will.

Being human, children – and babies too – enjoy obtaining a response from another human being, particularly the specific response they wish to obtain. Unless they find life enjoyable, they will fail to grow fully. Therefore, we emphatically do not 'spoil' a baby or a *small* child by allowing him to feel that he has power over us (Bettelheim). If, from the age of two, he is able to play freely among children of his own age who are also freely following their own desires and purposes, he will learn that it is necessary to take the desires and purposes of these children into account in order to obtain their co-operation in his games or in order that he may be able to ride a tricycle or push a doll's pram through the moving throng without mishap. (In spite of this, it may be several years before he comes to appreciate the fact that his parents have desires and purposes and rights of their own, which is one important reason for sharing parenthood rather than attempting it on one's own.)

A child does not distinguish between himself and his activity, and, if he finds that his spontaneous behaviour finds no favour in

262

his parents' eyes, may suffer from a devastating feeling of inadequacy. A child of a certain temperament may try to restore his battered self-respect by activity of a kind that upsets his parents even more and causes them to express their disapproval even more strongly (see p. 204). The vicious circle may continue until the child becomes labelled 'out of control' or 'delinquent'. Another child may sense what is required of him and may succeed in keeping the relationship harmonious but with an equally – if not more – disastrous effect on himself in the long run: if his parents have a very clear and consistent picture of what their child should be like, and he himself is sensitive and strong-willed, he may succeed in modelling himself on this picture as long as his parents are present to provide the incentive. As a result, many of his faculties will remain undeveloped, including his power of choice – in other words, his individuality. This may also occur when a child is exceptionally malleable. He may also have become so self-conscious through watching himself lest he put a foot wrong that he is incapable both of being aware of reality and of knowing his own developmental needs.

A human being's potentiality for awareness, judgment and creativity will be realized only if he *digests* specifically appropriate and sequential nourishment in the form of physical and mental activity and of experience, knowledge and knowhow.

A mature human being can be defined as a living organism that moves and thinks and feels and is moderately gregarious. This is not a complete definition but as far as it goes it is true. Therefore it follows from the above argument that a healthy but immature human being will want to develop his sensory discrimination, his judgment in the field of the movement of his body and its parts in space and time and his ability for mutually rewarding relationships with other human beings, both singly and in groups.

If we succeed in making it possible for children to satisfy these basic desires, they will be self-respectingly alert, aware, perceptive, responsive, resourceful, resilient and creative. The right kind of play environment can further the realization of a child's potentiality for these qualities and of his ability to act in a manner that is both true to himself as an integrated whole and specifically appropriate to the reality of the present situation as a whole.

But children will only get the kind of environment they need if adults are full of a keen interest and humble wonder before the most marvellous of all nature's marvels. Biologically speaking, the most important of all the occupations of men is the successful rearing of the next generation. In order to do this well in our technologically advanced, artificial and overcrowded environment, we need far more knowledge of the developmental needs of children than did our forebears. This book offers a synthesis of the discoveries of the Pioneer Health Centre team, Piaget, Robert W. White and others to those interested in making it possible for children to grow in wisdom, power and spontaneity.

Bibliography

Allen of Hurtwood, Lady, *Planning for Play*. London, 1968

Bettelheim, Bruno, *The Empty Fortress: infantile autism and the birth of the self*. New York, 1967

Burn, Michael, *Mr Lyward's Answer*. London, 1956

Crowe, Brenda, *The Playgroup Movement*. London, 1971

Groos, Karl, *The Play of Man*. London, 1901

Harlow, Harry F. and Margaret K., 'Social Deprivation in Monkeys' in *Scientific American*, Nov. 1962, pp. 136–46

Hebb, D. O., *A Textbook of Psychology*. Philadelphia and London, 1958. *Organization of Behaviour*. New York and London, 1949

Holme, Anthea, and Peter Massie, *Children's Play: a study of needs and opportunities*. London, 1970

Holt, John, *How Children Fail*. New York and Harmondsworth, 1964. Revised Edition, New York and Harmondsworth, 1982

Hunt, McVickers, *Intelligence and Experience*. New York, 1961

Laing, R. D., *The Divided Self* (particularly Chapter II, 'The Ghost in the Weed Garden: a study of a chronic schizophrenic'). London, 1950

Marshall, Sybil, *An Experiment in Education*. Cambridge, 1966

Mittelmann, Béla, 'Mobility in Infants, Children and Adults' in *Psychoanalytical Study of the Child*, vol. 9 (1954)

Padilla, S. G., "Further Studies in the Delayed Pecking of Chicks' in *Journal of Comparative Psychology*, 20 (1935), pp. 413–43

Pearse, I. H., and L. H. Crocker, *The Peckham Experiment*. London, 1943

Piaget, J., *The Origin of Intelligence in the Child*. New York and London, 1953. *Play, Dreams and Imitation in Childhood*. New York and London, 1951

Plowden Report, The: *Children and their Primary Schools*. The 1967 Report on Primary Education of the Central Advisory Council for Education (England) under the chairmanship of Lady Plowden

Raverat, Gwen, *Period Piece: a Cambridge childhood*. London, 1952

Scott Williamson, G., and I. H. Pearse, *Science, Synthesis and Sanity*. London, 1965

Shinn, M. W., *The Biography of a Baby*. Boston/New York, 1900. Reading, Massachusetts, 1985
Notes on the Development of a Child. Berkeley, 1909

Tudor-Hart, B., *Learning to Live*. London, 1963

Tustin, F., *A Group of Juniors*. London, 1961

Valentine, C. W., *The Psychology of Early Childhood*. London, 1942

Walk, R. D., and E. J. Gibson, 'A comparative and analytical study of visual depth perception' in *Psychological Monographs* (1961), vol. 75, no. 15

White, R. W., *Lives in Progress: a study of the natural growth of personality*. New York and London, 1966. 'Motivation Reconsidered: the concept of competence' in *Psychological Review* (1959), vol. 66, no. 5. Reprinted in E. P. Hollander and R. G. Hunt (ed.), *Current Perspectives in Social Psychology*. New York and Oxford, 1963

Index

abilities *see* powers
ability
  how it grows 13–14, 134
  why it grows 143–5
  confidence in 197, 205, 258, 262
  to be aware of others' needs 60–2, 163, 165–8
  to respond to reality 12, 121–4
  for social co-operation 165, 170–1, 227
  lost, to enjoy active play 199
  spotting 260
  needed by adult in playgroup 232
  waste of inherent 8
activity
  spontaneous and voluntary 7, 14, 144–6; beginnings of 16, 121–4
  characteristics of healthy 58, 75
  discriminating 102
  mental 73, 110, 113, 137–40
  appetite for 145
  avoidance of 16, 187
  chosen by schoolage children at the P.H.C. in Peckham 21–5
  as infants' functional food 123
  of jumping 15–16, 22–3
  of watching 21, 63
  of paying attention 58–9, 107, 129, 137, 284–9
  schemas of 137
  repetition of a new 112–13
  records of 29–102; in 2-year-olds 40–6, 163–5; in babies 104*ff.*
aggression 163–4, 169, 245–7, 250–2, 253–5
  biting 60–1
  in monkeys 59
Allen of Hurtwood, Lady 214
altruism 60, 166
apparatus *see* equipment
attention
  wholehearted 161
  sustained 22, 48–9, 106
  outward-directed 192–3, 197, 239
  distraction of 60, 245
  abstraction of 244
autism 186*ff*
autonomy 187, 190, 201–2, 236
  no opportunity to exercise 248
awareness 192–3
  growth of 29, 60, 117
  of reality 16, 58, 102, 190
  of total situation 23, 48, 58
  of one's learning-needs 29, 239
  of others' feelings 163, 165–8, 172–7

sensory-motor 166, 248
self- 178
  and self-confidence 201

balance in movement 31–7, 47–8, 150–4, 200, 254
  on a scooter 51
  on the slides 47
  on a bicycle 150
  on one's feet 151
  toddlers' interest in learning 40, 62, 151–4
behaviour
  of babies 103–14
  of toddlers 126
  of children in a new environment 29, 243–4
  individuality of 62
  eccentric 62, 190
  not typical of group 76
  superficially grown-up 200
  anti-social 236, 246–7
  see also activity
Bettelheim, Bruno 185*ff.*
bicycle riding 213
  at the P.H.C., Peckham 23
  in the playgroup 50
  and general sensory-motor judgment 150
Biography of a Baby, The 105–9
biology, laws of
  inherent in organism 119
  respect for 119
  and growth of power to feel 170
  operation of 170

capacity *see* ability
child
  healthy 143, 238
  'naughty' 137
  love to a 199, 204
  physically inactive 63–4
  strong-willed 246
  response of, to a suitable environment 74–5
childhood fifty years ago 210–12
child-rearing 208, 214
  science and technique of 261
children
  characteristics of, at the P.H.C., Peckham 201
  company of other 16
  rapidly moving 229
  autistic 186*ff.*

267

familiarity
  with environment 17, 192
  with a group of peers 18, 201, 258
  with widening environment 179
families, the society of whole 26
family
  circle 167
  need for 167
  need to get away from 167
  need for relationships outside the 178–9
  playgroups part of the experience of the 256
fear
  of inadequacy 15, 16, 195
  of experience 187–8
  of doing something unacceptable 235
  of loved one's disapproval 246
  in school playground 196
  a child's reaction to 204
  overcome 239
feeling(s)
  activity of 239
  growth of power to feel 114–17
  of power 104
  of inferiority, failure, incompetence 76
  of efficacy 126, 136, 234, 239
  of effectiveness 238–9
  of being capable of choice 203
  awareness of others' 167–8, 177
  experience of, in make-believe 172–4
  digestible amounts of 168
  respect for a baby's 189
  verbal expression of 47, 102
food see nourishment
free-choice pre-school playgroups 73, 75, 190–3, 220
  universal need for 205
  minimum useful size of 73
  large 230–1
  learning in 27ff., 74–5, 163–76, 192–3
  growth of awareness of reality in 190
  growth of individuality in 190
  growth of resilience in 102, 227, 233
  aggressive activity in 169, 250ff.
  passion in 169
  compassion in 167–8, 170
  make-believe games in 172
  educative experience of choice in 74–5, 193
  freedom in 168–9, 193, 232ff., 253–6
  feeling of freedom in 236
  mutual growth of child and environment in 73
  acquisition of social judgment in 168 and education 193, 205, 221
freedom 9, 18, 21, 75
  to play 214
  to choose what to do 18
  to do nothing 18, 20, 169, 205
  to learn from observation 26, 212, 238

to know one's learning-needs 26, 239
  in a free-choice playgroup 75, 222–45, 253
  children's feeling of 236
  main responsibility of supervisor 222–3
  to be aware 29, 205, 222
  organization that ensures 223–31, 236–9, 253–6
  vigilance that ensures 232ff., 251–4
  compulsive spoiling of others' 245–6
free will, 102, 117, 180, 245
  how to foster 237–45

game(s)
  compulsory 17
  invention of 62, 213
  make-believe 172–6, 177–8
  and acrobatic 'tricks' 27, 32, 48, 50 149
  of 'somersaults' 145
  of 'bridges' 145
grasping 128–34
  reflex reaction 128
  development of precision in 129–30, 132–4
Groos, Karl 12, 13, 103, 111, 151
group
  being oneself within a 147
  a familiar 18, 168, 258
  necessary for growth of individuality 16
Group of Juniors, A 177
growth 7–9, 258
  smooth 198
  nourishment necessary for 134
  essential opportunities for 256–8
  importance of play to 6
  mutual, of child and environment 73
  uniqueness of mental and emotional 9, 73
  quality of functional 13
  of diversity in environment 73
  of powers 116
  of faculty to suck 125
  of faculty to grasp 128–30
  of faculty to see 123–4
  of faculty to choose 236
  warped 246–7

Harlow, Harry 59, 124, 178
health (wholeness) 6, 9, 196
  of behaviour 237
  characteristics of 75
  encouragement of 238–9
Hebb, D. O. 125, 135, 262
Holme, Anthea, and Peter Massie 214, 219
How Children Fail 125n
Hunt, McVickers 122

imitation
  game of mutual 112, 140

imitation—*cont.*
  Piaget on 140–3; and pseudo-imitation 142–3
individuality 7, 223, 259
  growth of, in babies 180–1
  nourishment of, through digestion 180–1
  within a group 74
  of response 18
  failure to develop 183, 221
ingenuity 48, 253, 255
inhibition
  caused by fear of failing 15–16
  caused by self-consciousness 29, 240
  caused by awareness of reality 235
  of involuntary movements 124
  lack of, in babies 18
initiative 29, 260
instruction
  learning without 21
  need for 25–6
  and research into play needs 21
integrity 7, 8, 16, 74
  growth of, in babies 180–1
  nourished through digestion 180–1
intelligence 12, 113
  Piaget's definition of 117
  beginnings of 127
  the co-ordinating 192
  subnormality of, in chicks 119
  and ignorance 163–4
  sensory-motor 51, 113, 127
interaction between child and environment 126–9
  in free-choice playgroup 73, 233–4, 237
interest
  importance of 125, 137, 165, 263
  tactile 129
  in moving patterns 132
  of toddlers in balancing 151
inventiveness 30, 64, 137–40

joy 12, 15, 38, 152, 194, 198
  in power 22, 172, 226
  in 'being a cause' 136, 194, 196
  in obtaining a desired response 112
  in learning-activity 57, 112
  of babies in successful effort 107–9, 111–12
  in life 194, 202
  of a 2-year-old in successful co-operation 165
judgment 9, 14, 181, 206
  development of 103, 117, 192–3, 213
  sensory-motor 15, 23–4, 26, 48, 74, 146–61
  social 26, 74, 162–79
  interdependence of sensory-motor and social 146
  visual and manual 148
  auditory and vocal 148
  general sensory-motor 149ff., 153, 195, 255

familiarity necessary for 17, 192
specificity of 181
growth of confidence in 205
of the situation as a whole 170

knowledge
  body of 9, 14
  living tree of 134, 143, 159
  appetite for 9, 143, 258
  readiness to acquire 134
  growth of, in baby 109ff.
  desired by children 116
  through touch 131–2
  of learning-needs 116, 239
  sensory-motor 103, 110, 113
  synthesis of 103
  of persisting existence of object 142
  dead-end 161
  acquired in free-choice playgroup 102
  of self and others 102
  superficial 243

Laing, R. D. 186
language
  in the playgroup 47, 102, 169, 172, 258–9
  child's own 198
learning 114, 125
  in free-choice playgroup 74, 192
  several skills simultaneously 48–9
  adaptability 102
  realism 170
  the art of friendship 170–1
  to take decisions 57
  Piaget's theory of 116
  sequential 15
  through digestion or through conditioning 142–3, 161
  through voluntary repetition 14, 112
  through make-believe play 172–8
  through observation 26, 75, 179
  without instruction 21, 103
  by very active and very inactive child 63–4
  objectivity through subjective experience 172–4
  practice necessary for 103
  appetite for 143–4
  perseverance in 22, 26
  that is its own reward 126
learning-activity
  of babies 103–17, 120–45
  sensory-motor 27ff., 146
  social 27ff., 162–79
  to be oneself 27ff., 180–93
  at the P.H.C. 19–26
Learning to Live 198

Marshall, Sybil 232, 260
maturation 143
  limits of 125
  and judgment 161

mind 113
the co-ordinating 133, 142
and body 150
'Miss T', 9
Mr Lyward's Answer 183
Mittelmann, Béla 199
Montessori, Madame Maria 260
motivation 118–26, 143–4
R. W. White's theory of 124–6
Piaget on 121–3
'Motivation Reconsidered: the Concept of Competence' 124

natural selection 12, 261
need(s)
basic developmental 7
primary and fundamental 150
play 18, 29, 214–21
learning 26, 239
to become competent 126
to feel effective 187
to be effective 61, 189, 236
specific and present 244
well catered for 236
Notes on the Development of a Child 151
nourishment
mental and emotional 26
functional 10, 13
educational 75
necessarily sequential 134; and varied 113
produced in free-choice playgroup 73
of concepts 173
selection by child of specifically needed 9, 74–5
awareness of presently available 29
digestion of 8
nursery school 10, 168, 259
teachers 209

Origin of Intelligence in the Child, The 110n, 117
excerpts from 110–42

Padilla, S. G. 118
painting 31, 79, 42–3, 64
Peckham Experiment, The 23–4, 119
Peckham Health Centre (P.H.C.) *see* Pioneer Health Centre
Piaget, Jean 8, 110n, 112n, 116–17, 262
his theory of learning 116
his definition of intelligence 117
on motivation in babies 121–3
on activity as nourishment 123–4
on learning through digestion 129–30
on functional development 126–43
on the process of invention 137
on thinking 140
on imitation and pseudo-imitation 140–3

and G. Scott Williamson 117, 262
Pied Piper, being a 239–40
Pioneer Health Centre, the 6, 19–26, 40, 51, 59, 220, 249, 264
choice of play at 19–26
characteristic behaviour of children at 26, 201
opportunity for 'weaning' at 198
planning 214
Planning for Play 214
play
of children 12
of adults 13
possibilities of 16, 18, 116
Groos on 12
Piaget on 117
urge to 116
doorstep 216–17, 220
opportunity for, in the past and now 210–22
therapeutic, compensatory, aimless 17
as release of surplus energy 17
as the subject of this book 17
as treated in most books 17
quality of 13
unsupervised 19, 217–19
see also spontaneous play
playgrounds
adventure 178, 215
G.L.C. playparks 23, 215–16
G.L.C. one o'clock clubs 216, 220–1
an ideal natural 176
suitable sites for 178, 219
need for 177–8
unsupervised 217–19, 221
possible cause of under-use of 178
Play, Dreams and Imitation in Childhood 110n, 112n, 140
Play of Man, The 12
pleasure *see* joy
Plowden Report, the 244
potentiality(ies) 8, 263
of babies 14, 114
basic human 14, 180
functional 15
realization of individual 74
realization of mental and emotional 113
urge to realize one's 261
and play 18
power
emotional 8
healthy appetite for 136
to be oneself 181, 258
to discriminate and choose 193
to obtain a response from the environment 112
healthy and unhealthy urge for 246
through make-believe play 172
of communication 48–9, 102, 172
baby's enjoyment of 104
unconscious, of a supervisor 241
powers 7–9, 261–2

About the Author

Helen Alison Stallibrass (nee Scott) grew up in the country, the eldest of five children. In the years before World War II she was a student/assistant to the research staff of the Pioneer Health Centre in Peckham, London. The influential program of this family club *cum* research station was known internationally as The Peckham Experiment. Mrs. Stallibrass is at present a member of the Executive Committee of the Pioneer Health Center Ltd. which offers a consultative/advisory service and provides information about the Peckham Experiment. The address of the Pioneer Health Center Ltd. is 7, St. Bride Street, London EC4.

For fourteen years, Mrs. Stallibrass, the mother of five children, ran a pre-school play group in the front room and back garden of her own house. She thus became acquainted with a large number of the neighboring children of all ages and was able to watch them growing over a long period. Her notebooks from these years helped in the writing of this book. Mrs. Stallibrass is married to Geoffrey W. Stallibrass CB, OBE and they live at Turkey Island Corner, East Harting, Petersfield, Hants. GU31 5LT.

21.3.04